D1163246

The Effectiveness of Accounting Communication

PRAEGER SPECIAL STUDIES IN
U.S. ECONOMIC AND SOCIAL DEVELOPMENT

The Effectiveness of Accounting Communication

Abraham J. Briloff

Foreword by
Justice William O. Douglas

FREDERICK A. PRAEGER, Publishers
New York · Washington · London

The purpose of the Praeger Special Studies is to make specialized research monographs in U.S. and international economics and politics available to the academic, business, and government communities. For further information, write to the Special Projects Division, Frederick A. Praeger, Publishers, 111 Fourth Avenue, New York, N.Y. 10003.

FREDERICK A. PRAEGER, PUBLISHERS
111 Fourth Avenue, New York, N.Y. 10003, U.S.A.
77-79 Charlotte Street, London W.1, England

Published in the United States of America in 1967
by Frederick A. Praeger, Inc., Publishers

Second printing, 1968

Library of Congress Catalog Card Number: 67-16666

Printed in the United States of America

To Edith
Who Permitted Me to Explore This Path

and to Dean Emanuel Saxe
Who by Precept and Practice
Has Demonstrated That
a Path to the *Summum Bonum*
Passes Through Accountancy

Foreword

The Effectiveness of Accounting Communication should have an important and salutary effect on the practitioners of accountancy. Abraham J. Briloff has identified the underlying questions which are serious, even critical. They take me back to the days when corporation finance was my preoccupation and the teaching of accountancy a hobby. Of the questions posed by this book, the most fundamental is the accurate and true determination of the economic facts of corporate operations, and the interpretation, dissemination, and fair expression of such data to those who are entitled to know. The inability to determine the persons in interest to whom the attesting accountant holds himself to be responsible is alone destined to contribute to the deterioration of confidence in the accountant's product.

Looking back and beyond the present crises in accounting practice, this work searches for a definition of the true responsibilities of the auditor in terms of the economic society in which he practices. About a third of a century ago, Gardiner C. Means described the changes in the fundamental character of the "Modern Corporation" brought about through the growth of the corporate complex. This development has since been characterized by Adolf A. Berle as a "Power Without Property" dichotomy. It is in this context that the accounting profession must search for its ultimate identity. Unless it really comes to grips with these economic developments it will not be able to fulfill the role which is so vital to our society.

Nearly thirty years ago, while Chairman of the Securities and Exchange Commission, I advocated a system of paid directors to harmonize the various elements of public interest which converge in the modern corporation. I then observed that while "these elements may superficially appear to conflict, the fundamental interests of all social groups are identical over the long term." While the corporate officer should be expected to recognize these principles, he may be too close to his work to look beyond its immediate necessities. "But the paid director," I noted, "need not be afflicted with such nearsightedness. It would indeed be one of the defects which he would be paid not to have."

Mr. Briloff seeks to vest the independent auditor with a pervasive obligation—one which extends beyond his parochial relationship to his client per se, and to all those entitled to have access to the full and fair disclosure of the facts of corporate activity. This, then, is the logical extension to the independent auditor of the role which I suggested for the "paid director." To that end, Mr. Briloff urges his colleagues to parallel the historian in the ways in which he develops his commitment and pursues his "call," and to develop a philosophy going beyond the all too prevalent "vulgar pragmatism."

The author demands an understandably high price of the attesting accountant, who is preparing himself to fulfill this essential role. He expects him to undergo a "ritualistic purging" and to forego the rewards which may be derived from the rendering of management services and the other "peripheral services" which he describes.

The burdens which Mr. Briloff puts upon the profession are substantial; but, as he demonstrates, our economic society is in urgent need of this service. If the accounting profession does not respond effectively to the challenges presented, there may be little alternative but to have possibly a new profession fill the breach.

The functioning of our capitalistic society is rooted in confidence in those to whom power is delegated. That requires a functioning system of checks and balances; and that in turn demands the effectiveness of communication between and among the various elements in the society and system. In that communication the accountant should play a crucial role.

WILLIAM O. DOUGLAS

Preface

This book seeks a synthesis of what are believed to be the twin transcendentals of the professional accountant—his Being and his Doing; this synthesis is sought through the unitary theme, "the effectiveness of accounting communication," with particular reference to the fairness of the financial statements which have been the subject of review by the independent auditor.

The work is based principally on research undertaken for my doctoral dissertation by the same title accepted by the Faculty of the New York University Graduate School of Business Administration in the spring of 1965. The intervening months have at least confirmed the crises in professional identity and integrity described in the dissertation. As this book moves into the final stages, the prediction made in this earlier work that "the accounting profession is seriously vulnerable to attack by the financial community, which could then lead to stringent governmental constraints" is well on the way to being fulfilled.

The October 15, 1966, *Forbes* editorial entitled "Unaccountable CPAs" begins with the challenge: "It's past time certified public accountants were called to account for practices that are so loose that they can be used to conceal rather than reveal a company's true financial picture." The editorial then picks up the rhetorical question asked by Leonard Spacek a fortnight earlier as to whether the uproar over Westec's accounting practices will help bring about sweeping reform, to which he responded: "No, not unless the public demands it, as they did of the auto companies over the safety issue." The response from the editors of *Forbes* is angrier, and more direct:

> We do. Before government action is taken, the stock exchanges, industry groups and CPAs themselves ought to get together and establish accounting standards that will be standard, and a method of enforcement that will be enforceable.[1]

Within a month thereafter, with the revelation of several new accounting *causes célèbres,* lead articles in *The Wall Street*

Journal and *The New York Times* carried corresponding blasts at the profession. The former was captioned "CPAs Under Fire —Auditors' Critics Seek Wider, Faster Action in Reform of Practices" and began:

> A few months ago the nation's certified public accountants, hammered by criticism from all sides, were telling each other to cheer up—after all, things could have been worse. So they cheered up and, sure enough, things got worse.
>
> The independent firms that audit the books for American business are now under unprecedented attack, and their image of sober rectitude has already suffered damage that may take years to repair. Earlier this year, the CPAs were confident that they could make their own reforms in an orderly manner. The events of recent months, however, suggest that the Government, the courts, and the mounting pressure of adverse public opinion may force them to move faster and further than anyone expected—and in some cases, take the decisions out of their hands.[2]

The article proceeds to describe the proliferation of litigation brought by various aggrieved parties against leading auditing firms and notes that:

> The Securities and Exchange Commission, which has been growling over the accountants' alleged failure to adopt reform measures on their own, is now showing a sharp set of teeth; it threatens to force new rules of its own on the profession and is even talking about restricting the lucrative consulting services that many firms offer to managements.[3]

The lead financial article in *The New York Times* of the following Sunday carried a full-spread headline: "Accounting Profession, Vexed by Lawsuits, Weighs Responsibility to Shareholders." The article begins by observing that: "Concern is permeating the accounting profession in the wake of the indictment of two partners in one of the biggest and most respectable concerns in the industry," and then alludes to the "plethora of stockholder suits . . . seeking damages from accountants and company officials for disappointing business results of one sort or another."

The article then demonstrates that the dilemma is rooted in the communications gap:

> On the one hand, the accountant must certify the fairness of company accounting statements, while he cannot guarantee their accuracy or the actual worth of the assets. Still, he may be asked to answer in court if something goes wrong—as though he had in fact guaranteed his statements.
>
> Here are some important issues the accountants face:
>
> How can they revise "generally accepted accounting principles" and thus disarm critics who say present rules support distorted reporting?
>
> How can they educate the public to read carefully balance sheets and income statements?
>
> How can they avoid responsibility for management errors of judgment and outright fraud?
>
> How can they raise standards of their profession and avoid accusations that they bend to management's will?[4]

This, then, is the environment in which this book takes its final shape. This confirmation of the dire prophecy is not looked upon with any sense of real gratification; to the contrary, it adds to the sense of concern which originally motivated the research and the writing; namely, that forces which are perverse and pervasive are destined to make seriously vulnerable a most vital profession, a calling which is capable of rewarding us so felicitously—both materially and psychically.

Acknowledgments

While the pervasive theme of what the professional accountant stands for, and stands on, could be shown to have recurred in my previous writings, nevertheless, it was through the warm encouragement of Professor Michael Schiff, my sponsor and dissertation mentor, that the subject developed. It was he who, with tact and sensitivity, discouraged the pursuit of some lesser coin. It was Professor Schiff, in concert with Professors B. Bernard Greidinger, William A. Kopta, and Joseph A. Mauriello, constituting my dissertation committee, who through their challenge brought forth what is believed to be a better response. Through their persistence the thoughts here expressed were brought into sharper focus and with fewer digressions.

I have been fortunate to have a secondary "committee" comprised of two of my highly esteemed colleagues at the Baruch School of the City College of the City University of New York. Both Dean Emanuel Saxe, to whom this thesis is affectionately dedicated, and Professor T. Edward Hollander gave freely and generously of their time to consider early exposures of my views, and through their criticism and comments helped to shape and reshape my ideas.

I am very grateful to Justice William O. Douglas, not only for his generous Foreword to this work, but also for his philosophy which has so importantly shaped my ideas and ideals of our democratic society as a whole, and of the corporate society which must be deemed subsumed thereto. I am indebted to our dear, mutual friend Sidney M. Davis, Esq., for his having afforded me special insights into the views of this great jurist and humanist beyond those obtainable through readings.

My thanks to my amanuensis Antonia Mulett who added the aesthetic quality to this book through her typing and retyping, draft after draft, and rearranging tables almost without number —doing all this tirelessly and without complaint. Thanks, too, to Dinella B. Larman and Carmen D. Rivera who labored diligently on earlier stages of the work, and to Howard Ende who contributed to the mechanics of the research.

My appreciation to Alfred A. Knopf, Inc.; the American Accounting Association; the American Institute of Certified Public Accountants; Doubleday & Co.; *The Economist; Foreign Affairs; Fortune Magazine;* Harcourt, Brace & World, Inc.; Harper & Row; *The Journal of Accountancy;* Duke University *Law and Contemporary Problems;* Peat, Marwick, Mitchell & Co. *Management Controls;* Mentor Books; New York University Press; and Oxford University Press for their permission to quote from various works published by them.

My final acknowledgment is of a very special kind. It is to Edith, Leonore, and Alice, my beloved spouse and daughters, each of whom participated directly in the accumulation and verification of the data and of the writing. But even more importantly, they contributed in a very special and personal way by permitting me to undertake this expedition rather late in my career, thereby depriving them of some of the companionship which was so rightly theirs. I hope that the fulfillment, the exhilaration in fact, derived from this pursuit has somewhat compensated them for their important sacrifice.

CONTENTS

LIST OF TABLES

LIST OF FIGURES

The Effectiveness of Accounting Communication

1

> Go to, let us go down, and there confound their language, that they may not understand one another's speech. . . .
> Therefore is the name of it called Babel. . . .
> *Genesis, 11:7, 9*

Introduction

This work is being brought together at a moment when the accounting profession is confronted with a credibility gap; this gap (described by some as a crisis in integrity and confidence) is evidenced by criticism, even condemnation, from persons and groups within and without the profession and in its most virulent form in proliferating litigation. Many of the factors and forces leading to the criticism and condemnation are outside the frame of reference of this study; nevertheless, all of these factors (excluding possibly irresponsibility and fraud) can be seen to be related to the central and unitary process of "communication" here being considered.

Our study of the effectiveness of accounting communication is particularly concerned with determining the mutuality of understanding regarding the fairness of the corporate financial statements that have been the subject of the attest or audit function by the independent auditors. While this process of communication will be considered principally in terms of a common understanding between the auditors and the so-called financial community, we will also consider the effectiveness of communication between the various groups which comprise the accounting profession.

For our purposes the financial community includes all those persons who are responsible for making or guiding major investment decisions, and who are thereby capable of affecting significantly the allocation of the economic resources of our society. In fact, this "community" can be seen to be co-extensive with the world of "external users" of financial statements identified in the American Accounting Association's (AAA) *A Statement of Basic Accounting Theory;* this world includes "present and potential investors, creditors, employees, stock exchanges, governmental units, customers, and others [as well as] representatives of these users, such as security analysts, trade associations, credit rating bureaus, and trade union officers. . . ."[1]

Correspondingly, the accounting profession for present purposes comprises the principal financial officers of the corporate entities whose statements are the subject of the attest function, practitioners with accounting firms (who in turn may be subdivided into those with the major national firms, sometimes referred to as the "Big-Eight,"* and practitioners with other firms), and professors of accountancy.

Effective communication must be presumed to be an essential pre-condition of the fulfillment of the attest function, and to the functioning of our capitalistic society which is predicated on large-scale corporate enterprise, with its widely scattered ownership divorced from management. Such a condition of detachment presumes accountability by the management to the multiplicity of parties interested in the enterprise.

Throughout this work the terms "audit" and "attest" are deemed to be synonymous and are used interchangeably. The former term was defined officially by the American Institute of Certified Public Accountants (AICPA) as: "An examination intended to serve as a basis for an expression of opinion regarding the fairness, consistency, and conformity with accepted accounting principles, of statement prepared by a corporation or other entity for submission to the public or to other interested parties."[2] However, a subtle distinction between the terms has been drawn by John L. Carey, based on the writings of Herman Bevis, thus:

> The term "attest function" has been deliberately chosen . . . in preference to some term like "independent audit function." One reason is that the

* The term "Big-Eight" refers to the following firms: Arthur Andersen & Company; Ernst & Ernst; Haskins & Sells; Lybrand, Ross Brothers & Montgomery; Peat, Marwick, Mitchell & Company; Price Waterhouse & Company; Touche, Ross, Bailey & Smart; and Arthur Young & Company.

> latter may still be interpreted by some laymen as applying to a process of meticulous detailed checking, searching for fraud, and so forth. Moreover, the term "attest function" (the root of which means to bear witness) seems to be particularly descriptive of the independent auditor's relationship to data communications. While in the minds of some the term may be narrowly associated with "truth" or "facts," as used here it is also considered applicable to expressions of judgment.[3]

To the extent that there is a difference, the term "attest" implies that an even greater degree of responsibility is vested in the accountant since he is thereby asking that the users of the statements not only rely on his technical skills and abilities, but that they root their confidence in his judgment as well.

The data presented by us will demonstrate that our accounting communication is seriously deficient in several significant respects—sufficiently so, it is believed, as to make the accounting profession seriously vulnerable to the attack referred to initially; this might well lead to stringent governmental constraints. As will become apparent presently, this statistical evidence is in sharp contrast with the expressions of felicity, if not euphoria, coming from respected leaders of the profession.

The Vital Role of Communication in All Social Contexts

Every social context requires communication between those who are put into a position of responsibility and those to whom they are presumed to be accountable. Those who are in these positions of responsibility must be prepared to answer questions about what they are doing; correspondingly, those who have delegated responsibility must prepare themselves to ask the vital questions (or alternatively to designate those persons who are presumed to be competent to ask these questions).

In the political realm, the very concept of constitutional government presupposes the effective operation of a system of checks and balances so that the citizenry generally can limit the ambitions and power of those to whom they have delegated this responsibility. It is only such an enlightened citizenry (in a government, in a corporation) who will be capable of asking the critical questions and then punish or reward and, most important of all, be able to take their business elsewhere if they do not like the answers they receive. For this, there must be effective communication between those who perform and those who judge the performance.[4]

The Vital Role of Communication to All Professions

The very word "profess" demonstrates the central significance of communication to the professions generally. Professionals *profess*, Everett C. Hughes tells us. "They profess to know better than others the nature of certain matters. . . . This is the essence of the professional claim." Further, a profession "delivers esoteric services—advice or action or both . . . to whole classes or groups of people or to the public at large."[5]

In another dimension effective communication between members of a profession is essential for the advancement of the special branch of knowledge which the profession claims to know better than any other group. Their claim to this special expertise is predicated on their long study thereof, and initiation into the profession by their predecessors. Further, effective communication is vital within a profession, and between and among the professions, in order to obviate the "two-cultures" trap described by C. P. Snow; it is essential to permit the professional to adjust to his environment and to impress upon the society generally the wisdom which he has acquired through this long study and initiation.

The Vital Role of Communication to Accountancy

That communications is central to the accounting function was succinctly stated by Littleton and Zimmerman: "It is noteworthy that the tool of analysis that we call accounting has always had communication as an objective."[6]

Also emphasizing the vital link of communications to accounting we have Carey's assertion, writing as the *rapporteur* on the consultations of the Long-Range Objectives Committee of the American Institute of CPAs, that: "The idea that the accounting function embraces the measurement and communication of all financial and economic data is a breakthrough in the thinking of certified public accountants about themselves."[7]

This breakthrough which Carey has in mind must undoubtedly pertain to the "all" in the aforementioned comment. This presumption follows from the fact that in his work, which had already attained its eighth edition at the turn of this century, Pixley traces the etymological origin of the term "auditor" back to the thirteenth century and shows it to be rooted in communication.[8]

Breakthrough, or traditional, there is no question but that effective communication of financial data regarding the entity is absolutely essential to the accounting function. The vital role of accounting communication in our present-day corporate society was underscored recently by the Special Study of Securities Markets conducted under the aegis of the Securities and Exchange Commission (SEC). Chapter IX of the study, entitled "Obligations of Issuers of Publicly Held Securities," is introduced thus:

> The keystone of the entire structure of Federal securities legislation is disclosure. Making available to investors adequate financial and other information about securities in which they might invest or have invested is the best means of enabling them to make intelligent investment decisions and of protecting them against securities frauds.[9]

Along the same lines an earlier compendium of the discussions of the Long-Range Objectives Committee of the American Institute of CPAs considered the significance of communication to the profession (and for the functioning of our capitalistic society) and determined:

> A satisfactory system for communicating financial and other economic data is an essential condition for the accumulations of capital from widespread sources in

> single enterprises—i.e., for a successful industrial economy. Persons who have an interest in resources are in various stages of remoteness from them and from the factors affecting them. The greater this remoteness, the greater the need for communication of data. . . . *In fact, without assurance of reliable economic data, the remote investor or creditor probably would not supply capital to the enterprise. . . .*[10] [Emphasis in original.]

The same vital linkage was emphasized in the AAA 1966 *Statement* referred to above. In its section on "Guidelines for Communicating Accounting Information" we are told that:

> The development of accounting information is only part of the accounting function. A necessary companion aspect of the function is the development of the communication process so that information can be transmitted and so that those to whom information is provided understand it and its potential usefulness.[11]

Subsequently, the *Statement* seeks to discern the ways in which the scope and methods of accounting are likely to change in the future—changes which will be induced by technological changes and advances in knowledge of human behavior. After noting that accounting is essentially an information system the *Statement* continues:

> Accounting is also concerned with the effective transmission or communication of information. The committee believes the accounting communication method is in need of re-examination. The assumptions of the preparers of the statements and the reactions of the recipients of the information need to be explored. The problem may lend itself to systematic research, for recent developments in the behavioral sciences suggest that the reactions and needs of the people preparing and using reports are capable

> of study. This suggests that the study of accounting in the future may well include research on the behavioral aspects of accounting information.[12]

While it was undertaken some time before the promulgation of the AAA *Statement,* the study which is here being reported upon and analyzed can be seen to be responsive to their "call."

The Dilemma Discerned from the Literature—Evidences of a Sense of Relative Well-Being

Eminent leaders of the accounting profession have expressed themselves as being at least reasonably satisfied with the profession's effectiveness in fulfilling its communications function. The most definitive assertion in this regard was made by the Institute's Committee on Long-Range Objectives which (in its 1962 compilation) stated and reiterated the principal conditions that must be met for successful data communication and concluded: "These conditions are being satisfied, and the attest function is being discharged, on a constantly widening scale."

Also indicative of such a state of satisfactory adjustment are the observations by Leonard Savoie in his article "Accounting Improvement: How Fast, How Far?" Here he asks us not to lose sight of what is right with accountancy and why. While agreeing that "there is much room for improvement in the details of accounting," Savoie is sanguine because "there are many safeguards that ensure a high degree of usefulness in published financial statements."[13] The four cardinal safeguards which he sets forth in this connection are consistency, disclosure, conservatism, and integrity. (This quadrivium will be considered presently in this chapter.)

In the same vein we have the view of the late Weldon Powell that he is not disturbed at the prospect that further progress in developing accounting principles is going to take time. "After all," Powell tells us, "modern accounting is a very recent development in this world. . . . Let us continue to press on, but let us be patient."[14]

And Paul Grady, in making some significant points drawn

from the variety of alternative methods available in accountancy, observes that the investors may rest assured since "the management and directors of each enterprise adopt and apply the accounting principles and methods, which, in their judgment, will fairly present the financial position and results of operations of that enterprise." Grady then points up that the investor has yet another ring of protective insulation which is "inherent in the independent opinion of the certified public accountant that the statements are fairly presented in accordance with generally accepted accounting principles, which have substantial authoritative support and have been consistently applied, unless there are specific and clearly stated qualifications."[15] (That this last bit of comfort may, in fact, be illusory will be the subject of consideration in various contexts of this present study.)

Evidences of Dissent and Challenge from Outside the Profession

That this sense of adjustment and the sanguine air regarding the effectiveness of accounting communication, in the discharge of the profession's attest function at least, are not shared by all within our economic society will be the subject of extensive consideration in the succeeding chapters. Indicative of this dissent and challenge are the following:

From *The Wall Street Journal:* After commenting on the lack of comparability of financial statements from company to company (and sometimes even within a company from period to period; and even for a single period, depending on the function of the accounting communication), the *Journal* observed: "These variations . . . are drawing increasing criticism." It then cited the observation from a leading but confused accountant: "It's getting so bad you have to hire other experts to help you understand financial statements."[16]

From the testimony before a House Committee on bills before the Congress looking to added investor protection: Congressman Staggers had asked Mr. William L. Cary, the Chairman of the SEC, to file with the committee a statement regarding alternative practices in accounting together with a statement regarding "the significance of each such area." Mr.

Cary responded that while they could effectively compile a statement of the areas of divergence, he could not promise to "do a very satisfactory job" in the evaluation of their significance, nor with the statement demonstrating that the SEC considers "that investors who are considering and comparing various companies are adequately protected by [its] acceptance of these alternative practices."[17]

This indictment of the present state of the audit art was presented especially dramatically by J. Howard Laeri, Vice Chairman of the First National City Bank, when speaking before an American Bankers Association Committee early in 1966 on "The Audit Gap," thus:

> Altogether, there is a considerable audit gap, which unfortunately will not be filled by verbal reform. It may be heartening to the American Institute of Certified Public Accountants that of 600 companies surveyed, two per cent more than last year have found a more revealing substitute for the word "surplus." It is more likely heartrending to the investor who must confront a broadened vocabulary of confusion.
>
> The audit gap must be filled, nevertheless. In his book on the accuracy of economic statistics, Oskar Morgenstern wrote that "the investor should be the first to insist on the introduction of a modern spirit into this sadly stagnant field." But if auditing is a "stagnant field" in the Morgenstern sense, it is possibly because the investor has not so far been joined by the banker and corporate executive, for each defines the responsibilities of the auditor in different terms.[18]

And a former Commissioner of the Securities and Exchange Commission described the present state of affairs as follows: "I mean to suggest that a lay reader can read perfectly clear English and an orderly presentation of financial data and end up without a comprehension of the message sought to be conveyed."[19]

Evidences of Dissent and Challenge from Within the Profession

Correspondingly, there are many within the profession who have expressed their misgivings regarding the effectiveness of the communications function in accountancy and who thereby might be presumed to have some misgivings as to the appropriateness of the Institute's assurances that the conditions precedent to such effective communication have been fulfilled, and that "the attest function is being discharged, on a constantly widening scale." Indicative of such misgivings are the following:

Professor Dwight R. Ladd introduced his *Contemporary Corporate Accounting and the Public* by asserting that the coverage intended by the book "is broad enough to demonstrate the gap which exists between the needs of society for information about our large corporations and the quantity and quality of information being provided by contemporary accounting. This book is concerned with creating an awareness of that gap. . . ."[20]

From Professor David F. Hawkins, writing in *Business History Review:* After citing a two-year study of nearly 800 published annual reports of American industrial companies which demonstrated that "corporate reporting to shareholders is in some respects a financial fantasy," because the so-called generally accepted accounting principles have never been satisfactorily defined, Hawkins asserts: "The result has been that there is no general agreement among practicing public accountants as to the proper accounting treatment applicable in particularly important areas of financial reporting. . . ."[21]

Professor Greer makes the same point, thus: "There are two ways to make reported facts obscure or confusing. One is by saying too little. The other is by saying too much. Both practices are exemplified in present-day corporation financial statements."[22]

In his 1965 compendium John L. Carey is somewhat more cautious than in his earlier evaluation; he now observes: "There is some reason to doubt whether most individual investors, and even some of those who advise investors, understand accounting well enough to interpret properly the financial statements they receive in corporate reports." Carey then quotes with approval the 1963 remarks of Gerald L. Phillipe: "The public expects—and, in fact, really believes—that financial statements say a lot more, and more accurately, than they do."[23]

Weldon Powell also took note of the communications gap (although he generally then put the principal onus on to the statement users). Indicative of this assertion of responsibility:

> Ignorance about the financial statements and affairs of business is widespread. . . . Many investors, both large and small, do not read the reports furnished to them, or do not understand the reports. Some security analysts seem to be interested more in the quantity than the quality of available information and are not prepared to deal with unusual items that cannot be neatly compartmentalized. . . . Some financial writers do not have enough knowledge of accounting. . . . The suggestion has been made that the way to deal with this situation is to produce financial reports that are simple. I am afraid this is impossible.[24]

And then we have the entirely acerbic comments from the profession's satirist *qua non,* Leonard Spacek (to whom, in our opinion, the profession should be very much indebted). In his speech before The New York Society of Security Analysts, Spacek reviewed the centers of responsibility for the financial statements of the entity and then commented on the alternatives available in the development of these statements; he continues: "How my profession can tolerate such fiction and look the public in the eye is beyond my understanding. . . . My profession appears to regard a set of financial statements as a roulette wheel to the public investor—and it is his tough luck if he doesn't understand the risks that we inject into the accounting reports." And for his conclusion Spacek asserts:

> A successful free enterprise system demands that men live up to standards of integrity and trust. . . . Double standards of accounting are a license to mislead investors in comparing an investment in one company

> with another. This will result in killing the kind of business system we would like to preserve. This is true, just as freedom to speed on the highway is a license to kill.[25]

The Primary Study Here Undertaken

We are confronted, then, with the expressions of satisfaction if not felicity on the one hand, and indictments and jeremiads on the other. Despite this obvious polarization of opposing views there appeared to be no formal studies undertaken, either by the profession or by the SEC, to determine whether the message presumed to be conveyed by the financial statements was being effectively communicated; nor, correspondingly, has there been any empirical evidence to identify those for whom this communication was being made effective. That such studies are necessary was emphatically affirmed by Carey in his most recent volume, thus: "in planning for its future, the profession should sponsor research to discover the extent to which the auditors are succeeding or failing in getting their messages to those to whom they are directed."[26] And reference was heretofore made to the call for such research by the AAA Committee *Statement*.

So it is that in order to determine the appropriateness of the foregoing views of approbation or obloquy, and the extent of their fairness, that this research was pursued, principally in the spring of 1964, to ascertain the understanding by the financial community of the auditor's independent reporting function; of the nature of the economic environment in which the auditor fulfills his attest function; and of the structure of the accounting theory which underlies financial recording and reporting, as well as the way in which this theory is made to evolve. The research also sought to determine the extent to which the financial community understands, accepts, and is satisfied with the way in which the independent attest function is now being pursued. In addition to probing the present understanding by the financial community of the matters described above the research also requested the views of the financial community as to "what they thought *should be*" regarding the attesting accountant's involvement in the corporate society, as well as the theoretical, structural basis of the profession's pursuit, i.e., its "generally accepted accounting principles."

To determine the extent to which the financial community and the accounting profession have a common understanding of the "what is," and have corresponding views as to "what should be," these probes were also directed to practitioners and professors of accountancy.

This primary study or research was conducted by means of a questionnaire developed expressly for this purpose. The details regarding the development of the questionnaire, the determination of the several populations which were to become the subjects of this inquiry are set forth in Appendix A. The results obtained from this research will be considered in detail in the respective chapters on accounting principles, on the identification of parties presumed to be involved in the communications process, and on the degree of a mutual understanding regarding the attesting accountant's involvement in management services.

The Synopsis of this Work

It is believed to be entirely fair to assert that the research pursued herein would confirm the doubts and concern expressed by Powell, by Carey, and others, that the investors and even their advisers may be lacking in the apperceptive base presumed to be necessary for the proper comprehension of the financial statements on which they rely for their investment decision making. Further, this research has demonstrated a major failure on the part of the auditors "in getting their messages to those to whom they are directed." What may yet be an open question is whether the result would be salutary or inimical to the profession if the investors and their advisers were, in fact, in possession of this apperceptive base and if the full-blown message, with all of its nuances, were effectively communicated to those to whom it is directed.

The research and the inferences drawn therefrom, as well as those drawn from the readings comprising the secondary study, will be considered in this work as follows:

We shall turn presently, in this introductory chapter, to a

consideration of the pervasiveness of this deficiency in communication. This will be done by describing the results obtained from the questions relating to the "meaning of the auditor's certificate," and to certain other broad-based aspects of the accounting and auditing functions.

Chapter 2 will describe the way in which the language of accounting has been confounded. Thus, this chapter will present and discuss the data obtained from the research bearing on the special idiom of the profession, i.e., its generally accepted accounting principles.

Chapter 3 will review and evaluate the principal recommendations for mitigating if not eliminating the dilemmas created by the confusion regarding the substance, and the effective application in practice, of our generally accepted accounting principles.

Chapter 4 will consider the problem of research in accountancy and will describe and comment upon the way in which the profession is going about rebuilding its "tower" and the "city" and thereby hoping to free itself of the spell of Babel.

Chapter 5 will concentrate on one of the dilemmas which in our view contributes significantly to the communications gap, i.e., the failure to define the parties to the dialogue. Here we will consider such gnawing, pervasive questions as: "To whom are the accountants presumed to be communicating?" and "Who has the ultimate responsibility for these statements?" Again, extensive consideration will be given to the question as to whether there is a common understanding of these questions and responses between the two principal categories that were probed by this research. Further, the question as to whether there is a common understanding even within the profession will be the subject of analysis.

Chapter 6 will present the data obtained from the questions seeking to determine the mutuality of understanding by the financial community and the accounting profession regarding the range of accounting services which might be presumed to be compatible with the auditor's attest function. This chapter will then evaluate the position determined by the Council and various major committees of the AICPA regarding the expansion of the range of services which might be deemed to be so compatible.

Chapter 7, as will be seen, is a digression from the mainstream of this study. It will discuss the way in which another profession, that of the historian, has come to grips with its problems; these problems will be shown to be parallel *(mutatis mutandis)* with those of the accountant. If this is a fair statement, then the ways in which the historian's profession approaches the consideration and solution of its problems could be most informative for the profession of accountancy.

The principal work concludes with Chapter 8, a summary of our findings and recommendations. This will, however, be followed by a chapter on methodology, included as Appendix A. This appendix describes the sources on which the questions were based and the ways in which we determined upon the populations who were subjected to the questionnaire. The questionnaire as it was submitted to the respondents is included as Appendix B. The appendixes also include a tabulation of the results obtained by the questionnaire (Appendix C), and a roster of these respondents (Appendix D). Appendixes E and F represent two series of graphs developed from the research data.

A Consideration of the Effectiveness of Communication with Respect to Certain Pervasive Aspects of Accountancy

As was set forth above, the results obtained from this research will be considered in some detail in the respective chapters on accounting principles, on the parties presumed to be involved in the communications process, and on the common understanding regarding the attesting accountant's involvement in management services. For purposes of this introductory chapter, in order to point up the pervasive nature of the communications problem, the results obtained from two questions looking to what might be presumed to be the broad common base of comprehension of the nature of the accountant's function will be analyzed.

This introductory analysis of the data involves the questions which look for the degree of comprehension regarding the so-called opinion clause contained in the auditor's certificate associated with the financial statements, and the validity of the four cardinal safeguards presumed by Savoie, and referred to on Page 7 above.

The Respondents' Views Regarding "Present Fairly . . ." as Included in the Standard Certificate

So we direct our attention, first, to Question A-6 of the questionnaire which asked the respondents for their view regarding the meaning of the clause "present fairly . . . in conformity with generally accepted accounting principles," i.e., the clause which is undoubtedly the hallmark affixed by the profession to the financial statements which are the subject of its "attesting." In this connection we suggested several alternative inferences which might be drawn from the clause, to wit: in the auditor's opinion the statements were in fact *both fair and* in accordance with generally accepted accounting principles (sometimes referred to here and in the questionnaire by the mnemonic code "GAAP"); the statements were *fair because* they were in accord with such principles; or the statements were fair *only to the extent* that generally accepted accounting principles were fair.

The results obtained from this question are summarized in the following Table 1:

TABLE 1

Percentage Distribution of Responses
Regarding the Meaning of the Auditor's Certificate

	Accounting Profession Category				
	Practitioners				
	"Big-Eight" Firms	Other Firms	Professors	Entire Category	Financial Community Category
In the auditor's opinion the statements are:					
a) Both fair and in accordance with generally accepted accounting principles	47.2%	50.0%	14.3%	34.4%	44.4%

	Accounting Profession Category				
	Practitioners				
	"Big-Eight" Firms	Other Firms	Pro-fessors	Entire Category	Financial Community Category
b) Fair because they are in accordance with generally accepted accounting principles	11.8	35.8	33.3	29.7	22.2
c) Fair only to the extent that generally accepted accounting principles are fair	17.7	14.3	28.6	20.3	27.8

Source: Question A-6 of the Ouestionnaire

As is evident from the foregoing table, 34 per cent of the accounting profession category and 44 per cent of the financial community believed the fairness of the financial statements to exist essentially independently of generally accepted accounting principles (believing the statement to be *both fair and* in accord with those principles). Another 30 per cent and 22 per cent of the two categories respectively believed the statements to be *fair because* they were prepared in accordance with accounting principles (presuming, therefore, that adherence to such principles directs a fair presentation). From this it might be concluded that 64 per cent of the profession category and 66 per cent of the user category were willing to accept the statements as being fair, on one basis or another. The consistency of the two percentages (64 per cent and 66 per cent) might indicate that there is a common degree of acceptance (and correspondingly of misgiving) on the part of both the producers and the users regarding the fairness of the financial statements covered by the opinion clause which attests to the statements' fairness. Whether this fairness is established independently, or is subsumed in the principles of accounting, might be considered to be of secondary significance. However, as is evident from Table 1 there is serious doubt as to just what the opinion does in fact mean, emphasizing the lack of a consensus even with respect to this presumed absolute standard of the attest function, namely, the statements' fairness. Further, to the extent that the principles can, in fact, be demonstrated to be unfair, then those who presumed fairness from the presumptive fairness of the principles could be shown to have been deluded (if not deceived).

Proceeding further, subdivision of the accounting profession category into its several component groups finds that 47 per cent of the respondents from the "Big-Eight" firms and 50 per cent of the other practitioners opted for the first alternative (the fairness of the statements being established independently); but only 14 per cent of the professors so responded. The second alternative (whereby the statements are deemed to be fair because they were promulgated pursuant to these principles) was the one indicated by 12 per cent of the respondents from the "Big-Eight" firms, 36 per cent of the other practitioners, and by 33 per cent of the professors.

Proceeding to the third alternative indicated for this question, it is clear that significant numbers of respondents in both principal categories (and from among the respondents in the accounting profession, the academicians especially) had serious misgivings regarding the absolute fairness of the statements. Thus, 28 per cent of the user category, 20 per cent of the profession category as a whole, and 29 per cent of the professors refused to affirm the fairness *qua* fairness of the statements, preferring to make such fairness dependent on the degree of fairness of the principles.

Consistent with what was said above, if one were to conclude that accounting principles are not necessarily fair then those who responded with the second alternative could be considered to be in accord with those opting for the third possibility. In that event fully 50 per cent of the respondents in each of the categories (62 per cent of the professors) would have been shown to have voted that the quality of fairness to be attributed to the auditor's certificate is tenuous indeed.

Also informative in this connection are the comments supplied by several of the respondents who preferred the fourth alternative response to this Question A-6, which read: "None of the foregoing. (In which case would you describe the meaning of the clause as you see it?)" The meaning, as some of these respondents saw it, was as follows:

From an investment adviser and researcher: "Simply a hedge clause wherein the auditor attempts to absolve himself of his basic responsibility for full and complete disclosure."

From a CPA in public practice: "I am confused by what is

intended. Certainly GAAP does not always lead to fairness. I believe that one of 'fair' or 'GAAP' are redundant, but I reserve the right to alter my opinion."

From a "partner in a national CPA firm specializing in SEC matters": "The statements are fairly presented when considered in relation to the application of GAAP."

From a former professor of accountancy now the Director of Personnel of a major CPA firm: "The clause now means that in the auditor's opinion the statements are prepared in accordance with some generally accepted practice, although the clause was probably intended to mean more."

Other Evidence of the Confusion Regarding the Meaning of the Certificate

Thomas G. Higgins has identified the dilemmas as follows:

> [W]hen we independent public accountants report that financial statements are presented in conformity with "generally accepted accounting principles," we cannot be sure what we mean, because the expression "generally accepted accounting principles," has never been satisfactorily defined. . . . [T]hose who issue the financial statements on which we report, and those who use them, do not know what we mean either.[27]

This confusion has been mirrored by a Select Committee designated by The Council of the American Institute to study the opinions of the Accounting Principles Board. In its report the committee urged the board, "at the earliest possible time," to explain to the public the meaning of the terms of art used in its certificate: present fairly in accordance with generally accepted accounting principles. The report asks (without attempting an answer) just what the auditor means by this cliché.

> Is he saying: (1) that the statements are *fair* and in accordance with generally accepted accounting principles; or (2) that they are fair *because* they are in accordance with generally accepted accounting prin-

> ciples; or (3) that they are fair only *to the extent* that generally accepted accounting principles are fair; or (4) that whatever the generally accepted accounting principles may be, the *presentation* of them is fair?[28] [Emphasis in original.]

Since this report was promulgated a year after our research, our questionnaire did not include the fourth alternative interpretation of the auditor's certificate. Clearly, the committee's recommendations demonstrated that the confusion is pervasive even among the most sophisticated segment of the preparers as well as the sophisticated users of our financial statements.

In the light of the foregoing one is led to wonder how substantive and protective is the ring of insulation which Grady[29] saw in the independent opinion of the certified public accountant that the statements are fairly presented in accordance with generally accepted accounting principles. If the protective clause is incapable of definition the protection afforded by it can be seen to be ephemeral.

Some Results Bearing on the Presumed Four Cardinal Safeguards

In the quest for a common base of understanding regarding communications in accounting, consideration was given to the validity of the four conditions described by Savoie[30] as the four most important safeguards that "ensure a high degree of usefulness in published financial statements," to wit: those of consistency, disclosure, conservatism, integrity. In this pursuit the research sought to determine the extent to which the safeguards of consistency and conservatism were comprehended and generally accepted as common denominators for common understanding. (The transcendental virtue of integrity was deemed to be too abstract for effective probing through this questionnaire; the canon of disclosure will be considered in the subsequent chapters when such questions as: "What is disclosed?" "By whom?" "To whom?" and "With what degree of sophistication are these disclosures understood?" will be the subject of analysis.)

In any event, Question B–5(c) probed Savoie's principle of conservatism while Questions B–5(d), (e), and (f) his doctrine of consistency. The results of these probes are analyzed in Table 2:

TABLE 2

Percentage Distribution of Affirmative Responses
Regarding the Standards of Conservatism and Consistency

	Accounting Profession Category				
	Practitioners				
	"Big-Eight" Firms	Other Firms	Professors	Entire Category	Financial Community Category
Re Conservatism:					
5 (c) In the event that there is a doubt . . . the (alternative) that will show lesser earnings is to be selected.					
As Prevails at Present	11.6%	28.5%	52.4%	32.8%	18.1%
As Should Prevail.....	11.6	21.4	4.8	12.5	26.4
Re Consistency:					
5(d) More important than the particular principle selected is that the same principle be made applicable to all entities in the same industry.					
As Prevails at Present	18.4	21.4	4.8	14.1	34.7
As Should Prevail.....	53.3	64.2	38.1	51.6	62.5
5 (e) More important than the particular principle selected is that it be selected year-in and year-out.					
As Prevails at Present	41.7	85.6	80.9	60.9	58.4
As Should Prevail.....	70.8	100.0	61.9	71.9	68.1
5(f) The consistency rule assumes that companies will still be quite comparable because the turnover of items being accounted for tends to cancel out differences in method.					
As Prevails at Present	41.7	35.7	38.1	40.6	8.4
As Should Prevail.....	35.9	21.4	9.5	26.5	26.5

Source: Question B-5 (c), (d), (e) and (f) of the Questionnaire

These data demonstrate that the Savoie imperatives of conservatism and consistency cannot develop an effective consensus when subjected to a probe. Thus, Question 5(c) set forth a situation calling for the respondents' views on conservatism in accountancy, the doctrine which Savoie indicated as being "one of the oldest of underlying principles" and which is presumed by him to be "a comforting feature to most people who have a real interest in a business." The responses disclosed that only 18 per cent of the user category and 33 per cent of the profession recognized this comforting doctrine as now prevalent; only 26 per cent and 13 per cent of the two categories respectively indicated that this "oldest of underlying principles" should in fact prevail. When the profession was subdivided into the several groups of practitioners and professors there was an uneven response, again demonstrating a lack of consensus. Of the respondents from the major firms, 12 per cent recognized the applicability of the rule; 29 per cent of the other practitioners and 52 per cent of the professors so identified this "oldest" principle. As to whether this doctrine should prevail, we found 12 per cent, 21 per cent, and 5 per cent of the three groups, respectively, voting in the affirmative.

Questions 5 (d), (e), and (f) related to consistency; it should, however, be emphasized that the first two of these questions did not necessarily test the respondents' views of consistency as Savoie would comprehend it. These two questions pertained to *consistency between entities* in a particular industry (this is frequently referred to as comparability); and to *year-to-year consistency* for a particular entity. (Savoie's idea of consistency, as will be seen, was made the subject of the third of these questions, Question 5(f), explicitly.) Nevertheless, since the standards of consistency and comparability can be seen to overlap, it is appropriate at this point to note the results obtained from these first two questions also. Regarding intra-industry consistency (comparability), it is generally recognized that it *does not* prevail. Thus, there is something of a consensus in that only 35 per cent of the financial community and 14 per cent of the accounting profession categories indicated that it is the rule at present. (Subdividing the profession category indicates that 18 per cent of the major-firm respondents, 21 per cent of the other practitioners, and 5 per cent of the professors so asserted.) As to whether it *should* prevail, there is a marked tendency throughout for a shift in its favor; hence: 63 per cent of the financial community responded that it should be the rule, as did 52 per cent of the profession as a whole (53 per cent from the "Big-Eight" practitioners and 64 per cent of the other practitioners; but only 38 per cent of the professors thought that such a comparability rule should be established).

Regarding an internal consistency for the entity on a year-to-year basis, 58 per cent of the community and 61 per cent of the profession indicated that *it is* the standard, and 68 per cent and 72 per cent of the categories respectively thought that *it should be* the rule. It is significant to note that only 42 per cent of the "Big-Eight" respondents believed it to prevail currently (whereas 86 per cent of the other practitioners and 81 per cent of the professors so responded). As to whether it should be the rule: 71 per cent, 100 per cent, and 62 per cent of the three accounting groups respectively replied affirmatively.

It is to Question 5(f) that we turn to test the general acceptance of Savoie's safeguard, on his own terms. This question actually incorporated his assertions about the comparability and consistency coming about through the "turnover of items canceling out differences." Apparently, only 8 per cent of the users of the statements believed themselves thus comforted at present (and only 27 per cent thereof thought that they would in fact be put at ease by such a rule). Within the profession, 41 per cent of the category as a whole recognized this "balancing out" as now prevalent while only 27 per cent thought that it would be a good rule. Similarly, there were retrogressions, between the "is" and "should be," within each of the accounting groups analyzed herein; thus: from 42 per cent to 36 per cent for the major-firm respondents, 36 per cent to 21 per cent for the other practitioners, 38 per cent to 10 per cent for the professors.

It is to be emphasized at this point that our introduction of these data is not necessarily, nor principally, intended to express any disagreement with Savoie's views of what is right with accounting, nor with his views regarding the need for making haste slowly in effecting improvement in reporting standards. To the contrary: These data were here introduced essentially to demonstrate that there is an absence of a common understanding, that there is no consensus, even with respect to the supposed axiomatic, self-evident truths in accountancy presumed by the leaders within the profession.

This, then, was the principal thrust of this primary research: to determine whether there is a common understanding of the accounting function and the way in which it is being fulfilled. As has been demonstrated above, a consensus is absent both within the profession, and between the profession and the audience to which it is directing its communication, regarding such presumed basic underlying premises as those asserted by Savoie, and even more fundamentally, regarding the very hallmark of the audit function, i.e., the certificate associated with the statements. The communications process can thus be seen to be seriously deficient.

Conclusion

By way of a conclusion to this opening gambit and as a prologue for that which follows, it is our view that the research has confirmed that the language of accountancy has been most seriously confounded. Further, it is this confounding of our special language, coupled with the profession's announced determination to expand in dinosaurian fashion, which makes us seriously vulnerable to attack. Furthermore, the primary research and the collateral readings will be shown to have demonstrated a lack of a common understanding by the financial community and the accounting profession regarding the appropriateness of the auditor's involvement in the range of expanded services subsumed under the heading of "management services." This latter breakdown in communications will be shown to have a potentially adverse effect on the auditor's independence in the eyes of substantial numbers of the financial community and thereby put into jeopardy the profession's fulfillment of its traditional role, i.e., the attest function.

In various connections throughout the study there will be

shown to be an urgent need for the profession to move centripetally, rather than pursue its present centrifugal bent. This is because we believe that the solution lies in the profession's taking to heart the counsel of Père Teilhard to mankind generally, to recognize the need for an *"enroulement organique sur soi-même,"* a "convergent integration," to pursue (as Sir Julian Huxley urges) "more complex, and more integrated mental activity, which can guide the human species up the path of progress to higher levels of hominisation."[31]

In brief, and less metaphysically, we will be following in the path of Hermann Hesse's literary character, Siddhartha, who set out on a long quest in search of the ultimate answer to the enigma of man's role on earth. After a tortuous road he discovers that the answer was always within the self, and it is there that one is constrained to search for it.

2

"When *I* use a word," Humpty Dumpty tells Alice, "it means just what *I* choose it to mean—neither more nor less."

"The question is," said Alice, "whether you *can* make words mean so many different things."

"The question is," replied Humpty, "which is to be master—that's all."

Through the Looking Glass

The Basic Roadblock: The Gap in GAAP

In the initial chapter, communication was shown to be vital to all professional pursuits. While it was demonstrated to be essential to accountancy generally, it was shown to be especially significant in the fulfillment of its "attest" or audit function through which the profession discharges its responsibilities to third parties, to those who are the users of the financial statements to which the accountant has appended his opinion that the statements are "fairly presented."

It was for the purpose of testing the effectiveness of this accounting communication to various groups in the financial community regarding these financial statements that the primary research incidental to this work was undertaken; the data obtained therefrom are set forth in detail in Appendix C. As will be demonstrated below, a significant number of the questions related to the understanding by the financial community of the fundamental, special body of knowledge on which the accountant's dialogue with this community rests; this is the body of knowledge commonly referred to as "generally accepted accounting principles."

In brief, the questions relating to this phase of the study were intended to determine whether the "Keys to Successful Data Communications" set forth by the American Institute of CPAs Long-Range Objectives Committee had been met. These standards or "Keys" were described by them as follows:

> In any successful communication, a meeting of minds must exist between issuer and user as to the meaning of terms. Before there can be a meeting of minds in the communication of financial and other economic data, the following are among the conditions that must be satisfied:
>
> 1. The issuer and user of economic data must have an understanding as to standards for measurement and summarization.
> 2. The issuer must have the requisite knowledge and skills to carry out the antecedent steps leading up to, and to prepare, the communication.
> 3. There must be absence of bias in the communication (to a humanly feasible extent).
> 4. The communication must be intelligible to the user.[1]

Such a mutuality of understanding is patently essential if the profession is to merit the trust and confidence of the community; such a common understanding regarding the "meaning of terms" must precede the profession's expecting the community to recognize its claim as being a pursuit which "rests upon some branch of knowledge to which the professionals are privy by virtue of long study and by initiation and apprenticeship under masters already members of the profession." Only in that way will we satisfy the essence of the professional idea and claim that "we know better than others the nature of certain matters, and to know better than [its] clients what ails . . . their affairs."[2]

It is this very subject of the common comprehension (or the lack thereof) by the profession and the financial community, as to what are these generally accepted principles of accounting, which Andrew Barr described as the most basic problem confronting the profession.[3]

A Review of the Professional Literature Regarding the Gap

The existence of the "Gap in GAAP" was noted in many of

the references included in Chapter 1; clearly the expressions of Spacek, Savoie, Grady, Powell, Laeri and *The Wall Street Journal* to which reference was there made are all here also relevant. Further, a review of the literature in accountancy will demonstrate that the problem is not only of recent vintage. In introducing his *The Search For Accounting Principles,* Reed Storey wove together extracts from "A Statement of Objectives of the American Accounting Association" (vintage 1936), Maurice Stans' article "Accounting Weaknesses Which Inhibit Understanding of Free Enterprise" (1949), with Leonard Spacek's "Challenges to Public Accounting" (1948)—all of these extracts testifying to the fact that there is (in Spacek's words) "no general agreement as to the meaning of the phrase [in accordance with generally accepted accounting principles] or its applicability to the variety of situations in which it is used."[4]

Had he chosen to do so, Storey could have included in the warp and woof of his backdrop such classic references as "Accounting practices at present are based, in a large measure, upon the ethics and opinions of respectable accountants. . . . There is no unified body of opinion nor is there any official tribunal for the final determination of technical differences of opinion."[5]

"The directors have another powerful weapon," said Berle and Means; namely: "They have a large measure of control over the Company's income account. . . ." This weapon and control result from the fact that "accountants themselves have as yet failed to work out a series of standard rules."[6]

Passing along through time we have the Arthur Andersen "postulate" asserting that: "The public cannot permit the responsibility for reliable financial accounting to rest upon the initiative of individual accountants or of individual accounting firms or upon any particular part of the profession operating independently of the rest."[7]

And then we come to such recent jeremiads as Robert Anthony's opening gambit to his "showdown":

> The argument that accounting principles may end up eventually being prescribed by the SEC rests on two propositions:

1. If the American Institute of Certified Public Accountants fails in its present program for developing accounting principles, the Securities and Exchange Commission will act to develop these principles.
2. The AICPA effort is likely to fail.[8]

Professor Anthony's concern is mirrored by David Hawkins' view that: "Once more, the possibility of further government intervention in reporting matters is imminent, principally because of the accounting profession's inability to narrow the areas of differences in accounting principles. . . ." Professor Hawkins concluded his historical study by asserting that: "In any case, the historical evolution of acceptable standards of financial disclosure among American industrial firms is far from complete."[9]

And all of the foregoing is but prologue to the very heated controversy which raged at Boca Raton in early May, 1964, when the Council of the American Institute of CPAs debated a "white paper" previously approved by the Institute's executive committee intended to give greater and more definitive force and effect to the pronouncements of the Accounting Principles Board. (This controversy, revealing as it does the intensity of feeling generated by the subject of proliferating, if not tenuous, accounting principles, will be the subject of later consideration.)

In turn, this May, 1964, colloquy might well be considered to be a continuation, or a return bout, of the proceedings of the Institute held in Philadelphia during September, 1960. These earlier deliberations were described most dramatically by T. A. Wise in his compilation of articles on the accounting profession which had appeared in *Fortune* magazine; he there describes the intensity of the colloquy, generating much heat even with little light, regarding the nature of truth in accountancy and the manner of its pursuit and disclosure.[10]

As an aftermath of the 1964 Donnybrook a select Special Committee on Opinions of the Accounting Principles Board was designated by Council of the AICPA. Reference was heretofore made to the recommendation by this committee that the

Board consider the meaning of the auditor's certificate; in the same context the committee urged the Board, again at the earliest possible time, to consider: "What is meant by the expression 'generally accepted accounting principles'? How is 'generally' measured? What are 'accounting principles'? Where are they inscribed and by whom?" The committee then underscored the crucial nature of its recommendation, thus: "Until the profession deals with all these matters satisfactorily, first for itself and then for understanding by the consumer of its product, there will continue to be an awkward failure to communicate in a field where clear communication is vital."[11]

It is significant to note that this report of the Special Committee was promulgated some two months after the publication of Paul Grady's *Inventory* and yet the gnawing, fundamental questions indicated above are directed to the Accounting Principles Board and the profession generally. In taking note of the *Inventory* the committee observed that it is "a giant step forward" and that it does provide "a comprehensive statement of the accounting principles which appear to be generally accepted" and is "most of the raw material which the Board needs." But yet the questions asked by the committee remain—and they remain unanswered to anyone's satisfaction to the present.

That the *Inventory* must be less than a panacea is demonstrated by the series of alternatives catalogued in its Chapter 10,[12] which includes:

Transaction	No. of Alternatives
when revenue generally recognized	3
when revenue recognized for long-term contractors	2
accounting for unfunded pension cost	2
accounting for funded pension cost	3
charging of real and personal property taxes to income	8
treatment of tax vs. financial accounting divergencies	3
methods of depreciation	4

inventory methods	5
accounting for discounts	2
fixed asset acquisition	4
fixed asset construction	3
developments costs in extractive industries	3
etc.	

In all, the study lists thirty-one separate kinds of transactions with an aggregate of eighty different alternatives.

Nor is Grady chagrined by this enumeration and the absence of uniformity which it implies. To the contrary, he asserts that: "Members of the Board, in common with most experienced accountants, recognize that diversity in accounting among independent business entities is a basic fact of life."[13] He acknowledges that: "There is a minority view which urges uniformity in accounting as the panacea for all accounting and reporting deficiencies," but Grady is not moved because he then cites various factors to indicate the "unreality" of the suggestions and expectations of this minority.

This very retelling of the continuing controversy regarding the nature and substance of our generally accepted accounting principles, and the realization that during the third of a century that this controversy has continued the accounting profession has survived (better still, has moved to even higher levels of affluence and of general felicity), might well induce a sense of apathy. We might even brush the subject off with a quip like: *"Plus ça change, plus c'est la même chose."* This might in fact appropriately describe the attitude of Leonard M. Savoie, who takes cognizance of the controversy and counsels that we move only very carefully, and only with deliberate speed. Thus, Savoie recognizes the existence of major areas of divergence in accounting but then concludes:

> After one analyzes each item [of divergence] and then steps back and looks at the hypothetical example as a whole, he cannot help being impressed by the ease with which differing accounting methods among companies can be illustrated. . . . However, this country to date seems convinced that the welfare of its people is better served by the progress which comes from

> the interplay of a large number of diverse individual judgments than centralized decisions arrived at by the few.[14]

Earlier in that article Savoie had counseled caution in improving accounting principles and practices especially because the "managerial rights" of the owners and managers of business enterprises "actually are at stake."[15] Also among those urging a more deliberate approach to change we find the late Weldon Powell,[16] the first Chairman of the Institute's Accounting Principles Board. (It might be noted in passing that the relatively sanguine attitude which Powell thus recently expressed is not readily reconcilable with the sense of urgency manifested by him several years earlier when speaking before the 1960 meeting of the American Accounting Association.)

Recent Criticisms Because of the Gap in GAAP

But this sanguine air cannot continue for long; the indictments against the present relatively amorphous state of our underlying body of knowledge, our generally accepted accounting principles, are coming forth so loudly, and from so many important sources, that any sense of complacency fostered by the historical retelling should well be exorcised. These indictments come from both within and without the profession.

First from within the profession itself, we have John L. Hennessy telling us that the profession might be faced with legislative action setting up rules and regulations requiring conformity if "the public, stockholders, labor unions and Congress understood the wide differences that presently exist in accounting."[17] Similarly, Professor Drebin traces the "cash flow" controversy to the source of confusion on the part of the financial community, that is: "information anemia." The only hope for this real ailment is "to eradicate the germ that causes the dread disease: inconsistent accounting practice."[18]

In his May, 1966, presidential address to Council of the American Institute, Robert M. Trueblood used his "privilege of the floor" to talk "quite personally—on a subject which I know all of us regard as extremely important." His remarks took notice of this gap and the intensity of criticism as follows:

> For the past few years I've been concerned, as you have surely been, about the matter of accounting principles; about the questions and criticisms appearing in the press; about the doubts which such comments must arouse among people outside our profession; and about the possible divisive influences which could develop within the profession over the philosophical issues which seem to be of concern.[19]

Then from outside the profession we have indictments like the following:

A financial analyst warns: "Unless greater comparability is accomplished, it is probable that the demand for action to force uniformity will increase. Such an eventuality would certainly prove distasteful to most accountants." He recognizes that complete uniformity cannot be obtained, but "it should be possible to minimize inter-company variations."[20]

And in a front page article in *The Wall Street Journal* captioned "Bookkeeping Battle: SEC Auditors Drive for More Uniformity in Corporate Reports," we are told that variations in financial statements "are drawing increasing criticism." The article then observes: "Even some accountants confess they get confused at times. It's getting so bad you have to hire other experts to help you understand financial statements says one of the country's leading certified public accountants."[21]

That the confusion regarding the profession's underlying body of theory, its generally accepted accounting principles, has become a matter of concern for our Congress is evidenced by the questions asked of Chairman William L. Cary of the SEC, by Congressman Staggers, as Chairman of the Subcommittee on Commerce and Finance of the Committee on Interstate and Foreign Commerce, in connection with the bills pending in early 1964 before the Congress seeking added investor protection. As reported in the transcript of the hearings, Congressman Staggers asked:

> Can you file with this committee setting forth what you consider to be the areas of accounting where alternative practices could produce materially different

> results under generally accepted accounting principles? [And] if you would, with your conclusions as to the significance of each such area and with the reasons why you consider that investors who are considering and comparing various companies are adequately protected by your acceptance of these alternative practices.[22]

(It is significant that the aforementioned Report of the Proceedings then discloses that Andrew Barr, the Chief Accountant of the SEC, entered a demurrer to the second question reported above. So it is that he advised his chairman that while they could supply the committee with the examples, the cases, the situations, where there are divergencies, they would find it difficult to measure the impact of the divergence. Chairman Cary indicated that they would do their best but "cannot promise to do a very satisfactory job on that second phase." It might well be asked preliminarily that if the Chairman of the SEC and his Chief Accountant "cannot . . . do a very satisfactory job" in evaluating the significance of alternative accounting practices then who can or should do such an essential job satisfactorily?)

Later, when speaking before the Financial Executives Institute, Chairman Cary counseled the accounting profession to move toward the narrowing of differences in alternative principles. He manifested an understanding of the dilemmas which confront the profession; nevertheless his words were unmistakably firm. He acknowledged that the question of uniformity in accounting principles was controversial; he went on to recognize that there were limitations on accounting, "that absolute certainty is a chimera—impossible to achieve." Nevertheless, Cary observes (after first referring to the remarks by his predecessor, Judge Jerome Frank, on this question):

> Despite any difficulties, you and we should direct our efforts toward accelerating the move toward uniformity. At the same time, we should strive to make our disclosures more meaningful so that differences in accounting treatment are clearly brought out and

better comparison of companies is possible.[23]

These words of friendly counsel to the profession were preceded by the assertion that the government does have the power to set the rules of accounting; and advancing the carrot (to avoid the stick) Cary tells the profession that we can help in "preventing the encroachment of government by participating directly in steps towards agreement upon accounting principles."

But most recently Cary's successor related a circumstance where the stick could not be avoided. When speaking before the Financial Analysts Federation, SEC Chairman Manuel F. Cohen cited the example of the Commission's Accounting Release No. 102 to illustrate the way in which stronger leadership by the SEC is being asserted in order to goad the profession forward toward the goal of uniformity. This release related to the proper method of reporting deferred income taxes arising from installment sales. Cohen gives us this background:

> At the time the release was issued, no fewer than four different reporting methods were used by companies for which the item was of considerable importance. Some treated it as a current liability. Others classified it as a long-term liability. . . .
>
> The American Institute of Certified Public Accountants had not ignored the problem but had up to then been unable to resolve it. Without going into detail, I can say that the problem was studied and restudied; suggested opinions were sent to committee and resubmitted to committee. Another year-end was approaching, and the diversity of treatment seemed bound to continue. There were two additional reasons for Commission action. One was a formal "Petition" by a leading accounting firm, which recited the several ways in which the deferred tax item was being reported and requested that the Commission issue a release requiring consistency in treatment. The other was a belief that some companies, put at a disadvantage when compared with other companies

> reporting deferred taxes differently, were about to change their reporting methods, and the Commission wanted to ensure that change, if any, would be for the better.
>
> A formal expression of opinion by the Commission seemed called for, and we obliged.[24]

Lest this precedent become the hobgoblin of the profession the Chairman again lets us smell the carrot:

> Although Accounting Series Release No. 102 was used to resolve one problem of uniformity, I do not believe it will be necessary for us to use that device with great frequency—although the option is always open to us. The extent to which action on our part is required will depend in large measure on the vigor and determination of the Accounting Principles Board of the American Institute of Certified Public Accountants, which has the principal responsibility of defining accounting principles to be used in financial reporting.[25]

It is clear, then, that many persons who are important to the promulgation of financial statements or their use in vital decision making have expressed their concern in more or less urgent terms over the confusion which prevails presently regarding the nature and substance of our underlying body of knowledge, our generally accepted accounting principles. To the extent that this confusion regarding the special language of our profession prevails, then the standards for successful data communication urged by John L. Carey could not be met. If our very language is amorphous or ephemeral, then there could not be the "meeting of minds [which] must exist between issuer and user [of the financial statements] as to the meaning of terms."

The Gap in GAAP as Disclosed by Our Study

How does our research furnish the empirical data bearing on the problem under consideration in this chapter? It is the "C" series of questions to which we turn to discern the extent to which there is justification for the present concern about the lack of uniformity in accounting principles and the inimical impact this may have on the effectiveness of accounting communication to those who are entitled to know (and who are generally presumed to know). It is in this series that the questionnaire sets forth:

> [V]arious accounting transactions and business events in areas which are now considered to be the subject of significant study by the accounting profession. While the questions in this section are, of necessity, technical in nature, they are not designed to test [the respondent's] technical background in accountancy. Instead, they are intended to help ascertain whether the financial community shares the concern of the accounting profession regarding these areas; further, these questions should help to determine whether the profession has effectively communicated the financial and accounting implications of these transactions and events to this community.

The responses to this series of questions (i.e., Questions C-1 through C-15) have been summarized in Appendix C so as to show the affirmative and negative responses from both the financial community and accounting profession categories, as to whether the accounting treatment accorded the particular transaction is deemed to be in accordance with generally accepted accounting principles, and whether it ought to be so deemed.

Because the frame of reference for this study was to evaluate the effectiveness of communication rather than to judge the respondent's technical knowledge of accounting principles and practice, no attempt will here be made to compare the various alternatives suggested by the questions with what may have been reflected by published financial statements. Instead, for present purposes, the responses will be analyzed to determine whether there is the meeting of minds between issuer and user as to the meaning of terms so as to permit an effective dialogue to occur.

For the particular purposes of this chapter there are included herewith, as Table 3, the data summarizing the *affirmative responses only* to each of the "C" series of questions tabulated for the two principal categories of respondents. While these data are consistent with those shown in Appendix C, Table 3 also discloses separately such affirmative responses from the academic sector of the accounting profession category, the practitioners with the so-called "Big-Eight" firms, and from practitioners with other firms within the profession category.

Table 3 follows:

TABLE 3

Percentage of Affirmative Responses Regarding Alternatives of Accounting for Selected Business Transactions

In this section various accounting transactions and business events will be set forth. In each case various alternatives for financial statement presentation are indicated. You are than asked with respect to each such alternative:

(A) Whether you believe the alternative indicated is in accordance with "generally accepted accounting principles" (GAAP), and

(B) Whether you believe the alternative indicated should be in accordance with such principles.

		PERCENTAGE RESPONDING AFFIRMATIVELY					
		Accounting Profession Category					Financial Community
		Practitioners					
		Big Eight	Other Firms	Combined	Professors	Entire Category	Entire Category
Frequencies:		(17)	(14)	(31)	(21)	(64)	(72)
C-1 The corporation has realized a very substantial and extraordinary gain from the liquidation of an investment. This gain is shown:							
a) On the income statement as a part of the corporation's income for the year	A*	29.5	21.5	25.9	28.6	25.0	23.7
	B*	23.6	21.5	22.6	23.8	23.5	9.8
b) On the income statement, but only after the income for the year is determined	A	94.2	78.6	87.1	90.5	89.1	72.3
	B	76.6	85.7	80.6	76.2	78.1	77.8
c) Not shown on the income statement at all	A	58.9	42.9	51.6	80.9	57.8	20.9
	B	41.3	14.3	29.0	23.8	25.0	26.5

*A—indicates response to subpart (A) to this question; i.e., whether respondent believed the alternative indicated is in accordance with "GAAP".

*B—indicates response to subpart (B); i.e., whether respondent believed the alternative should be in such accord.

Source: Responses to Series C Questions of the Questionnaire.

		PERCENTAGE RESPONDING AFFIRMATIVELY					
		Accounting Profession Category					Financial Community Category
		Practitioners					
		Big Eight	Other Firms	Combined	Professors	Entire Category	
C-2 The corporation has a substantial loss for the year: a) This loss is reduced by any tax refund to which it is entitled by reason of the carry-back of such loss	A*	94.2	92.9	93.5	71.4	82.8	73.6
	B*	88.4	92.9	90.3	47.6	75.0	69.4
b) A carry-back is not available; however, the reported loss is reduced by reason of the fact that the corporation expects to have taxable income in the future (to which the loss could be carried forward)	A	11.8	0	6.4	14.4	7.8	5.6
	B	17.7	14.3	16.2	33.4	25.0	7.0
C-3 The corporation has very substantial earnings during the current year. However, no income taxes are required to be paid this year because of a substantial loss carry-forward. a) The current year's income is stated without any provision for income tax	A	100.0	100.0	100.0	71.5	87.6	69.4
	B	70.7	78.6	74.2	38.1	61.0	54.1
b) The current year's income is reduced by the amount of tax which would otherwise have been payable (and the tax being saved is credited to earned surplus)	A	5.9	28.6	16.2	52.4	29.8	19.5
	B	29.5	28.6	29.1	42.8	36.0	39.0
C-4 Stock options have been granted to an executive entitling him to purchase shares at 100 (when they are worth 100) exercisable at any time within five years. The option is exercised when the shares are selling for $140. a) The $40 differential is additional compensation and is deducted as a cost on the income statement for the year when the option is exercised	A	5.9	7.2	6.5	23.8	12.6	4.2
	B	17.7	42.9	29.1	38.1	29.7	16.7
b) The option is valued by a "Put and Call" option dealer and is deducted as a cost of the year when the option is granted	A	5.9	14.3	9.7	23.8	15.7	0
	B	17.7	28.6	22.6	38.1	26.6	4.2
c) While the option is deemed to be a method of compensating the executive, it is nevertheless properly ignored in the determination of income	A	88.4	64.3	77.4	81.0	76.6	57.0
	B	35.4	35.8	35.5	19.0	34.4	55.5
d) In order to prevent dilution of the corporation's stock the corporation goes into the market place and buys its shares at 140 (which it then resells to the executive at 100). The $40 differential is then shown as a cost for the year (thereby reducing its income)	A	17.7	42.9	29.0	23.8	28.2	20.9
	B	47.2	71.5	58.1	33.3	46.6	29.3

* See legend at bottom of first page of this table.

		PERCENTAGE RESPONDING AFFIRMATIVELY					
		Accounting Profession Category					Financial Community Category
		Practitioners				Entire Category	
		Big Eight	Other Firms	Combined	Professors		
C-5 This question relates to the problem of accounting for long-term leases.							
a) Whenever the circumstances indicate that a long-term lease is (by its nature or terms) essentially equivalent to a purchase of the property, the transaction is required to be shown as such a purchase (with the related liability disclosed)	A*	82.5	92.9	87.1	61.9	71.9	19.4
	B*	100.0	92.9	96.8	90.5	89.1	55.6
b) Such an accounting treatment (i.e., as though it were a purchase) is especially prevalent where it is apparent that the leasing (rather than actual purchase) was determined upon in order to avoid showing a debt in the balance sheet	A	41.3	85.7	61.3	9.5	34.5	15.3
	B	58.9	78.6	67.8	61.8	59.4	44.4
c) This treatment (i.e., as though it were a purchase) is particularly urgent where various debt restriction covenants are contained in bond indentures (and where the "purchase" might indicate a breach of these covenants)	A	41.3	78.6	58.0	28.6	39.1	16.7
	B	53.0	78.6	64.5	62.0	56.3	52.8
d) This treatment (i.e., as though it were a purchase) is particularly urgent where it is apparent to the auditor that the rentals in the early years are especially reduced in order to permit greater income to be shown in these early years	A	41.3	64.3	51.6	14.3	32.3	11.1
	B	70.7	64.3	67.7	52.4	55.7	50.0
e) This treatment (i.e., as though it were a purchase) is particularly urgent where it is apparent to the auditor that the rentals in the early years are especially high in order to permit a reduction in income in these earlier years (and correspondingly greater amounts in the later years)	A	41.3	64.3	51.6	14.3	34.4	9.7
	B	70.7	64.3	67.7	57.2	35.4	52.2
f) Regardless of the manner of accounting treatment, the rental for the ensuing year is required to be shown as a current liability (just as the ensuing year's debt amortization would be thus shown)	A	5.9	21.5	12.9	38.1	25.0	25.0
	B	35.4	42.9	38.7	90.4	57.8	57.0
g) This reflection of the current liability is especially urgent where the auditor sees that the working capital ratios would be vitally affected by such an inclusion of additional current debt	A	0	35.8	16.1	19.0	18.8	19.4
	B	29.5	42.9	35.5	61.9	45.4	52.7

* See legend at bottom of first page of this table.

		PERCENTAGE RESPONDING AFFIRMATIVELY					
		Accounting Profession Category					Financial Community Category
		Practitioners				Entire Category	
		Big Eight	Other Firms	Combined	Professors		
C-6 An important silver producer carries its inventories of metals on the Last-in, First-out (LIFO) basis. These inventories aggregate $120 million as of the close of 1963.							
a) Inasmuch as there had been a very precipitous rise in silver prices during the year 1963, the market values of the inventories at the beginning and end of the year are required to be shown	A*	11.8	0	6.5	0	6.3	19.4
	B*	70.7	28.6	51.7	81.0	62.6	59.7
b) Assuming that the silver is really worth $250 million the management can, in its sole discretion, realize income of $130 million (or any portion thereof), subject, of course, to the applicable income taxes. The income so realized would be included in the annual income statement	A	82.5	35.8	61.3	61.9	65.6	30.5
	B	47.2	21.5	35.5	42.8	45.3	23.6
c) If management determined that it desired earnings of $4.50 per share but saw the corporation realizing only $4.00 from operations otherwise, it could dispose of enough of its silver inventories so as to produce the additional 50¢ per share. The income for the year would then be stated at $4.50 per share	A	94.2	78.6	87.1	95.2	85.1	45.9
	B	53.0	64.3	58.1	42.8	51.6	40.3
C-7 This question also relates to the Last-in, First-out (LIFO) method of inventory valuation and assumes that price levels are increasing.							
a) The balance sheet of a company which carries its inventories on the LIFO basis is more conservatively stated than its competitors' which use the First-in, First-out (FIFO) basis	A	94.2	78.6	87.1	85.7	85.9	68.1
	B	58.9	57.2	58.1	28.6	46.9	64.9
b) The annual income statement of a company which carries its inventories on a LIFO basis is more conservatively stated than its competitors' which use the FIFO basis	A	94.2	78.6	87.1	81.0	84.5	66.7
	B	58.9	57.2	58.1	38.1	50.0	62.5

* See legend at bottom of first page of this table.

PERCENTAGE RESPONDING AFFIRMATIVELY

		Accounting Profession Category					Financial Community Category
		Practitioners					
		Big Eight	Other Firms	Combined	Professors	Entire Category	
C-8 This question relates to the accounting problems of the oil and gas industry.							
a) Where the corporation incurs costs for Intangible Drilling Costs of productive oil and gas properties these costs are charged to expense in the year when incurred	A*	88.4	71.5	80.7	95.2	84.3	44.4
	B*	17.7	21.5	19.4	23.8	23.4	44.5
b) These costs are entirely capitalized and then amortized over the expected productivity resulting from these costs	A	82.5	71.5	77.5	76.1	59.5	45.8
	B	53.0	71.5	61.3	66.7	43.8	44.4
c) These costs are first to be reduced by any immediate tax saving resulting from the cost, the excess is then amortized over the expected productive life of the facility	A	76.6	21.5	51.6	57.1	51.6	16.7
	B	64.8	28.6	48.4	38.1	39.2	25.0
C-9 In order to acquire the entire capital stock of the S corporation which owns a very valuable patent (carried on the S books at $10,000) and nothing else, the P corporation issues 1,000 shares of its $1 par value stock which then has a market price of $40 a share (hence an aggregate value of $40,000.							
a) In accounting for the transaction on the consolidated balance sheet of P, the patents thus acquired will be carried at $10,000 (i.e., their book value on the S books)	A	70.7	35.8	54.9	66.7	56.3	36.2
	B	41.3	50.0	45.2	0	23.5	34.8
b) In accounting for the transaction as above, future operations will be charged with amortization of patent cost of $10,000	A	70.7	42.9	58.1	71.4	61.0	34.8
	B	41.3	42.9	42.0	9.5	26.5	37.5
c) This accounting for $10,000 would be possible for P even though, in order to avoid any dilution of its shares, P went out into the open market and bought in 1,000 shares at $40 (hence for $40,000)	A	58.9	42.9	51.7	71.4	48.9	19.5
	B	23.6	35.8	29.0	0	15.6	18.1
d) In all future comparative financial statements, the previous year's operations will be restated so as to reflect the combined operations of both P and S during these previous years	A	70.7	42.9	58.0	38.1	48.4	38.9
	B	53.0	50.0	51.6	33.3	42.2	47.1
C-10 This question relates to problems of consolidated financial statements.							
a) The C company is a major producer of silver, copper and other metals. It owns a "more than 50%" interest in the Z corporation which owns major mines in Australia. The financial statements of C and Z are undoubtedly to be presented on a consolidated basis	A	41.3	28.6	35.5	47.6	40.6	22.2
	B	70.7	57.2	64.4	76.2	65.6	41.6
b) The D corporation, engaged in food retailing, owns 100% of the outstanding shares of T (a trading stamp company). The operations of D and T are undoubtedly to be presented on a consolidated basis	A	53.0	71.5	61.3	47.6	51.6	47.2
	B	76.6	92.9	73.9	76.1	75.0	68.0

* See legend at bottom of first page of this table.

PERCENTAGE RESPONDING AFFIRMATIVELY

		Accounting Profession Category					Financial Community Category
		Practitioners					
		Big Eight	Other Firms	Combined	Professors	Entire Category	
C-11 The A corporation desires to obtain for itself competent management now with the X corporation. To accomplish this result A exchanges 100,000 of its shares (representing a 25% interest in itself) for all of the X corporation shares and thereupon obtains this management together with inventory worth $100,000 (but with a book value on the books of X of $15,000). At the time of the exchange the shares of A are quoted on a stock exchange at 7 (hence $700,000 in the aggregate for the 100,000 shares).							
a) This transaction will be reflected on a consolidated statement of A so as to show: Inventories $100,000; Goodwill (the amount presumed to represent the value of the management taken over) 600,000; Total (the amount equal to the value of the shares given up by A) 700,000	A*	58.9	57.2	58.1	76.2	65.6	37.6
	B*	53.0	50.0	51.6	76.2	61.0	44.5
b) The Goodwill shown above will undoubtedly be written off over the years when the newly acquired management will be making its contribution to the consolidated income	A	23.6	21.5	22.6	47.7	32.9	40.3
	B	41.3	35.8	38.7	66.7	48.5	59.7
c) In all future comparative financial statements, the previous years' operations will be restated so as to reflect the combined operations of A and X	A	35.4	57.2	45.1	19.1	37.5	38.9
	B	47.2	57.2	51.6	38.1	48.5	50.0
C-12 Oil company B has a 50% interest in petrochemical company Y which uses B's product for the manufacture of various consumer and industrial commodities.							
a) 50% of profits earned by Y will be reflected year-by-year in the B financial statements	A	64.8	50.0	58.0	57.2	56.3	26.4
	B	88.4	50.0	70.9	81.0	71.8	40.2
b) It may be that B management will determine that it will pick up its share of the profits only when it receives a dividend from Y	A	94.2	92.9	93.6	95.1	92.3	65.3
	B	35.4	57.2	45.2	19.0	34.4	56.9
c) It may be (assuming that there are no significant dividends paid over the years) that the B management might determine to reflect the bulk of its share of Y income in a particular year through a disposition of its interest in Y	A	82.5	78.6	80.7	85.6	78.1	50.1
	B	29.5	50.0	38.7	23.8	36.0	37.6
d) A very substantial gain on the disposition or liquidation by B of its investment in Y would be credited directly to B's earned surplus (and not to the year's income)	A	76.6	71.5	74.2	85.7	78.1	55.5
	B	23.6	57.2	38.7	38.1	42.2	54.2

PERCENTAGE RESPONDING AFFIRMATIVELY

		Accounting Profession Category					Financial Community Category
		Practitioners					
		Big Eight	Other Firms	Combined	Professors	Entire Category	
C-13 This question relates to the problems of accounting for pension cost.							
a) Corporation E has an established pension plan entitling its employees to a stipulated pension on attaining retirement age. Assuming that E does not have a prefunded pension plan, no charge need be made to annual operations until it is called upon to make payments to retired employees	A*	64.8	28.6	48.5	62.0	51.6	27.7
	B*	11.8	14.3	12.9	9.6	11.0	19.4
b) Assuming that F does have a prefunded pension plan with some discretion allowed to the corporation in making contributions under the plan. The amount charged to annual operations will be equal to the amount which management determined to fund that year	A	70.7	50.0	61.3	61.9	64.1	59.7
	B	17.7	21.5	19.3	14.3	20.3	38.9
c) Because the pension fund referred to in (b) above will have earnings and capital appreciation, the annual charge to operations for F's pension cost will be affected by such earnings, etc., of the fund	A	88.4	64.3	77.4	85.7	78.2	47.2
	B	76.6	71.5	74.2	76.2	71.9	50.0
d) Company G has no pension plan but is in an industry where most other major firms do have such a plan. Company G's operations will be charged with an amount equal to what the pension cost would be if the company had a plan consistent with that common in the industry	A	5.9	0	3.2	0	3.2	0
	B	17.7	7.2	12.9	4.8	9.5	13.9
C-14 During 1958 company H acquired an extensive new plant at a cost of $100,000 which had an estimated life of ten years. The replacement value of this plant is now considered to be $200,000 (new). Price levels have increased by 50% between 1958 and the present. The company uses the declining-balance method of depreciation for income tax purposes. The depreciation charged on the 1963 financial statements will be:	A	94.2	92.9	93.7	95.2	89.0	40.3
a) $10,000 (one-tenth of the cost)	B	70.7	92.9	83.8	38.1	64.1	36.2
b) $6,600 (the amount deductible in 1963 for tax purposes)	A	76.6	85.7	80.7	85.6	79.6	55.6
	B	53.0	71.5	61.3	33.3	51.5	48.6
c) $20,000 (one-tenth of the $200,000 replacement value)	A	0	0	0	4.8	3.2	2.8
	B	5.9	0	3.2	14.3	12.5	8.3
d) $15,000 ($10,000 multiplied by 150%—the current price index in relation to 1958)	A	0	0	0	4.8	3.2	2.8
	B	23.6	14.3	19.4	42.8	28.2	12.5
C-15 Company J is engaged in aircraft manufacture. It expended $500,000 in costs for Research and Development in the development of a prototype of a new supersonic aircraft. Company J will:							
a) Charge this $500,000 against the current year's operations	A	82.5	57.2	70.9	90.6	79.7	48.7
	B	47.2	35.8	41.9	28.6	40.7	50.1
b) Capitalize this $500,000 and amortize it over a period of years	A	88.4	64.3	77.5	85.7	78.2	50.0
	B	58.9	42.9	51.6	61.9	54.7	43.0
c) Capitalize this $500,000 and write if off when the aircraft design produces revenue	A	76.6	92.9	83.8	76.3	79.7	36.1
	B	70.7	85.7	77.4	71.5	73.5	30.5

The Series of Graphs Developed from the Data Regarding the Gap

From the data in Table 3 there was developed a series of graphs (included in Appendix E as Figures 1 through 10) designed to demonstrate the degree of relationships of the responses received from the Series "C" questions. Figures 1, 5, and 9 each charted the relationships between the responses from two populations to the first probe of these questions, i.e., whether they believed the alternative *to be* in accord with generally accepted accounting principles. Figures 2, 6, and 10 each charted the relationships between two populations of respondents for their answers to the second probe of these questions, i.e., whether they believed the alternatives suggested *should be* in accord with such principles.

The remaining figures numbered 3, 4, 7, and 8 are each for a single population and show the shifts or divergence between that population's responses to the "it is" and "should be" probes.

Specifically, and in greater detail, the relationships shown by these ten graphs are the following:

> *Figure 1,* reflects the relationships between the affirmative responses received from the financial community and accounting profession categories to the first probe of the Series "C" questions, to wit: "Whether you believe the alternative indicated is in accordance with generally accepted accounting principles."
> *Figure 2,* reflects the relationships between the same categories with respect to the second probe of the Series "C" questions, to wit: "Whether you believe the alternative indicated should be in accordance with such principles."
> *Figure 3,* shows the relationships between affirmative responses received from the financial community category to the first probe of the Series "C" questions (whether the alternative is in accordance with GAAP), with responses received from the same category to the second probe thereof (whether the alternative should be in accordance with GAAP).

Figure 4, reflects the same relationships as Figure 3, except that they are here shown for the accounting profession category.
Figure 5, shows the same set of relationships reflected by figure 1 (i.e., the "is it" probe), except that the populations here being compared are the accounting practitioner and accounting professor groups (both of which are included in the accounting profession category).
Figure 6, shows the same relationships reflected by Figure 2 (i.e., the "should it be" probe) except that here again the populations being compared are the practitioner and professor of accounting groups.
Figure 7: This graph is consistent with Figures 3 and 4, excepting that the relationships between the "is it" and "should it be" responses are here being shown for the accounting practitioner group.
Figure 8: Correspondingly, this graph shows the "is" and "should be" affirmative responses for the professor of accounting groups.
Figure 9, reflects the relationships between the affirmative responses received from practitioners with the national ("Big-Eight") firms and such responses received from other practitioners with reference to the first probe (i.e., "is it in accord with GAAP"). This graph is consistent with Figures 1 and 5.
Figure 10, reflects the relationship between the affirmative responses received from the practitioners with such "Big-Eight" firms and from other practitioners, with reference to the second ("should it be") probe. This graph is, accordingly, consistent with Figures 2 and 6.

A 45° curve (solid line) has been superimposed on each graph; any point along this curve would reflect agreement in the affirmative responses received with respect to the particular question from the two populations being measured (or for the two probes from the same population as the case may be). The extent of departure from this 45° curve would measure the degree of divergence of one population from another (or where appropriate, measure the divergence between the "it is" and "it should be" responses from a single population).

In addition, broken lines paralleling this 45° curve have been drawn to measure "20 percentage point" deviations from the aforementioned "identity of agreement" curve. For purposes of the analysis of the graphs and the underlying data any deviation or divergence in excess of such "20 percentage points" (and therefore causing the relationship to fall outside these "broken lines") was presumed to be a "major divergence."

Inferences Drawn from These Graphs

From Figures 1, 5, and 9: The specific major divergencies noted by these three graphs (each of which charted the relationship between two populations to the "Is it in accord with GAAP" probe) have been described in conjunction with each of the graphs.

The degree of such divergence may be recognized from the following:

Figure 1, reflected the responses from the financial community as contrasted with those from the accounting profession category as a whole—divergencies were recognized in twenty-four instances out of the fifty cases presented.

Figure 5, reflected the responses from the accounting practitioner groups as contrasted with the professors of accountancy, and showed twelve major divergencies in the fifty cases suggested by the questions.

Figure 9, reflected the responses from the practitioners with the national firms (i.e., the "Big-Eight" firms) contrasted with those from the other practitioners; such major divergencies were discerned in nineteen cases out of the fifty.

These data and the graphs derived therefrom do confirm the serious breakdown in communication between the users of the financial statements and the accounting profession which plays such an important role in their promulgation. This breakdown is especially apparent from the fact that there were twenty-four major divergencies (out of a possible fifty) between the financial community and the accounting profession categories charted on Figure 1, as to whether the accounting treatments suggested by the Series "C" questions were in accord with generally accepted accounting principles. Evidences of such a breakdown might well have been anticipated by the responses to Question B-1 (which will be considered in the digression which follows).

A Digression to Consider the Responses to Question B-1

Among the "Keys to Successful Data Communications" determined by the Long-Range Objectives Committee, and set forth at the beginning of this chapter, we were told that the "communication must be intelligible to the user" and that accordingly "a meeting of minds must exist between issuer and user as to the meaning of terms." Such a meeting of minds, specifically, must extend to a common understanding "as to standards for measurement and summarization."[26] This meeting of minds, this condition precedent to the effective discharge of the attest function, was presumed to prevail, because the committee concluded that "the attest function is being discharged, on a constantly widening scale."[27]

If what the committee thus determined does in fact prevail then it must be because the committee was satisfied that the users were knowledgeable with respect to these "standards for measurement and summarization" which undoubtedly would embrace our generally accepted accounting principles. That the committee may well have been mistaken is indicated by the divergencies reflected by Figure 1 (among others); also indicative of the inappropriateness of the committee's conclusion are the answers furnished by the respondents to Question B-1 of the questionnaire. Here the respondents were asked whether, in their views, the body of generally accepted accounting principles was reasonably well known to various important user groups in our economic society. The results obtained from this question, to the extent herein significant, are summarized in the following Table 4:

TABLE 4

Opinions of Respondents As to Whether They Believe the Body of GAAP to Be Reasonably Well Known to Selected "User" Groups in the Economic Society

	PERCENTAGE RESPONDING AFFIRMATIVELY	
	From the Financial Community	**From the Accounting Profession**
To "User" Groups		
f) Certified (sic) Financial Analysts	70.8%	54.7%
g) Investment Advisers generally	40.3	17.2
h) Individual Investors generally	4.2	3.1
i) Accountants with the SEC	93.1	93.8
j) Economists generally	23.6	4.7
k) Governmental Personnel responsible for . . . fiscal policy	40.3	15.6
l) Governmental Personnel with regulatory agencies	40.3	28.0
m) "Customers'Men" with stock brokerage firms	2.8	1.6

Source: Responses to Question B-1 of the Questionnaire

Clearly, if the attest function is being discharged, and on a constantly widening scale, then in the eyes of the accounting profession it must be to groups other than investment advisers generally, to economists, to government personnel responsible for fiscal policy and those with regulatory agencies. This follows from the fact that only 17 per cent, 5 per cent, 16 per cent, and 28 per cent of the respondents from the profession asserted that the body of principles was known to these user groups, respectively. Nor could this attest function be presumed to be satisfied on any scale (constantly widening or otherwise) for the individual investors and the customers' men who are presumed to guide the masses toward the astute investment decision. This last conclusion follows from the fact that only

3 per cent of the accounting profession thought the investor was thus knowledgeable, and fewer than 2 per cent attributed such wisdom to their apparently "blind guides."

So it may well be that the divergencies reflected by Figure 1 might well have been expected. In brief, the lack of knowledge regarding the standards for measurement and summarization in accountancy, the lack of understanding of our body of generally accepted accounting principles, frustrates any meeting of minds which is synonymous with effective communication.

Inferences Drawn from These Graphs (continued)

We return now to the consideration of the inferences which may be fairly drawn from the graphs developed from the responses to the Series "C" questions.

> *From Figures 2, 6, 10:* The specific major divergencies noted by these three graphs (each of which charted the relationship between two populations to the "Should it be in accord with GAAP" probe) have been described in conjunction with the respective graphs.

The aggregate number of divergencies thus defined were:

> *Figure 2,* reflected the responses from the financial community as contrasted with those from the accounting profession category as a whole—divergencies were recognized in eleven instances out of the fifty cases presented.
>
> *Figure 6,* reflected the responses from the accounting practitioner groups as contrasted with the professors of accountancy, and showed sixteen major divergencies in the fifty cases suggested by the questions.
>
> *Figure 10,* reflected the responses from the practitioners with the "Big-Eight" firms contrasted with those from the other practitioners; such major divergencies were discerned in twelve cases out of the fifty.

The relationships and contrasts disclosed by these three

graphs are believed to be especially responsive to the condition for effective accounting communication set forth by the Long-Range Objectives Committee that "whenever data regarding the quantity of and changes in resources are required for a continuing enterprise conventions must be established to guide the measurement."[28] If in the determination of these conventions it appears that there is a difference of objectives between the issuer and the user of data, then the committee asserts "the attest function cannot fully be discharged until issuer and user come into agreement." Consistent with the foregoing the committee stated that there must be: "Familiarity, on the independent auditor's part, with the purposes of the communication, including appreciation of the user's needs."[29]

Proceeding within this frame of reference, it is of course gratifying to observe that while there were twenty-four instances of divergence between the financial community and the profession noted in Figure 1, regarding the "is it" probe, the number of such divergencies was but eleven in Figure 2 regarding the "should it be." This narrowing of the areas of difference could demonstrate that the users and the profession are closer to a consensus regarding that which *should* prevail; somehow when it comes to the actual implementation the gap widens.

Interestingly when the divergencies noted by Figures 6 and 5 are compared, it becomes apparent that the professors' views as to the "should be" diverge from the corresponding views of the practitioners more frequently than their divergencies as to "what is" (the frequencies being sixteen and twelve, respectively). This undoubtedly is some further manifestation of the differing views of the "town" from the "gown."

> *From Figures 3, 4, 7, and 8:* These four graphs are not especially informative regarding the effectiveness of communication, *per se,* between or among the groups who were the subjects of the study. Instead, each of these graphs shows the relationships between the affirmative responses received from a single population of respondents to the first probe of the particular Series "C" question (i.e., whether the alternative

suggested is believed to be in accordance with generally accepted accounting principles) with that same population's responses to the second probe of that question (i.e., whether the alternative should be in accordance with such principles). In brief these four graphs reflect the respondents' sense of adjustment or satisfaction with that which they believe to prevail presently; these major disparities are indicative of areas of significant dissatisfaction with present accounting practices or assumptions. Because the very recognition of these areas could be an important first stage in the reappraisal of the particular principle, practice, or method, they are summarized in Table 5 which appears on succeeding page.

Summary

This chapter evaluated the extent to which the profession was meeting the standards for successful data communication which were advanced by the Long-Range Objectives Committee of the Institute as conditions precedent to the fulfillment of the accountant's attest function. As was indicated above, these standards call for a meeting of minds between the issuer and the user of the financial statements which are promulgated with the help of the auditor, if not under his aegis. Such a meeting of minds must be presumed to extend to the body of principles of accountancy since they are the "standards for measurement and summarization in accountancy."

The Institute's committee saw these standards as being met, so that "the attest function is being discharged, on a constantly widening scale." This optimistic conclusion was put in question, first by the reference to the published views of various persons importantly situated both within and without the profession regarding the sad state which prevails by reason of the multiplicity of accounting alternatives, all of which may qualify as generally accepted accounting principles. Second, this sad state was confirmed by the results of our research. Further, our study defined the areas of accounting principles or conventions where the lack of meeting of minds was most acute and also

TABLE 5

Divergencies in Excess of "20 Percentage Points"
Between the "IS It in Accord" and "SHOULD It Be in Accord" with Generally Accepted Accounting Principles

Divergencies Tending Toward the "SHOULD BE"

Transaction	Question	Population Where Discerned*
Stock Options	C-4(a)	7
	C-4(d)	7
Long-Term Leases	C-5(a)	3, 8
	C-5(b)	3, 4, 8
	C-5(c)	3, 8
	C-5(d)	3, 4, 8
	C-5(e)	3, 8
	C-5(f)	3, 4, 7, 8
	C-5(g)	3, 4, 8
LIFO Inventories	C-6(a)	3, 4, 7, 8
A Consolidation Situation	C-10(a)	4, 7, 8
	C-10(b)	3, 4, 8
A Jointly Held Entity Situation	C-12(a)	8
Depreciation Accounting	C-14(d)	4, 8

Divergencies Showing Regression from "IT IS"

Transaction	Question	Population Where Discerned*
Extraordinary Income	C-1(c)	4, 7, 8
Income Tax Accounting	C-2(a)	8
Income Tax Accounting	C-3(a)	4, 7, 8
Stock Options	C-4(c)	4, 7, 8
LIFO Inventories	C-6(b)	7
	C-6(c)	4, 7, 8
LIFO Inventories	C-7(a)	4, 7, 8
	C-7(b)	4, 7, 8
Oil and Gas Accounting	C-8(a)	4, 7, 8
A Pooling-of-Interest Situation	C-9(a)	4, 8
	C-9(b)	4, 8
	C-9(c)	4, 7, 8
A Jointly Held Entity Situation	C-12(b)	4, 7, 8
	C-12(c)	4, 7, 8
	C-12(d)	4, 7, 8
Pension Cost Accounting	C-13(a)	4, 7, 8
	C-13(b)	3, 4, 7, 8
Depreciation Accounting	C-14(a)	4, 8
	C-14(b)	4, 8
Research and Development Cost	C-15(a)	4, 7, 8
	C-15(b)	4, 7, 8

* Numerical references are to the graphs included as Appendix E wherein relationships were charted as follows:
Figure 3—For the Financial Community Category   Figure 4—For the Accounting Category
7—For the Accounting Practitioners   8—For the Accounting Professors

Source: Appendix E, Figures 3, 4, 7, 8

set out those areas where the various groups comprising the population probed by us indicated a need for change.

It is this research which might well be considered to be responsive to the question raised by Carey: "How well do [financial statements and auditor's opinions] convey to readers what they are intended to communicate?"[30] In his view there is evidence that they are widely misunderstood, even by sophisticated persons; he based this assertion on the fact that in other fields where research in communication has been conducted such a breakdown has been discerned; the results reported in this chapter have confirmed Carey's foreboding for our special area of expertise.

The succeeding chapter will review and evaluate the principal programs which have been advanced to cure this serious condition of a lack of common comprehension as to what are the profession's generally accepted principles of accounting—to cure the condition which was described by Andrew Barr as the profession's "most basic problem."

3

"Cheshire-Puss," said Alice, "Would you tell me, please, which way I ought to go from here?"

"That depends a good deal on where you want to get to," said the Cat.

"I don't much care where—" said Alice.

"Then it doesn't matter which way you go," said the Cat.

Alice's Adventures in Wonderland

Bridging the Gap in GAAP

What are some of the major recommendations for change which have been proposed by those who have deliberated upon this dilemma regarding the basic roadblock to effective communication in accountancy, i.e., the profession's failure (or inability) to define GAAP?

There are those who say "give them the facts," and then let the users reach their own conclusions. Others, with more proselytizing fervor, are determined upon "educating the users to understand" the meaning, and to grasp the nuances of the financial statements. Then there are those who would root the accountant's pursuit in "objectivity" and thereby avoid controversy and confusion. There is, of course, the leadership within the Institute which is determined to proceed with the present apparatus, i.e., through the Accounting Principles Board (APB), with the view that they will yet develop the required solution. And at the other end of the spectrum there are those who are determined to develop something of a catechism in accountancy, a body of authoritative principles, so that the accountant's responses to a particular problem would be categoric and lacking in equivocation.

So it is that we turn to a consideration and evaluation of these several alternatives to bridge the gap in GAAP.

The "Give Them the Facts" Recommendation

There are those who are of the opinion that improvement can best be effected through the dissemination of more information, possibly more loudly. This is the principal recommendation made by Professor Corliss D. Anderson in his compendium, *Corporate Reporting for the Professional Investor.*[1]

Similarly, Professor Alan Robert Cerf's *Corporate Reporting and Investment Decisions* recognizes that there are divergent accounting procedures in such areas as inventories, accelerated depreciation, tax allocation, accounting for the extractive industries, leasing, long-term contracts, and price-level change ramifications. He asserts that: "Reported income may be affected by alternative accounting procedures. . . ." He is then quite satisfied to accept as the answer to this uncertain and indeterminate state the response: "Investors should know how alternative procedures affect profits, the current position, and other factors they consider."[2] Regrettably, since he does not tell us how the investors should become knowledgeable it is difficult to accept Professor Cerf's response as anything but a palliative. If, as noted above,[3] Chairman Cary of the SEC and his Chief Accountant, Andrew Barr, were unable to measure the "impact" on the financial statements of the divergencies in accounting principles, it is impossible to conceive of the way in which ordinary mortals (e.g., the investors to whom Professor Cerf was referring) could discern how these "alternative procedures affect profits, the current position, and other factors they consider." Conceivably, the investor might infer that they are not getting the answers they need; then what? Profits might be presumed to be overstated or understated, depending on the nature of the divergency; again, then what?

That Professor Cerf may have been carried away by his thesis, "give them the facts and they'll come up with the right answers," is especially evidenced by his observation: "The analyst can make a rough approximation of fixed and variable costs if separate cost-of-goods-sold figures are given."[4] That this attribution of omniscience to "the analyst" is undoubtedly something of an exaggeration can be demonstrated by the learned papers coming forth in increasing frequency on the subjects of break-even point determination, direct costing, flexible budgeting, and the like. All of these areas of accounting for decision making address themselves to management, who presumably do have all of these separate figures suggested by Cerf, and even more, for their determination of fixed and variable costs; and yet even the making of these "rough approximations" is the subject of controversy. Further, if the "separate cost-of-goods-sold figures" which would be given are in turn predicated on one or another of the several inventory alternatives, or leasing arrangements, etc., to which Professor Cerf makes reference, how is the analyst supposed to make the "rough approximation" if he doesn't even know the nature and extent of the impact of the alternative procedures on the statements as a whole?

No inference should be drawn from the preceding critical remarks that there is any disagreement with Professor Cerf in his insistence (repeated at several points in his monograph) that the investors are entitled to additional data regarding: (a) sales breakdowns, (b) capital expenditures both current and planned, (c) research and product development both current and planned, (d) information on management and their policies, (e) long-term summaries of important financial items, (f) information on the outlook, (g) disclosures of accounting procedures.[5]

However, these data must be meaningful data, presented in a manner and in terms consistent with the standards set forth by Carey.[6] Until, and unless, we address ourselves to these standards it would appear that we are not facing up to our underlying fundamental dilemmas; and probably thereby even indulging ourselves in a myth, that if we give them more data we will thereby be communicating more "truth."

Correspondingly, there are those in the financial community who are of the opinion that the accountants are not responding to the community's fair requirements, and have therefore determined that the accounting profession should be responsible only for getting "all the facts" and for their dissemination to the community. It would then be the responsibility of the analysts and others in the financial community to digest the data and develop appropriate configurations therefrom. This was evidenced by the view of one of the respondents to the questionnaire, whose firm and credentials would indicate that his is an authoritative and informed opinion, who stated in his "notes and comments": "In my opinion most practicing security analysts *simply want all the facts* regarding controversial transactions and will make up their own minds irrespective of the attitude of the accounting profession toward the matter."

This view, which is clearly a repudiation of much of what the attesting accountant believes to be among his prerogatives, might best be met by the retort that there is no assurance that the new configurations formed by the financial community from the facts thus laid bare before it would necessarily be superior to those currently being formed by the profession; in fact it may very well be a mere transfer of the burdens of discovering "generally accepted accounting principles" from the profession to this community.

Another possible response to the advocates of this approach is suggested by a writer on the meaning of art (which could be generalized to embrace the meaning of any expression) who observed: "Raw feelings, like raw facts, are unintelligible and meaningless. A work of art is feeling objectified, organized, conceptualized. . . ."[7]

So it is that even if we could somehow throw up all of the facts (an assumption which is believed to be unwarranted both in theory and in practice, in any significant area of inquiry, including accountancy), they would then be raw facts, meaningless, unintelligible, indigestible. Instead, it is urged, the financial statements developed for use by intelligent users should represent the facts of the entity brought together on an "objectified, organized, conceptualized" basis; a creation in significant "symbolic forms . . . presented to an audience . . . to state a conception of . . . experience which can be appreciated only by understanding"—the standard suggested by Walker for the artists.[8]

The "Educate Them to Understand" Recommendation

As a corollary to this "give us (them) the facts" school of

thought, we are presented with the view that the financial community needs to become better informed about accounting principles, and that the profession has the responsibility for disseminating this enlightenment. This view was expressed most succinctly by the late Weldon Powell, who, as was noted above, complained that ignorance about financial statements and business is widespread. Only through a major effort whereby the profession sees to it that the decision makers acquire the required knowledge, will the presumption for financial reporting put forward by the American Accounting Association, that the statements are "prepared for use by interested persons having a working knowledge of business methods and terminology," be capable of fulfillment.[9]

The results of our research confirm Powell's assertion that: "Ignorance about the financial statements and affairs of business is widespread." This ignorance has been shown to exist among businessmen and investors (both large and small); that "some financial writers do not have enough knowledge of accounting" has also been confirmed by the data.* This is, of course, fine as far as it goes. Clearly this understanding of subject matter, jointly by the disseminator and receptor, is essential to effective communication. But it still does not address itself to the failure on the part of the communicator first to comprehend for himself the nature and substance of that which he is seeking to communicate.

So it is that the data developed by us, as well as the literature of accountancy generally, demonstrate that the profession has not clarified even for itself the very knowledge which Powell asserts is its responsibility to impart to others. Clearly, it is mere platitude to urge the wider dissemination of "the good doctrine" as the solution for the accounting profession's basic problem unless and until it clarifies for itself the subject matter which is to be thus indoctrinated.

Further, it might very well be that if the enlightenment

* See especially in this connection the data developed by Questions A-3(b) and (c) and B-1. Thus, A-3(b) indicates that only 46 per cent of the profession believes that the shareholder is getting the information essential for his effective performance in our economic society; A-3(c) shows that over 60 per cent of both categories believe that the shareholder is not generally capable of comprehending and utilizing the data which he is getting. As was pointed up on page 49, Question B-1 shows the very low grades assigned to some very sophisticated segments of our economic society with respect to their presumed comprehension of the body of generally accepted accounting principles.

which Powell espouses were to become effective it would have an inimical impact on the profession. This conjecture stems from the aforementioned observation of Hennessy that: "If the public . . . understood the wide differences that presently exist in accounting, the profession might be faced with legislative action. . . ."[10] It is confirmed by the transcript of a dialogue at a seminar sponsored by the AICPA during the spring, 1965, where a sophisticated practitioner is quoted as having said: "There is a danger to over-educating people as to . . . the CPA's capability. Our economic value in society is based on certain beliefs and relationships, and if you over-educate them, they are liable, likely to feel that our contribution is much less than they think it is today."

The record of the proceedings discloses that a leading spokesman for our profession replied by referring to an article by a financial columnist criticizing the shortcomings of the auditors in one of our *causes célèbres;* the spokesman is quoted as follows:

> We had a meeting with our public relations people right after the . . . article came up. I was burning about it. My boys were being abused. My God, we are going to tell . . . what the facts were, and I wrote on the airplane coming back from Colorado, I wrote a statement to the press that I thought . . . [might be issued] so that the public relations people would look at it and say: What good is an auditor. I was telling everybody what accountants didn't do and why they shouldn't be held responsible for anything. We didn't publish it, of course.[11]

The "Let Us Be Objective" Recommendation

Another important pattern of recommendations for improvement comes from those seeking to emphasize standards like consistency, objectivity and independence. This view was most fully developed by Curtis Holt Stanley in his *The Role of Objectivity in Accounting.*[12] Professor Stanley's thesis is essentially directed to a consideration of the mechanistic aspects of our subject matter, seeking to make certain that the inputs for the accounting stream are freed from personal bias, thereby helping to establish the truthfulness of accounting information. Central to Stanley's position is his assertion that "objectivity is the requirement that the procedures adopted . . . should result in reports which reflect the readily measurable facts of business operations in such a manner that other reasonably skilled accountants would be able to achieve substantially the same results given the same situation."[13]

This making of "objectivity" the *summum bonum* of accountancy (or of any discipline) has a number of major flaws.

To achieve such objectivity, Stanley is constrained to limit the communication to "the readily measurable facts of business operation." Such a concentration on the "readily measurable" would, of necessity, limit the range and breadth of the spectrum of the facts of business operations which should be the subject matter of the accountant's reporting. True, by narrowing the range of observation (in a metaphoric sense) to that which is "readily visible," or "readily audible," we might be made to agree on the readily measurable facts of the business operations; but it may very well be that the significant communication may lie in the reporting of the "buzzing" which is outside the range of ready measurement or definition. Again, the scientist recognizes that "the physical sieves of our sense organs" will perceive "only one part in ten thousand million" of the spectrum of light, and are sensitive to sounds the pitch of which lies within about ten octaves, "out of the infinite range" in nature. The scientist realizes that he cannot, therefore, take the "readily measurable" data at their face value, but instead must search far beyond such measurement.[14]

Implicit in Stanley's quest for objectivity in accountancy is the presumption that the facts of the business operation will confront the accountant. After a long history extending over two centuries when the scientists presumed that this was the case in their "pursuit of truth," they have now resigned themselves to a far more modest responsibility. This is the view expressed by philosophers of science including Bronowski, Jeans, and Heisenberg; it was most lucidly stated by Heisenberg, thus:

> Nor is it any longer possible to ask whether or not

> these [elementary] particles exist in space and time objectively, since the only processes we can refer to as taking place are those which represent the interplay of particles with some other physical system, e.g., a measuring instrument.
>
> Thus, the objective reality of the elementary particles has been strangely dispersed, . . . into the transparent clarity of a mathematics that no longer describes the behavior of the elementary particles but only our knowledge of this behavior. The atomic physicist has had to resign himself to the fact that his science is but a link in the infinite chain of man's argument with nature, *and that it cannot speak of nature in itself*. Science always presupposes the existence of man and, as Bohr has said, we must become conscious of the fact that we are not merely observers but also actors on the stage of life.[15] [Emphasis in original.]

Walker supplies a consistent view as a philosopher of art: "All knowledge of reality is derived from experience. Experience is generated by an interaction between the human organism and its environment, and is therefore determined at the same time by the nature of the human organism and by the nature of the external world."[16]

So it is in accounting. The "readily measurable facts of business operations" are not readily measurable at all. Instead, they are there to be determined and measured by accountants; it follows, then, that the accountant "cannot speak of nature in itself," he must become conscious of the fact that he is not merely an observer of the facts but is, in fact, an "actor on the stage of life" of the business.

The first two arguments suggested in rebuttal of Stanley's thesis related to his concentration on "readily measurable facts." We turn our attention next to the end result of this concentration, which is to permit "other reasonably skilled accountants . . . to achieve substantially the same results given the same situation." In this important respect Stanley's concept is essentially consistent with what the late Professor J. Robert

Oppenheimer described as the "different notion of what we mean by objectivity," thus:

> All over the world, in France, in Japan, in New Zealand, in [Communist] countries, we talk about atomic physics, and we check each other's experiments. In that sense it is a most objective part of our knowledge, and a most well-verified one. These comparisons are possible because we can tell each other how we have gone about an experiment and what we saw and what we found. Mistakes are made, but they are found very quickly. The objectivity which we see . . . is a characteristic of the way we can talk with others about it, of the lack of ambiguity and of the reproducibility and the verifiability of our communication with each other.[17]

This may be all to the good in science; but then a distinction, invidious to accountancy, must be made; the critical condition precedent in Oppenheimer's "different notion" is the way in which scientists can talk with each other about an experiment after "we . . . tell each other how we have gone about an experiment." Only because they can thus tell each other can there be the "lack of ambiguity" leading to objectivity. In accountancy, the nature of the relationship with the entity which is subject to the "experiment," and the profession's code of ethics, would prevent the "reproducibility and the verifiability of our communication with each other."

And there are signs that even this "different notion of what we mean by objectivity" in science may no longer prevail even in science. A report to the American Association for the Advancement of Science begins by defining this integrity, this "ultimate source of strength," as "the system of discourse which scientists have developed in order to describe what they know and to perfect their understanding of what they have learned." The report goes on to document major events in recent scientific history where the scientists were required to operate under rules of secrecy so that the "normal self-correcting procedures of scientific discourse cannot be brought to bear." The report then warns that: "Under the pressure of insistent social demands, there have been serious erosions in the integrity of science. This situation is dangerous both to science and society."[18]

It should be emphasized that the foregoing is not being recited in rejection of a standard of objectivity in the sense that it presumes that the attesting accountant is turning to the facts with independence and seeking their meaning apart from himself and from the peculiarities of his experience, or of his environment. Presumably such an accountant would have the habit (as suggested by Bronowski) of "testing and correcting the concept by its consequences in experience . . . by turning to the world of sense to ask, is this so? This is the habit of truth. . . ."[19] Certainly, such objectivity is to be presumed as being consistent with such a habit of truth-searching. But this is presumed to be a habit, and cannot be characterized as the *sine qua non* for a learned profession. The thrust of this argument, then, is opposed to such an obsession with objectivity, as to lead to a concentration on the readily measurable, thereby losing track of just what is being measured, and the presumed purpose of all this measurement. Further, to the extent that objectivity emphasizes the merely consensual, rather than the independence of the viewer, it serves to detract from, if not destroy, the professional image.

Similarly, no inference should be drawn from the foregoing remarks that we disagree with the basic standard proposed by the *AAA Statement of Basic Accounting Theory* that the accounting information be freed from bias; this "freedom from bias" is there defined to mean "that facts have been impartially determined and reported." It also means that techniques used in developing data should be free of "built-in bias." While we concur in this standard, and especially the objective sought thereby, we are afraid that it is addressing itself to a situation which no longer prevails. This feeling, that the standard relates to a more bucolic era, is confirmed by the contrast drawn by Caplan between the behavioral assumptions of the "traditional" management model of the firm and those drawn from "modern organization" theory. Thus, while the former presumed that the "accounting system is 'neutral' in its evaluations—personal bias is eliminated by the objectivity of the system," the modern view is that:

> Objectivity of the management accounting process is largely a myth. Accountants have wide areas of discretion in the selection, processing, and reporting of data. In performing their function within an organization, accountants can be expected to be influenced by their own personal and departmental goal in the same way as other participants are influenced.[20]

Some Results from Our Research Bearing on This Question

Significantly, and ironically, the data obtained by the research herein indicate that the term "objectivity," and the phrase "free from bias" may have become something of a shibboleth. This inference might fairly be drawn from the responses to Questions B-5(a) and (b) where the respondents were asked to give their views regarding the following situations:

> a) Since management knows of the various alternative principles in advance of entering into a transaction, it can so structure the transaction that it will correspond to that principle which it believes will be most desirable for its purposes.
> b) The independent auditor (who will ultimately be the one to perform the audit function) may describe in advance the several alternative principles which can be made to apply to a particular kind of transaction and emphasize for management the particular principle which will apply, dependent on the form of the transaction.

The responses to these questions, summarized in Appendix C, reveal that 50 per cent of the financial community category and 84 per cent of the accounting profession recognized that management may now so "structure the transaction that it will correspond to that principle which it believes will be most desirable for its purposes." Nor does such a condition create any sense of concern, for 53 per cent of the financial community and 61 per cent of the profession believed that this should be the case.

Similarly, 75 per cent of the community and 89 per cent of the profession recognized that the auditor may now "describe in advance the several alternative principles . . . and emphasize for management the particular principle which will apply, depending on the form of the transaction." And 82 per cent and 77 per cent of the two categories respectively asserted that this should prevail.

Clearly both of these questions were directed toward determining whether the respondents recognized (and then whether they approved) that accounting principles may be made applicable in a particular circumstance after the manner of Procrustes; further, the questions sought to determine whether the independent auditor (who will ultimately be the one to perform the audit function) should be permitted to involve himself in this expedition. The responses, as summarized above, indicate that the respondents considered it fitting and proper for this condition to prevail. Now, however true and virtuous the Good King Procrustes may have considered himself to be, and however objective were his standards for determining the manner of "adjusting" the objects of his bounty, the term Procrustean has not generally been analogized with truth, virtue or objectivity.

Implications of the Foregoing

It may very well be that a major defect in accounting practice is exposed by the foregoing discussion of the responses to our Question B-5(b); as was noted the respondents quite generally understood, and were entirely sanguine about, the fact that management looks to their independent auditors to describe for them in advance the several possible accounting alternatives which might apply for a contemplated transaction; they saw that management may then pick and choose the form of the transaction which best corresponds with its objectives.

It may be that it is this anticipatory, declaratory judgment of the independent auditor which deprives the financial statements of a dimension of objectivity which they might otherwise have; it may be that this very practice diverts management from pursuing its goals with a view toward their optimal achievement (however defined) independent of their eventual reflection in the financial statements. This "declaratory judgment" process extends to permitting management and their independent auditors to confer with representatives of the Securities and Exchange Commission and of the stock exchanges to obtain their anticipatory blessings for the accounting treatment; and if the blessings are not immediately forthcoming then to agree upon the reshaping of the proposed transaction so as to permit the desired accounting treatment to become effective.

These procedures run counter to the "predictive function of the law" which Mr. Justice Holmes asserted to be the very meaning of the law; as he put it: "The prophecies of what the courts will do in fact—and nothing more pretentious, are what I mean by the law."[21]

In brief, it may very well be that our present procedures obviate a need for management to aspire toward the very best possible conduct and, instead, they permit management to shape their conduct and the transactions, so as to accommodate the desired accounting presentation. These practices thereby encourage something of a Gresham's law approach to business transactions; but most important for present purposes these practices at least warp the concept of objectivity in accountancy.

Let the Accounting Principles Board Proceed

As had been noted heretofore the Board was handed a mandate in late 1964 to review the accounting research bulletins theretofore promulgated by the Institute and to determine which shall be considered to have continuing force and effect. The Board's Opinion No. 6 was promulgated the following October as an initial step in fulfilling this mandate;[22] by this opinion it effected the amendment of some few of these earlier bulletins and then decreed that the older bulletins were to continue in effect with the same degree of authority as Board opinions. In the view of most observers the Board has thereby essentially perpetuated the spectrum of alternatives which theretofore prevailed (and in the opinion of some this Opinion No. 6 represents a serious step backward since certain disclosure requirements theretofore in effect were eliminated).

That the actions of the Board to date have not met with unanimous acclaim is evidenced by its defense by Robert M. Trueblood in his presidential address to the Council of the AICPA in May, 1966. He first expressed his complete confidence in the potential effectiveness of the APB in the bridging of the gap in GAAP; after then observing that standards of financial accounting are essential in our society and that it was imperative that these standards be set by the Institute "and that means by the APB," he proceeds to the justification of this view:

> This is so, I believe, because there is no other nongovernmental agency that can do the job. And certainly no thoughtful person, familiar with the problems, would be happy to have government undertake the job. Accountants would not be pleased with such a solution. Business certainly would not be. And, according to statements of its spokesmen over the years, the SEC would not desire to have the assignment thrust upon it.[23]

The leadership expected of the APB in this connection means: "identifying and exposing problems; researching them; suggesting solutions; giving everyone a fair hearing; weighing all views involved; and publishing clear-cut, well-reasoned, and well-documented decisions."

Trueblood then interposed the following plea for a general vote of confidence in the APB:

> I am persuaded that the Board has the will and the means to do all of this—and I earnestly suggest that unless and until the opposite is proved true, there be a moratorium on internal criticism. I suggest that the Board be allowed—at least for a time—to pursue its

> work unhampered by a need to defend itself among its own colleagues. Self-criticism is good to a point. But at some point it is better to save our energy, in order to get on with the job.[24]

As was implicit in President Trueblood's remarks the alternative seen by some critics of the Board (or by the Jeremiahs, as was noted in the preceding chapter) is that the principle-promulgation responsibility will be undertaken by the SEC. That this may be feasible, and that it has been undertaken in some restricted areas, was also considered in the preceding discussion of the prevalent gap in GAAP. That the SEC will not undertake this responsibility with relish (and probably will not undertake it as a unitary project) can be demonstrated by reference to some of the especially acute observations by Grant McConnell regarding the collaboration between government agencies and business. In his *Private Power and American Democracy* he notes the curious irony of American politics whereby the forces of reform and progressivism have brought about results remarkably similar to those of the orthodoxy. These results, in Professor McConnell's view, have appeared most clearly in the independent regulatory commissions; the outstanding fact about these commissions is "that they have in general become promoters and protectors of the industries they have been established to regulate."

This political fact evolves from the characteristic life cycle of these commissions, thus:

> In the period of a commission's gestation, agitation develops for reform of a condition that is causing widespread distress. The agitation is denounced as "socialistic" and a heavily ideological struggle occurs. Ultimately, however, the fervor for reform reaches a peak and the regulatory agency is established with a very vague and general Congressional mandate. Such were the origins of the ICC and the SEC, for example.
>
> In its youth the commission has a crusading spirit. It encounters, however, the by now well-organized resistance of the industry it has set forth to control.

> The industry has superior knowledge of matters relating to itself and is determined to defend itself day in and day out against the apparent threat. Moreover, the legal standing of the commission may be uncertain and serious action may have to await Court determination of its validity. Even more serious, public concern over the problem quickly wanes and the commission is left without the strong political support that had brought it into being. Congress is happy about the disappearance of agitation and conflict, and the President is presumably freed of responsibility. In its maturity devitalization characterizes the commission. It achieves acceptance and loses its reforming zeal. . . . In old age debility sets in and the primary task of the commission degenerates into maintenance of the status quo in the regulated industry and the commission's own position as the industry's recognized protector.[25]

We are in essential accord with Professor McConnell's views in this context; we don't see the SEC taking on the burden here under consideration with any greater alacrity (nor with any greater effectiveness) than the APB. We are constrained, then, to look elsewhere.

The "Ultimate" Solution: A Body of Authoritative Accounting Principles

Having considered critically four of the solutions suggested for the profession's communications dilemma, insofar as it stems from the failure to define generally accepted accounting principles, those of (a) greater dissemination of facts, (b) spreading enlightenment among the statement users, (c) concentrating on objectivity in measurement, and (d) let's stick with the APB, we turn to a consideration of the fifth such solution, to wit: that we promulgate a body of authoritative accounting principles. Such a body of principles would serve the needs of all those entitled to have information regarding the corporate entity which is the subject of the attest function.

Undoubtedly the leading present-day spokesman (if not proselytizer) for such an integrated, uniform, authoritative, codified body of accounting principles is Leonard Spacek. (We have heretofore expressed our approbation of his willingness to take dissensual views, and to put forward these views publicly and forthrightly despite the obloquy which they attract toward him.) *The Postulate of Accounting,* promulgated by Spacek's firm, includes a most complete and extensive presentation of this plea for an authoritative codification; the single postulate to which the exposition leads is set forth emphatically, as follows:

> Thus, the one basic accounting postulate underlying accounting principles may be stated as that of fairness—fairness to all segments of the business community (management, labor, stockholders, creditors, customers and the public), determined and measured in the light of the economic and political environment and the modes of thought and customs of all such segments—to the end that the accounting principles based upon this postulate shall produce financial accounting for the lawfully established economic rights and interests that is fair to all segments.[26]

How is this ideal state of ultimate fairness to be attained? Through making financial accounting and accountability rest "on the laws governing the economic interests established by the people." This is because: "Law determines what rights exist and to whom they belong." After drawing a parallel between the judicial process as it sees it (i.e., where the jury ascertains the facts and the judge then applies the law) and the attest function (where once the facts are determined the auditor must apply the established principles), the monograph asserts: "The law and the accounting principles must be specific and must be applicable in any cases where they fit the facts."[27]

Before considering the feasibility and appropriateness of a definitive and authoritative code of principles for accountancy, it might be well for us to comment on Spacek's very apotheosis of the Law (and it must be spelled with a capital "L" in view of the qualities which Spacek attributes thereto). Thus, we find the monograph setting forth without equivocation that:

> The Law makes decisions regarding a given state of facts.
>
> The decisions of our judges flow from the Law, not from their personal views.
>
> The American way of life is governed by fairness administered by a government of Laws, not by the personal dictates or likes of men in important positions.
>
> A judge, once presented with the facts, must apply the Law which the public has enacted.
>
> Once the facts are established, the Law becomes axiomatic.
>
> The Law must be specific and must be made applicable in any cases where it fits the facts.
>
> Law cannot be one thing for one entity and something else for another entity.

Complementing this reliance on the Law, we find Spacek, again under the aegis of his firm, urging that the profession give consideration to the establishment of a Court of Accounting Appeals which would have jurisdiction over all accounting regulations promulgated by the Federal agencies, including the SEC. Implicit in this proposal is his (or his firm's) view that the APB will not succeed timely in the fulfillment of its role; this inference is drawn from the following comments in the monograph setting forth the proposal:

> The APB . . . is facing the same formidable obstacles which have faced other AICPA committees in the field of accounting principles. All of them have found it difficult to cope in an effective manner with the problems arising from the rapid changes in our society, or to meet the needs arising from the dynamic developments in the business community.
>
> . . . .
>
> While the APB may have needed some period of

> time to organize the research program and to get started in fulfilling its purpose, the time for accomplishments no longer can be delayed. The APB will demonstrate by its actions, for all to see, whether it *will* or *will not* carry out its assigned responsibility on behalf of the profession.[28] [Emphasis in original.]

An Analysis of Spacek's Assumption of Certitude in the Law

Morris Raphael Cohen has observed that satirists, like other human beings, "had their own sentimental weaknesses which have made them believe things no less illusory than those they have attacked."[29] Professor Cohen cited Juvenal, Voltaire, and Veblen to illustrate his point. So may it be that Spacek, the satirist in accountancy, has his own sentimental weakness which has made him believe that the Law is as he presumes it to be; this belief may well be no less illusory than those which he is attacking in accountancy.

It may very well be a failing of each of us to see the Achilles' heel in our own pursuits with which we are so familiar and love so dearly, and yet put some other calling onto a pedestal, and then bestow a halo thereon. Before pointing up the fact that the law had not come through as unblemished to many who have reflected deeply thereon from their positions as distinguished jurists and philosophers of law, let us note some expressions of sublime approbation for accountancy and accountants. So it is that we can see Sir James Jeans asserting that Leibniz was trying to devise a precise technical language and to construct a calculus for philosophy; the reason: "Leibniz considered that such a calculus would settle disputes between philosophers as easily as arithmetic settles disputes between accountants; if two disagreed, they would simply say 'let us reckon it out,' and sit down with their pens."[30]

It was, however, Ludwig von Mises, the highly sophisticated economist and economic philosopher, who undoubtedly expressed the ultimate rhapsody for accountancy. In his *Bureaucracy* he makes double-entry bookkeeping the very nirvana toward which mankind should be striving; it is this process which makes the entrepreneur effective; and because of the lack of double-entry bookkeeping, government leads to "bureaucracy" which is, for Professor Mises, a pejorative. In the course of his eulogy, Professor Mises quotes Goethe who called bookkeeping by double-entry "one of the finest inventions of the human mind."

This characterization by Goethe "hit the core of the matter" because accountancy can provide the entrepreneur with a faithful image of all his operations. The books and the balance sheets are the conscience and compass for the businessman.[31]

Having thus seen accountancy exalted by non-accountants, and the law by a non-lawyer, let us return to see whether Spacek's vision of the law is consistent with that of philosophers of the law. Dean Roscoe Pound, after examining the various springs from which law might be seen to have evolved, concludes that it cannot be circumscribed by any circumspect code because "the significant thing is not the fixed rule but the margin of discretion involved in the standard and its regard for the circumstances of the individual case." This must be so because of the three characteristics implicit in legal standards, thus:

> (1) They all involve a certain moral judgment upon conduct. It is to be "fair," or "conscientious," or "reasonable," or "prudent," or "diligent." (2) They do not call for exact legal knowledge exactly applied, but for common sense about common things or trained intuition about things outside of everyone's experience. (3) They are not formulated absolutely and given an exact content, either by legislation or by judicial decision, but are relative to times and places and circumstances and are to be applied with reference to the facts of the case in hand. They recognize that within the bounds fixed each case is to a certain extent unique.[32]

Judge Jerome Frank stated his views regarding the tenuous nature of the law even more affirmatively, thus: "But the law as we have it is uncertain, indefinite, subject to incalculable changes." He continued:

> The truth of the matter is that the popular notion of the possibilities of legal exactness is based upon a misconception. The law always has been, is now, and will ever continue to be, largely vague and variable. And how could this well be otherwise? The law deals with human relations in their most complicated aspects. The whole confused, shifting helter-skelter of life parades before it—more confused than ever, in our kaleidoscopic age.
>
> . . . .
>
> Our society would be strait-jacketed were not the courts, with the able assistance of the lawyers, constantly overhauling the law and adapting it to the realities of ever-changing social, industrial and political conditions; although changes cannot be made lightly, yet law must be more or less impermanent, experimental and therefore not nicely calculable. Much of the uncertainty of law is not an unfortunate accident; it is of immense social value.[33]

It might be interesting to observe, in passing, Judge Frank's analysis (or is it psychoanalysis) of the reasons why the myth of certitude prevails in the minds of many regarding the law. In his view this stems from the infant's striving to retain something like his prenatal serenity. He passes from stage to stage in his development seeking peace and security and "satisfies" that craving, in large measure, through his confidence in and reliance on his incomparable, omnipotent, infallible father. Then, when father's image tarnishes: "The law can easily be made to play an important part in the attempted rediscovery of the father. For, functionally, the law apparently resembles the Father-as-Judge." This is because the myth "that law is, or can be made, unwavering, fixed and settled" makes of the Judge the infallible father whose judgments and commands appear to bring order out of chaos. In short: "Grown men, when they strive to recapture the emotional satisfactions of the child's world . . . seek in their legal systems the authoritativeness, certainty and predictability which the child believed that he had found in the law laid down by the father."[34]

Whatever the contributory factors and forces, we see mankind pursuing its Quest for Certitude, expecting to realize this goal through a Code of Laws "sufficiently complete to settle all future controversies." This is illusory, Frank tells us, because:

> Codification, whatever its real worth, cannot create a body of rules which will exclude judicial innovation and thereby guarantee complete predictability. In attempts to achieve a perfect code covering all imaginable cases, we encounter again the old dream of legal finality and exactitude. Once this dream took the form of a belief in a list of rules directly God-derived. Belief in a man-made code, which shall be exhaustive and final, is essentially the same dream in another form, but a form which hides from superficial study the nature of the dream. But a dream it is, nevertheless. For only a dream-code can anticipate all possible legal disputes and regulate them in advance.[35]

Judge Frank buttresses his views on this myth of certitude by citing Mr. Justice Holmes decrying the tendency of many to deal with law as if it were a "theological working out of dogma." Further (quoting Holmes): "Certitude is not the test of certainty. We have been cocksure of many things that were not so."[36]

Mr. Justice Cardozo expressed himself along the same lines in his *The Growth of the Law:* "We must spread the gospel . . . that there is no gospel that will save us from the pain of choosing at every step. . . ." Then, "We seek to find peace of mind in the word, the formula, the ritual. The hope is our illusion."[37]

The Return to the Controversy Regarding Certitude in Accountancy

It should be evident from the foregoing that the quest for certitude is destined to be illusory, at least in the law, and apparently also in the sciences (natural as well as behavioral).

It should follow, then, that Spacek's search for an absolute definitive code of accounting principles must also lead to frustration. Would this then justify the position implicit in Savoie's suggestion that we "should permit many flowers to grow"? This question was incorporated in our questionnaire as Question B-7, wherein the respondents were asked:

> It has been suggested that the welfare of the various groups comprising our economic society is best served by having a multiplicity of alternative principles permitting a diversity of individual judgment rather than through having centralized decisions arrived at by the few. Do you agree with this statement?

The responses, as shown by Appendix C, indicate an almost equal division from both major categories between the affirmative and negative responses to this question. Thus, 43 per cent of the financial community respondents indicated "Yes" thereto; 40 per cent responded "No." The accounting profession's responses were 44 per cent and 45 per cent respectively. These data point up that which has already been discerned in the literature—the essential deadlock as to whether there should be a unitary code, or a pluralistic body of principles to be applied in the particular circumstances, when and as appropriate.

It might also be interesting to note that those who favor such a pluralistic body of principles are reasonably satisfied with the way in which the individual judgment is being exercised at present. This is indicated by the following subsidiary question:

> If you have responded "Yes" to the preceding question, do you believe that the "individual judgment" is being well exercised at present?

Of the thirty-one respondents from the financial community who answered affirmatively to the principal question, fourteen (45 per cent) responded that they were satisfied with such exercise; eight (26 per cent) said they were not; five did not know and four failed to respond to this subsidiary question.

With reference to the twenty-eight of the profession category who responded affirmatively to the lead question, seventeen (61 per cent) were presently satisfied; six (21 per cent) were not; the remaining five did not know.

As had been indicated above the controversy between the "absolutists" and the "pluralists" has raged with intensity at least since 1960; this is evidenced by the proceedings of the American Institute of CPAs in September of that year so fully described by Wise. While there may have been something of a change in the *dramatis personae* (but with Leonard Spacek retaining his role as the Constant Absolutist), the intensity continues unabated. Among those seeking to refute the Spacek view we find the late Weldon Powell using the following restrained terms to derogate the proposal put before the Spring, 1964, meeting of the Council of the AICPA (and possibly also to deprecate those supporting the proposal):

> The advocates of this proposal, of course, denied that it was compulsive. They said that it would not compel anyone to follow accounting principles enunciated by the Institute, but would only compel members to direct attention to departures from such principles. If these persons had not been known to me to be both sophisticated and honest, I would have thought they were being either naive or deceptive in taking this approach. It patently was an attempt to capitalize on the status which the opinions of independent accountants have achieved in the business community, and to secure the adoption by the business community of practices favored by the Institute, by requiring the members to take exception to practices opposed by the Institute. This requirement of the proposal, if it had been put into effect, would have tended either to cause controversies between accountants and their clients, the Securities and Exchange Commission, and other users of corporate reports, or to downgrade the reports of the accountants and the position of the American Institute of Certified Public Accountants.[38]

Powell then quotes from a plea for uniformity made by a New York securities dealer in a brochure issued a "few years ago." Powell's retort is peremptory: "This is nonsense. Uniformity is not attainable."

With corresponding intensity, Savoie sees in this advocacy of a definitive body of principles, in this "criticism from within the profession," something of a "fifth column" fomenting an insidious plot to undermine the fair prerogatives of management. After first calling to task the false prophets, those men prominent in the accounting profession (and whose views therefore carry great weight), for taking a "black-or-white approach, which is particularly unsuitable when the world we live in is a shade of gray," Savoie concludes:

> As a result of widespread publicity of the most destructive type, we have a false crisis precipitated by false prophets. Perhaps there was a time when this criticism could have been interpreted as an attempt to stimulate interest in accounting problems, but it is now apparent that the real intention of these critics is to remove from business management the right to participate in development of accounting principles and place this important function in the hands of an external regulatory body, either within the accounting profession or, failing that, within the government.[39]

A more moderate view was stated by Alvin R. Jennings. Speaking before the Hayden Stone Accounting Forum, Jennings made the following points regarding the accounting profession's responsibility in determining accounting principles:

1. Financial reporting loses much (if not all) of its utility without standards by which fairness of presentation may be judged.
2. The most useful criteria for the purpose is a body of coordinated accounting principles.
3. While such principles must necessarily always be general statements, they must be precisely defined

so that their applicability is clear to reasonably well-informed people and so that they will serve the disciplinary function for which they are created. Criteria which lack definition and reasonable precision are really worse than useless because they give an appearance of dependability when none exists.

4. The need is not for uniformity without regara to circumstances. Rather, it is the elimination of variations which cannot be justified by differences in circumstances, including, naturally, significant differences in basic facts or in the environment in which an applicable transaction occurs. This does not imply a single solution for every accounting problem. Nor does it require that in every case there must be two or more alternative choices.[40]

What is the present posture of the "Uniformity Controversy"? As had been pointed up by the various recent speeches and articles, the controversy shows no signs of abating and it is unlikely to abate despite pleas for a moratorium. A remarkably clear perspective of the current status of the controversy can be discerned from the Editor's Foreword to a most recently published compendium of fourteen separate papers on the subject of "Uniformity in Financial Accounting." After carefully considering the contributions, the editor concludes:

> The conclusions reached by our contributors on the hopefulness of the current situation are startlingly divergent. While widespread agreement exists in the profession on the need for progress in narrowing the availability of alternative accounting methods, differences persist over the ultimate goals and the methods, and urgency of achieving them. Many of what appear to be the true issues in the controversy have been largely avoided in accountants' intramural discussions. The following are among the questions that appear to require better answers than have yet been given: What degree of uniformity is actually desired?

> What scope would uniformity leave for the exercise of enlightened professional judgment? Given the necessity for a degree of arbitrariness in almost any accounting decision, what is lost by adopting uniformity as a paramount value, overriding unavoidable (and possibly disingenuous) differences of opinion? Will uniformity necessarily produce artificial biases against particular industries on the part of investors or against particular business practices on the part of business managers? Granting that "circumstances" must control the choice of accounting methods, should a circumstance such as management optimism or other subjective corporate policy be given weight? Can accounting theory provide a workable series of principles or not? Can academic accountants, presumably more interested in and adept at developing accounting theory make a contribution that will be accepted by practitioners?[41]

An Alternative to the "Ultimate" Recommendation

What might be deemed to be a fair response regarding this controversy? It has already been emphasized that a body of absolutes is not capable of attainment; this, then, might very well ally us with Powell's position. We are, however, determined to avoid this alliance because we could not, in any reasoned professional dialogue, describe another person's considered views as "nonsense," nor could we even by implication characterize these considered views as being deceptive. Probably even more critically, we must disavow ourselves from any position because to do otherwise "would have tended . . . to cause controversies between accountants and their clients."[42] In another context in this work, consideration will be given to the question as to "who are our clients"; for present purposes we seek to dissociate ourselves from any view which is centered principally on the obtaining of a consensus, and the creation of an atmosphere of cordiality. It appears to us that it does not require a dedicated group, hence a profession, to move in such a consensual realm; this is the area where ordinary mortals in great numbers can move entirely comfortably and effectively. No, a profession must determine the standards toward which it shall aspire even where such standards attract serious controversy. It is through the process of "Challenge and Response" (Toynbee tells us) that civilization moves forward; it is not through a process of expeditious accommodation.

What are our views on this major controversy? Several years ago we set forth the following as one of our principal recommendations for responding to this gnawing dilemma:

> [W]e need an Accounting Principles Commission comprised, principally, of our own Accounting Principles Board, but expanded to include representatives from the banking, labor, investment and governmental areas of our society. Such a Commission would be charged with the reviewing of current developments and research and to promulgate their determinations. These determinations should then be presumed to be the "generally accepted accounting principles" as generally comprehended by the members of our profession. While divergence from such determinations should be feasible, any such divergence would be presumed to call for an explicit statement of the circumstances which prevail, and an affirmation by the accountant that the departure results in a fairer presentation of operations and financial condition than would otherwise prevail.[43]

This, then, could be considered to be consistent with the Spacek position urging the adoption of a code from which to measure deviation. The differences in our respective positions might be summarized as follows:

1. The Accounting Principles Commission which we urge would be made to include persons from outside the profession to a far greater degree than is afforded by the present Accounting Principles Board. In our opinion such a pluralistic composi-

tion is essential to recognize the multiplicity of interests involved in the principles to be determined. Possibly of equal importance is the desire to see the pronouncements carry force and weight through the very auspices under which they were caused to be promulgated. It is believed that a Commission would give such force and weight in a measure far greater than is feasible with the present structure.

2. It is then urged (for reasons which will be considered in detail elsewhere in this work) that the selection of the particular alternative principle (or the deviation in an appropriate case from the principle, per se) should be determined by the attesting accountant rather than by the entity's management as prevails at present.

Each of the foregoing differences, or extensions, from Spacek's position is deemed to be significant. Thus, the emphasis on the pluralistic composition of the Commission is consistent with the great hopes and aspirations held by Mr. Justice Cardozo for the Restatement of Law as envisaged by him when the program sponsored by the American Law Institute was yet in its infancy. In his view the completeness of the promulgation, the fact that it would be prepared and reviewed by the leading jurists, professors, philosophers, and practitioners of the law, all will invest the Restatement with unique authority. This authority would not be to command, but to persuade. "It will embody a composite thought and speak a composite voice."[44]

And then, our charging the attesting accountant with the responsibility for the selection of the particular alternative principle (or the determination to deviate from the presumed principle) would, in fact, further the parallel between the judicial and attest functions sought to be made by Spacek. In his *The Nature of the Judicial Process,* Mr. Justice Cardozo described the duty of judging as envisaged by some judges as comparable with the matching of "the colors of the case at hand against the colors of many sample cases spread out upon their desk." Observing that some judges seldom get beyond this process, Justice Cardozo continues: "But . . . no system of living law can be evolved by such a process, and no judge of a high court, worthy of his office, views the function of his place so narrowly."[45]

Wherein and how does the judge ultimately fulfill his high function? It is "when the colors do not match . . . when there is no decisive precedent, that the serious business of the judge begins." For then he must fashion the law for the litigants before him conscious of the fact that in so "fashioning it for them, he will be fashioning it for others."[46]

In brief, then, the center of gravity which Spacek envisages to be in the Code of Accounting Principles would, in the process urged by us, be centered within the attesting accountant. True, the accountant would be possessed of such a Code, but it would be he (rather than management) who would be responsible for the selection. Further, it would be the accountant who would be permitted to innovate, or extend, where he considers this discretion necessary. Some of the standards suggested by Cardozo could be informative in determining the measure of this discretion. Thus, the accountant (like the judge) would not be "a knight-errant" roaming at will. He would "draw his inspiration from consecrated principles"; he would not "yield to spasmodic sentiment, [nor] to vague and unregulated benevolence"; he would be constrained "to exercise a discretion informed by tradition." With all of these constraints there remains a wide field of discretion—"wide enough in all conscience."[47] This shift of the decision-making center from management to the attesting accountant will also be considered in some detail in Chapter 5.

Conclusion

So it is that we have here presented and considered the several principal proposals advanced for the curing of the "most serious condition" which was demonstrated in the preceding chapter and developed to some extent in this chapter. After considering these several alternatives it was concluded that none of them is the ultimate panacea (undoubtedly, even the program advanced herein can be shown to be something less than such a nostrum). It is because such a panacea is nowhere to be found (and if it were, it would soon be seen to be no longer appropriate) that the ultimate answer is here centered in the "habit of truth" of the attesting accountant. It was this centripetal interest, centered within the accountant himself, to which reference was made at the close of the introductory chapter; this central interest will also become evident in the succeeding chapters.

The burdens which are here being imposed upon the attesting accountant, and the profession generally, are indeed awesome. But (to adapt Judge Frank's ode to the law), if that view of the profession brings to the accountant "a large sense of the burdens of the responsibility, it may also bring its pleasures—the pleasures of self-confidence, self-authority, of the conscious use of one's abilities in one of the most important areas of human activity."[48]

It is to prepare ourselves to meet our professional responsibilities (and to become entitled to the encomium which a profession affords) that we must move to perfect the special body of knowledge in which we profess expertise, to clarify the special idiom in which we express this body of knowledge, and to identify our place in the dialogue relating to this special body of knowledge. Such a process of "perfecting," "clarifying," and "identifying" presumes an important commitment to research; it is this commitment, and the problems encountered in the process of its fulfillment, to which we move in the succeeding chapter.

4

"You can't scratch
if you don't itch."
Albert Einstein, on Research

The Quest for Eureka

The preceding chapters described the failure on the part of the profession to come to grips with the defining of the special body of knowledge which it professes to know better than anyone else, and the ways in which this failure contributed to the communications and credibility gaps. If, as Everett C. Hughes puts it, the professional asks of his clients and the community that he be trusted, that he be granted "the exclusive right to practice, as a vocation, the arts which [he professes] to know, and to give the kind of advice derived from [his] special lines of knowledge,"[1] then the presumption must prevail that the professional is determined to comprehend fully and effectively this special body of knowledge. Only if this presumption is fair can there be the shift to the underlying relationship for a profession, as Hughes sees it that of *credat emptor,* from the converse, which is the rule of the market place, namely *caveat emptor.* Because of this shift in the relationship: "the client is to trust the professional . . . the professional asks protection from any unfortunate consequences of his professional actions . . . only the professional can say when his colleague makes a mistake."[2]

All of these presumptions make it mandatory that the profession stake out with some precision the particular area of knowledge which is to be the basis for the professional license, and wherein the profession claims the exclusive right to practice. That this body of knowledge which is deemed to be within the special realm of the profession's expertise cannot be a static body of knowledge was asserted unequivocally by Whitehead, when defining a profession as "an avocation whose activities are subjected to theoretical analysis, and are modified by theoretical conclusions derived from that analysis."[3] The analysis and criticism required by a profession must be relevant "to the purpose of the avocation and to the adaptation of the activities for the attainment of those purposes." It must be "founded upon some understanding of the natures of the things involved in those activities, so that the results of action can be foreseen." In brief, a profession must be possessed of "foresight based upon theory, and theory based upon understanding of the nature of things."

Failing such foresight and the forward thrust of theory, Whitehead continues, we have but a craft which he considers to be the antithesis of a profession. In his view: "Pure mentality easily becomes trivial in its grasp of fact." The craft is an "avocation based upon customary activities and modified by the trial and error of individual practice."[4] This act of creation, this advancement of the frontiers of theory, this better comprehension of the nature of things, this anticipatory foresight, is generally considered to result from research dedicated to the fulfillment of these lofty objectives.

That there is a serious anemia in research in all areas of knowledge is evident from Père Teilhard de Chardin's lament that though we exalt research and derive enormous benefit from it yet "with what pettiness of spirit, poverty of means and general haphazardness do we pursue truth in the world today." To emphasize this point Père Teilhard continues: "We behave as though we expected discoveries to fall ready-made from the sky, like rain or sunshine. . . ." If, he continues, we were to relate the proportion of our nation's revenue allotted to research, "we should be staggered." We are so parsimonious in this respect that "surely our great-grandsons will not be wrong if they think of us as barbarians."[5]

It is this anemic condition, especially insofar as it pertains to accountancy, which will be the subject of definition and analysis in this chapter.

Research Within the Major Accounting Firms

How, and to what degree, has the accounting profession recognized and responded to these expressions of the need for research for all learned professions? To begin with we find that each of the major national accounting firms (i.e., the so-called "Big-Eight") does engage in a program of formal research. This kind of research might be said to correspond to the research and development type of activity conducted by major corporations as an incident to their creation of new products and the improvement of old products in order to enhance its sales and profit position. Research under such conditions "has to be characterized as useful or within a company field of interest to be considered desirable." Research so conceived and pursued may have a salutary effect for the scientific community (the profession); this is, however, tangential since "basic research holds an unstable position in the laboratory." In brief, the most effective utilization of research in the corporate laboratory (and the firm) is in applied research. While the corporation (like the firm) "needs and depends upon basic research [it] looks to the university for much of it."[6]

The foregoing observations based on a study of research in industry is consistent with the conclusions found by G. Edward Philips in his study of "Research in Major Public Accounting Firms." He there found that: "The research department . . . performs as a staff function. It accumulates, analyzes, and summarizes information and ideas as a service to the operating sections of the firm." He predicated this conclusion on his findings that:

> Research activities of the firms are quite complex and difficult to classify. The firms engage in little "basic research" although there are growing efforts in this direction. It does not appear likely that public accounting firms will devote much formal effort to constructing an accounting theory which can be used as a basis for evaluating the soundness of alternative accounting practices. Most of the firms' research activities are oriented toward keeping the firm aware of cur-

> rent practices and developments, providing a basis for establishing policies in accounting and auditing matters, and resolving urgent questions that arise in the course of practice.[7]

Here too, as in the case of the industrial laboratory, there may be a "fall-out" benefit to be derived by the profession as a whole; this follows from the fact that the research staff of the firm will review and respond to "exposure drafts" of Institute bulletins, opinions, and the like. However, there is not much sharing of unpublished research findings with the profession as a whole; this cloistering of the research staff prevents its making an optimum contribution to the "most pressing research task facing accountants . . . the need for clarification of the theory and principles of financial reporting. . . ."[8]

The History of the Institute's Accounting Research Program

While this research by the accounting firms themselves can be shown to be most useful to the respective firms, and incidentally to have a salutary effect on the profession as a whole, the most ambitious program of the accounting profession is that which was undertaken in the decade of the sixties under the aegis of the American Institute of CPAs. In his *The Search for Accounting Principles,* Reed Storey dates this major undertaking from late 1957 when "a number of events occurred which returned accountants' attention to the problem of formulating accounting principles." The causal factors enumerated by Storey were Spacek's prodding in August, and Alvin R. Jennings' call (in late October): "for the establishment of an expanded and independent Institute research program based on the premise that the development of accounting principles was more in the nature of basic rather than applied research."[9]

It may very well be nothing more than an historical coincidence that Jennings' call for a new and greater commitment followed so closely in the wake of Sputnik's launching. In any event history will undoubtedly recite that "late 1957" was a period which found educators, politicians and the professions generally, engaged in the process of rededication and a new commitment to higher ideals; it was a period of transcendent vows. With what persistence this dedication, these vows, and commitment were pursued generally, must be left for future history to relate.

The "late 1957" dating by Storey is not inconsistent with the benchmark determined by Hawkins who sees the new departure stemming from 1959, when the profession was "faced with growing discontent over current financial reporting practices."[10]

The need for new departures for accounting research was most effectively and eloquently underscored by Alvin Jennings. We hear him telling the 70th Annual Meeting of the Institute of the "Restrictions of Existing Research Methods":

> In the field of medicine pure research is largely in the hands of biochemists and other specialists and not in the normal province of the practicing physician. Techniques exist to test new drugs before they are offered to the public. At law, the continued acceptability of established concepts is tested each time a case goes to trial.
>
> We have no comparable laboratory in which the new may be examined and tested against the old. This is a serious handicap to creative thinking.[11]

To justify his indictment, he asserts that: "Present methods of accounting research give no opportunity to test new ideas—in fact there is some justification for a belief that they tend to stifle creative thinking."[12]

Jennings reiterated the foregoing indictment of the Institute's research practices when addressing the 1958 Annual Meeting of the American Accounting Association; to demonstrate this insistence that the Institute and the membership should prepare itself to "think about the unthinkable," he there said:

> Another problem inherent in our present methods of research is the difficulty of reversing positions previously taken. The need for doing so gives rise to awkward questions of procedure and protocol and tends to encourage procrastination. I believe that a research

> organization which, in a sense, would be independent of the Institute would have less difficulty with problems of this kind.[13]

This, then, was the new program launched so eloquently and sincerely by Jennings; we then see the responsibility for moving the program further along on its path to its apogee passing to the late Weldon Powell, the first chairman of the new Accounting Principles Board. Speaking before the 1960 meeting of the American Accounting Association, he reported that the new research plan had become effective in September, 1959, and that "we are now engaged in making it operative." By this he meant that there were six projects which were then in progress and there were plans for a seventh. Because of their importance in this development, we recite his enumeration of these projects:

> As for specific research projects, to date we have begun six of them and have plans for a seventh.
>
> The first two are those recommended by the special committee, namely, studies of postulates and principles. Maurice Moonitz, formerly professor of accounting at the University of California at Berkeley, had agreed to direct the staff work on both these projects before he was appointed Director of Accounting Research, and he still plans to do so, with the assistance of Robert T. Sprouse of California.
>
> The third is a study of the accounting for income taxes. Homer A. Black of Florida State University is the director of this project.
>
> The fourth research project concerns the accounting for long-term leases. This study is in the charge of John H. Myers of Northwestern University.
>
> The fifth has as its subject the accounting treatment of business combinations. Arthur R. Wyatt of the University of Illinois is directing it.
>
> The sixth and final research project now under way relates to the accounting of non-profit organizations. Emerson O. Henke of Baylor University is conduct-

> ing the work on this.
>
> The seventh project will be a study of the accounting for pension costs. . . .[14]

And to confirm the high aspirations articulated by Jennings, Powell declared:

> [W]e shall try to do some bold thinking about our problems. If we are to succeed, we shall have to be willing to consider new ideas in developing theory, and to reach out towards new methods not tried before in developing relevant practices and procedures. There are those who think we need a major overhaul, not a minor repair job. George O. May in writing to me recently, said: "It is no time for patching up; it is time for viewing the system as a whole and developing, if not a philosophy of accounting, at least a mode of thought that visualizes the problems as a whole."[15]

So much for this dedication and commitment. What has become of this new program since those awesome days in late 1957 or 1958 or 1959 or 1960? It might be interesting to point out in passing that the program may be seen to have passed its zenith some time in 1964, because it is then that Powell (who in 1960 had concurred in Jennings' sense of urgency) was asserting: "Further progress in developing accounting principles is going to take time. There are some who are disturbed at this prospect, but I am not. I do not understand the emphasis on speed." While it is unlikely that the nadir has yet been reached, nevertheless, the apogee appears to have been attained. It is to the demonstration that the new and dramatic program has begun the descent to which we next turn.

The Results to Date of This Bold Program

Between 1961 and the time of this writing (fall 1966) nine Research Studies have been promulgated under the sponsorship of the Institute's Research Division. As described by Storey in *The Search:* "The quality of the research studies to date, each of which is undeniably a contribution to the literature of accounting, indicates the soundness of the Institute's new approach to research";[16] the studies to which he referred were:

No. 1. *The Basic Postulates of Accounting* by Professor Maurice Moonitz.
No. 2. *"Cash Flow" Analysis and the Funds Statement* by Professor Perry Mason.
No. 3. *A Tentative Set of Broad Accounting Principles for Business Enterprises* by Professors Robert T. Sprouse and Maurice Moonitz.
No. 4. *Reporting of Leases in Financial Statements* by Professor John H. Myers.
No. 5. *A Critical Study of Accounting for Business Combinations* by Professor Arthur R. Wyatt.
No. 6. *Reporting the Financial Effects of Price-Level Changes* by the Accounting Research Division of the AICPA.

Subsequent to his writing, three additional studies were promulgated; inasmuch as these were published under Professor Storey's supervision and control the approbation expressed regarding the first half dozen would undoubtedly carry over to these later three:

No. 7. *Inventory of Generally Accepted Accounting Principles for Business Enterprises* by Paul Grady.
No. 8. *Accounting for the Cost of Pension Plans* by Ernest L. Hicks.
No. 9. *Interperiod Allocation of Corporate Income Taxes* by Professor Homer Black and assisted by the Research Division of the AICPA.

In the intervening years Professor Moonitz, who was theretofore described by Powell as "formerly professor of accounting at the University of California at Berkeley," found that he was only on leave from the University, necessitating his return thereto in 1963. His position as Director of Accounting Research was filled on an interim basis by Paul Grady, who had theretofore retired as a partner in Price Waterhouse & Co.; Storey then replaced Grady on a regular basis.

The Broken Covenant

It is significant to point up at this juncture the marked contrast between the centers of responsibility for the initial projects outlined by Powell in 1960 and for the projects thereafter undertaken and pursued. Each of the six initial projects was to be pursued by a professor of accountancy who undertook the responsibility as such a professor. It is here believed to be significant that Powell stressed the fact that Moonitz had agreed to direct the first two projects *before* his appointment as Director of the Institute's Accounting Research Division, hence while he was a professor.

In sharp contrast, most of the studies initiated thereafter were put in the charge of practitioners who continued in the active association of their firms; the subsequent studies thus authorized are:

> *Accounting for the Cost of Pension Plans,* undertaken by Ernest L. Hicks of Arthur Young & Co. (and published as ARS No. 8, as noted above).
> *Accounting for Goodwill and Business Combination,* being pursued by George R. Catlett and Norman O. Olson of Arthur Andersen & Co.
> *Accounting for Research and Development,* assigned to Oscar S. Gellein and Morris Newman of Haskins & Sells.
> *Accounting Problems Peculiar to Extractive Industries,* being studied by Robert E. Field of Price Waterhouse & Co.
> *Concept of Materiality,* undertaken by Kenneth Stringer of Haskins & Sells.

There are also two additional studies in process, viz:

> *Intercorporate Investments,* being brought to completion by Professor Samuel R. Hepworth and Reed Storey.

Accounting for Foreign Operations, also being brought to fruition by Professor Hepworth.

(These last two studies were assigned to an academician in August, 1961, hence before the promulgation of Research Studies 1 and 3, and the resultant shock of recognition.)

It is difficult to reconcile this centering of research in active practitioners with the aforementioned 1957 observations of Jennings making an invidious distinction between research in the field of medicine and that which prevails in accountancy.[17]

Nor does this shift appear to be readily reconcilable with Powell's covenant to: "try to do some bold thinking about our problems [and if] we are to succeed, we shall have to be willing to consider new ideas in developing theory, and to reach out towards new methods. . . ."[18]

That there has been at least an apparent reversal in the orientation of the research program is undoubtedly evident from the foregoing. The Institute's concern that the research studies were producing some unexpected, seriously dissenting views, can be demonstrated by the fact that a more traditional view of the probing of the business combination problem, particularly the "pooling vs. purchase" dilemma, was bound into Study Number 5, along with Professor Wyatt's analysis, thereby blunting his thrust. Also significant is the fact that while Study Number 2 (on "Cash Flow") did find its way into a formally promulgated opinion of the Accounting Principles Board, yet there is serious question as to its impact on reporting standards. Opinion numbered 5, while predicated on Study Number 4 ("Reporting of Leases in Financial Statements") nevertheless severely limited the applicability of the study's recommendations and its effect; this opinion essentially sustains the position heretofore expressed in Accounting Research Bulletin Number 43, "Restatement and Revision of Accounting Research Bulletins," Chapter 14. While it does require more extensive disclosure of lease rental requirements, and sets forth more specific criteria for determining capitalization of leases in particular cases, the research study's recommendations are severely attenuated.

This transition from the university scholars to the practitioners might well be explained in terms of the traditional, and possibly natural, conflict between the "gown" and the "town." The roots of this conflict were described especially succinctly and sensitively by Professor John William Ward when concluding his essay on the role of the intellectual in the university as follows:

> So we . . . are caught finally in the unsettling posture of being inside and outside our society, passionately committed to it, yet by that very passion inevitably somewhat alienated from it. . . . Little wonder that the society that supports us should be uneasy about what we are up to and little wonder we cannot easily say whether the main function of the University is the preservation of the old or the discovery of the new, whether the intellectual in the University is to be cleric or critic.[19]

Implications of the Foregoing

A careful study and close analysis of this brief period in the history of research in accountancy can point up some very important object lessons for guiding the accounting profession, and professions generally, toward a more effective fulfillment of their research objectives. Thus, this study and analysis demonstrate first, that a professional organization, as such, is not the appropriate center of research regarding the theoretical infrastructure of that profession. Further, it can be shown that a person or a firm actively engaged in the practical pursuit of a professional avocation cannot be fairly expected to develop the forward thrusts anticipated from theoretical research while continuing such a "practical pursuit."

Turning to the first of the conclusions drawn from the study of this recent history, it is well to re-emphasize the observations of Jennings in his "keynote address" regarding the stifling effect of the research practices in accountancy. These premonitions are entirely comprehensible; it is probable that all of these observations could be applied to a major pure theoretical research endeavor under the aegis of any professional organization representing an affluent body of practitioners. The reason for this is implicit in the Einsteinian aphorism cited at the headnote to this chapter: "You can't scratch if you don't itch." An affluent profession isn't compelled to scratch, or if it does, it prefers not to scratch too deeply (at least not to the point where blood is made to flow, and especially not where the blood be blue).

Further, one is led to wonder what became of the commitment implicit in Jennings' criticism of the then prevalent methods of research which made difficult the reversing of positions previously taken. This, we were told, was to be corrected by "a research organization which, in a sense, would be independent of the Institute" and thereby have less difficulty on that score. The reversal (or breaking) of this clear commitment becomes evident from a statement by Savoie in *The Price Waterhouse Review* wherein he characterized the AICPA Research Division as the operating staff of the Accounting Principles Board.[20]

In short, as Jennings recognized so clearly, any research program which is structured so that new ideas cannot be examined independently, and with fresh outlooks and new insights, cannot produce the essential breakthroughs. Where the environment in which this program is implemented puts a premium on questions of procedure and protocol, procrastination ensues inevitably; this might well be summarized by the observation that a program so conceived and pursued will not "give change a chance."

This Reluctance to "Give Change a Chance"

That affluent professions (e.g., accountancy) might well prefer to concentrate on the world of appearance (as contrasted with the whole world which extends far below and beyond) is the very condition, in the generalized case, which was so very cogently and effectively articulated by Senator J. W. Fulbright in his opening gambit in *Old Myths and New Realities:*

> There is an inevitable divergence, attributable to the imperfections of the human mind, between the world

> as it is and the world as men perceive it. As long as our perceptions are reasonably close to objective reality, it is possible for us to act upon our problems in a rational and appropriate manner. But when our perceptions fail to keep pace with events, when we refuse to believe something because it displeases or frightens us, or is simply startingly unfamiliar, then the gap between fact and perception becomes a chasm, and action becomes irrelevant and irrational.[21]

So it is believed to be with those responsible for making the policy decisions of the AICPA regarding its research program. Where the results from its initial thrusts into pure research consistent with the Jennings vision were displeasing, if not frightening (at least startlingly unfamiliar) to the leaders of the Institute, it caused them to pursue some other approach to what might still be called "research." By so doing the Institute demonstrated the tendency of avoiding the thinking about "unthinkable thoughts." Instead of daring to disabuse itself of old myths (still in the Fulbright idiom) and "to act wisely and creatively upon the new realities of our time," it preferred to submerge the voices of dissent, and to proceed with an "inventorying" pursuit, and to a transfer of the centers of inquiry from the universities to the active practitioners.

These shifts on the part of the Institute could also be shown to be entirely consistent with the familiar Platonic parable of the cave: In this parable mankind is chained in a cave; the legs and necks of the men dwelling therein are chained so that they cannot move; they can only look on the wall which forms the back of the cave. They cannot see the life of the world outside, but only the shadows which the objects moving in the sunshine outside cast on the walls of the cave. For the dwellers in the cave, the shadows on the wall constitute the whole world, while the world of reality (as it is usually envisaged) lies forever beyond their ken.

And when one of the prisoners does work himself loose and gets to the outer, the "real," world and (after a difficult process of adjustment) sees the world of "reality," he returns to the other dwellers in the cave to tell them of their delusion or illusion. As we know, his erstwhile colleagues are certain that the ascent has caused him to lose his senses; if he were to persist in his endeavors to spread the message of the truth of the real world they would kill him.

The reasons are not hard to find. Every society, be it a nation or a profession, even a family, acquires a vested interest in its "shadows" or "realities" as the case may be. It is just these "vested interests" which John Gardner was warning all institutions against; these interests are "among the most powerful forces producing rigidity and diminishing capacity for change."[22] Organizations and societies which fall prey to these diseases are destined to die. Gardner laments that all too few understand how essential flexibility and changes of direction are for the process of continuous renewal. The same point is described in an historical and scientific context by Page Smith when describing the observations by Yang and Lee in their experiments on nuclear particles.[23]

There, then, is the key: the "vested interests" (and like Gardner's usage of the term it is not here used in a pejorative sense); when represented in an organized professional body like the American Institute of CPAs they are disposed toward opposing anything which threatens the principles to which the group has given its loyalty, on which its stature may, to a large degree, be founded. Where the new pursuits may tend to overthrow these traditional beliefs, and leave the profession adrift upon uncertain seas, the "vested interests" react to forestall the processes which might give change a chance.

So it is that the brief history of the research program undertaken by the Institute on the threshold of the sixties has already adequately demonstrated the dangers pointed up by Plato's parable, and by Gardner and Fulbright in their respective contexts. The analysis of this history, however brief, leads to the conclusion suggested above: A professional organization, as such, is not the appropriate center of research regarding the theoretical infrastructure of that profession.

The second of the conclusions premised above, that a person or a firm actively engaged in the practical pursuit of the professional avocation cannot be fairly expected to develop the forward thrusts anticipated from the theoretical research, is actually implicit in the foregoing discussion; such a person or firm, like the professional organization, is saddled with the "mind-forged manacles," the "vested interests" to which Gardner alluded. However, the transition effected in the Institute's research program, from contracts with professors to contracts with practitioners, necessitates special attention.

A Case in Point: The Study of Goodwill

An aspect that needs first to be considered relates to the inevitable subjectivity implicit in all research, especially basic research; if we acknowledge this unavoidable condition, then it should direct the Institute to adopt a policy which would militate against, or at least mitigate, this subjective involvement. Instead, as we see it, the recent policies or practices of the Institute tend to aggravate the problem. A most dramatic manifestation of this crucial question is presented by the current research study of Accounting for Goodwill by George R. Catlett and Norman O. Olson of Arthur Andersen & Co., under the aegis of the AICPA Research Division. No fault can be found with our colleagues' dedication to our profession; their independence is unquestioned; and as had been noted heretofore the profession is very much indebted to their firm for its endeavors to move the profession forward and upward. Yet it is believed to be entirely regrettable that Catlett and Olson undertook this assignment; as members of the same firm in which Leonard Spacek is an elder statesman there will undoubtedly be a special strain on their objectivity and independence of research; the strain will become particularly intense when the results are promulgated. This is because Spacek had already entered his absolute judgment regarding this subject under review.

Without now presuming to judge the merits of his views, Leonard Spacek made known, in most unequivocal terms, his considered recommendations on the proper accounting treatment of goodwill when speaking before a meeting held at the New York University Graduate School of Business Administration in November, 1963. When his remarks were thereafter published in *The Journal*[24] they brought forth an extremely large volume of mail,[25] much of the correspondence taking on the tone of a polemic. While such a colloquy is undoubtedly essential to the promulgation of any new concept, Spacek did not expose his findings as a research scholar who is engaged in an academic expedition. Instead, he concluded the statement of his views on the following urgent note:

> In my opinion, the principles of accounting I have proposed would help to restore the balance sheet and income statement to a position of usefulness in presenting factual data to the public. . . . I would like to urge the accounting profession to consider these proposals seriously, as I have asked each of my partners to do.[26]

And then, in the dialogue with several of the correspondents commenting on his recommendations, Spacek is moved to an even more extreme position. So it is that when he replied to a letter from Robert Kahn (who in turn had commented on an earlier interchange of correspondence between Professor Hylton and Spacek) Spacek asserted:

> It is wrong to tell stockholders that they have equity in a corporation when that equity represents only the value of estimated future earning power of the company. . . . Just because the facts are unusual or shocking to a reader is no excuse to hide those facts. Amortization of goodwill against earnings is the most misleading presentation we can possibly give to stockholders. . . . if a deficit results from writing off goodwill in an acquisition, it will in fact exist until the earnings have replaced it.[27]

Clearly, the foregoing categoric conclusions that "it is wrong . . . ," "no excuse to hide those facts," "the most misleading presentation," "will in fact exist . . . ," etc. might well be associated with the views coming *after* research rather than from a research scholar embarking upon an exploration. It would indeed be a most herculean effort for Spacek's associates to move to a dissociation or refutation of his absolute determinations as heretofore set forth by him; and if their research were to justify Spacek's views fully, there would be those who would understandably cast doubts thereon.

In brief, recognizing that bias cannot be exorcised even under the best of circumstances, it would appear to be especially and peculiarly rational and logical to avoid any further entangling alliances. Such a disentanglement or disengagement is deemed to be most difficult in the consideration of any major, pervasive problem within the context of the firm; it appears to be an especially impossible pursuit in a case where a principal associate has already made his categoric views on the issue publicly known, and has made them known in no uncertain terms.

No consideration has been given in these discussions to the question as to whether the compensation (if any) paid to the researcher is in turn remitted by him to the firm with which he is associated. This question, as well as those regarding the procedure for compensating the principals or any of their associates who may have devoted time to the project, and the procedures whereby members of a major accounting firm are given access to the views (and papers) of others in the profession (who might look at such a researcher with an air of suspicion born of a competitive environment), might themselves be the fair subjects of research.

Also in this context we have serious misgivings regarding the assignment of two major research studies to an accounting firm (we are not here alluding to Arthur Andersen & Co.) which is presently seeking to justify its activities in three accounting fiascos of major proportions. Thus, we believe that it is an unfair and excessive burden to impose on a firm so situated to further dissipate its energies and resources, and to do so at a time when the firm is undoubtedly constrained to reappraise its own current practices and procedures. Further, to the extent that the researchers' findings, conclusions and recommendations relate to the problems involved in these *causes célèbres* the objectivity and validity of the resultant studies might fairly be challenged.

In sum, all of the foregoing leads to the conclusion that regardless of the sponsorship of the theoretical research in accountancy it should not be centered in a person or firm then actively engaged in the practical pursuit of accountancy. To the extent that the Institute has determined on such a centering for its research program we believe that it has embarked on a practice inimical to the research objectives of the profession.

Research Must Be Centered Within the Universities

Where, then, should this extensive research activity be centered, especially that research relating to the probing of the theoretical infrastructure or the special body of knowledge which the accountant professes to know better than anyone else? In the present scheme of institutions existing in our society we believe that such center should be within the universities, and their schools of business. This follows from the belief that only the universities are presently capable of avoiding the inner contradictions which are considered to be indigenous to the centering of research in the major accounting firms and the Institute. Further, if those preparing for admission to the profession are to acquire their academic background under optimum circumstances then a major, possibly a crash, effort needs to be made for diverting more, and more significant, research to the universities.

This was the need spelled out by R. K. Mautz in his address before the 1963 meeting of the American Accounting Association. In the course of his speech Professor Mautz emphasized the compatibility of research with education (and its incompatibility with professional practice). This is because "the opportunity, the freedom, the stimulus, the time are all available to the teacher." Is this propitious circumstance exploited in accountancy for the benefit of the profession? Mautz replies with a categoric negative, thus:

> So far as I know, we do not have a single research professor of accounting in this country. We have had only a scant handful of research efforts considered worthy of publication by the American Accounting Association in its monograph series, and except for

> these we have had little substantial research production. In the last twenty years or more, very little has been accomplished by the academic side of accounting to increase our understanding of accounting as a field of knowledge.[28]

Further, recent and important surveys of the higher education for businessmen (and the business professions) underscored the anemia of research in the schools of business and pointed up the inimical effect of this condition on the quality of the educative experience in our schools. Thus, Gordon and Howell observe that "there is a critical need to develop in the business schools a more stimulating intellectual experience"; they then conclude: "if the business school belongs in the university, then research belongs in the business school."[29]

Correspondingly, the Pierson report asserts: "Research, or the lack thereof, sets the whole tone and direction of a field." It is the contribution, we are told, which each generation of scholars makes to the predecessors in the field and which, in turn, provides the base on which the succeeding generation will build.[30]

Most recently the Committee for Economic Development undertook a study to consider whether the collegiate schools of business, in their present condition, were equipped to make their needed contribution to the development of business leaders. An important part of this study was to determine the extent to which the criticisms and recommendations in the two previous reports had effected an improvement in the schools. The CED report notes that one of the principal charges levelled by the Gordon-Howell and Pierson reports was that: "Research in most business schools was weak; in consequence, educational programs suffered, and the schools of business failed to do enough to advance knowledge and thereby serve practitioners in the field."[31] And after all is said and done the Committee is constrained to conclude that: "Research in the business schools still needs more support—and more first-rate minds."[32]

It should be evident, then, that the diversion of research to the firms or even to a division (however autonomous) of the Institute contributes to a corresponding anemia in the universities; such a diversion not only diverts the vital and exciting subject matter which would be the fair subject of study but also thereby diffuses two other scarce resources—scholars and finances.

So much for the contribution to the university which would be afforded by this deliberate centering of research therein. Reciprocally, what can the university contribute to the fulfillment of the objectives of the research program for the profession of accountancy? While he was identified with the Harvard School of Business, Professor Alfred North Whitehead told the American Association of the Collegiate Schools of Business that a university must be imaginative "or it is nothing—at least nothing useful." This imagination, Whitehead continues, is contagious; further: "It cannot be measured . . . and then delivered to the students by members of the faculty. It can only be communicated by a faculty whose members themselves wear their learning with imagination."[33]

Professor Whitehead gives this description of the university environment which makes it so propitious to the act of creation, to the achievement of the breakthroughs considered to be so essential to the evolution of a profession in an evolving society: "The combination of imagination and learning normally requires some leisure, freedom from restraint, freedom from harassing worry, some variety of experiences, and the stimulation of other minds diverse in opinion and diverse in equipment."[34]

Then, adding emphasis to the point made by Mautz regarding the compatibility of research and education, Whitehead asserts that research and teaching must be tied in tandem if an efficient faculty is to result. The mutual attraction between the two is described by him with his inimitable clarity and eloquence and resultant beauty, thus:

> Do you want your teachers to be imaginative? Then encourage them to research. Do you want your researchers to be imaginative? Then bring them into intellectual sympathy with the young at the most eager, imaginative period of life, when intellects are just entering upon their mature discipline. Make your researchers explain themselves to active minds, plastic

> and with the world before them; make your young students crown their period of intellectual acquisition by some contact with minds gifted with experience of intellectual adventure. Education is discipline for the adventure of life; research is intellectual adventure . . . shared in common by young and old. For successful education there must always be a certain freshness in the knowledge dealt with. It must either be new in itself or it must be invested with some novelty of application to the new world of new times. Knowledge does not keep any better than fish. You may be dealing with knowledge of the old species, with some old truth; but somehow or other it must come to the students, as it were, just drawn out of the sea and with the freshness of its immediate importance.
>
> It is the function of the scholar to evoke into life wisdom and beauty which, apart from his magic, would remain lost in the past. A progressive society depends upon its inclusion of three groups—scholars, discoverers, inventors.[35]

The same point regarding the presence of both good teaching and important research in good measure as conditions precedent to an effective university education is made, but much more recently, by John R. Platt,[36] Nathan M. Pusey,[37] and James A. Perkins.[38]

In our view, then, it is only within the university that the various disciplines which are required for the discerning and the resolution of the major problems which confront any learned profession, like accountancy, are made to converge. It is there that each of the other disciplines is capable of making an unexpected even unpredictable contribution to such a discerning or resolution of a research problem in accountancy; reciprocally the process of cross-pollination of ideas may move from the faculty in accountancy to those of law, economics, the natural and social sciences, to philosophy. That this is not a mere rhetorical conceit can be demonstrated by the remarks of Whitehead cited above, and the very circumstances in which they were conceived and spoken.

The Further Advantage of Continuity Provided by the Universities

There is yet another distinct and important advantage to be derived from this shifting of the center of research from the Institute to the universities—it is the phenomenon of continuity. A look at the subjects determined as subjects of study by the Research Division of the Institute, and its marshalling of researchers and advisory committees, demonstrates the essential discontinuity of the research process. The team is brought together very much like a baseball team to play a particular game (or season); upon the fulfillment of the contract or commitment (hopefully with a victory) the team is disbanded. The legacy in the form of a study is, of course, not inconsequential; however, there is no continuing cohesiveness to the team which was thus brought together, nor is there the chain reaction process whereby the team undertakes dimensions and departures not contemplated by the contract; absent, then, is the environment where these dimensions and departures are pursued with some new infusion of younger scholars replacing those who have moved elsewhere. In brief, the very reference to the comparatively recent turbulence in the Research Division of the Institute, and the review of the dozen or so programs undertaken to date, demonstrate this lack of continuity.

How should it be? This process of continuity in research was most dramatically presented in *The Structure of Scientific Revolutions* where Thomas S. Kuhn defines the term "normal science" (or "paradigm") as presuming an example of scientific practice, which includes "law, theory, application, and instrumentation together," from which spring particular coherent traditions of scientific research. Such "paradigms" share two essential characteristics, viz: "Their achievement was sufficiently unprecedented to attract an enduring group of adherents away from competing modes of scientific activity. Simultaneously, it was sufficiently open-ended to leave all sorts of problems for the redefined group of practitioners to resolve."[39]

It is this open-endedness of university research, the legacies of the recognition of problems, hypotheses, false starts, but then some small positive steps, even those short of breakthroughs, which research in the university environment permits to be passed on to changing bodies of professors and scholars. Such a gradual process involving infusion and transfusion, possibly even of osmosis and mitosis, is the process through which breakthroughs in learning are achieved.

Because of its lack of continuity, believed to stem from its determination to concentrate on the solving of discrete problems facing the profession, the research program centered in the AICPA doesn't encourage groups of adherents away from the existing paradigms. Nor does the Institute give to these apostates sufficient resources or encouragement (in material and psychic terms) to pursue the open-endedness of the new problems which may have been brought to light by these newer developments. In brief, the Institute's approach to solving problems *qua* problems, rather than transferring the over-all burden, and the opportunity, to the universities, exerts on research in accounting an atavistic (albeit benign) hand.

How should the profession move in order to institute a research program which might be less vulnerable to the indictments and contingencies considered above?

Recommendations for the Financing and Structuring of Research

First, the manner of the financing of research in accountancy needs to be changed. As had been indicated above, accounting research in the universities is suffering from anemia—in the degree of responsibility vested in them for effecting the breakthroughs in knowledge, but also in, possibly because of, the available financing. Thus, the American Accounting Association, as representative of the academic branch of the profession, does not have any formal machinery (excepting for the appropriate committees comprised of professors performing this function entirely as volunteers, and merely as an adjunct to their academic burdens) for the cultivation, seeding, and cross-pollination of ideas, and the sponsorship of new and exciting and imaginative research projects.

The channelling of funds through limited outlets by the Institute's Research Division, with its superstructure and lines of responsibility, produces a canalizing of ideas which can lead to an apathy (if not an atrophy) in creative tendencies. This dimension of the indictment was most effectively underscored by Gardner when he observed that in addition to recognizing the need for renewal, a society (e.g., a profession) must also develop the institutional arrangements that make orderly change a possibility. He then states as a mathematical truism that: "In an organization with many points of initiative and decision, an innovation stands a better chance of survival. . . ."[40] In brief, a pluralism is an essential quality of the arrangements required of a society to help it to escape the cycle of growth and decay.

Accepting the principle of pluralism in the determination and administration of the research programs, there then follow such subsidiary questions as: "Who is to pay for this research?" "Who should be the patron?" "How should the funds be administered?"

The answer to the first and second queries might well be "principally the accounting profession." However, to assure the pluralistic support required to permit greater independence, support should also be forthcoming from the securities and commodities exchanges, labor unions, chambers of commerce, associations of financial analysts, and from the government.

Turning to the administration of these collective funds: In order to afford the maximum degree of autonomy in their administration it would appear that a foundation should be established with such sponsorship as would permit a most propitious functioning. The standards for the structuring of such a foundation might well be consistent with those set forth in the Report of the Commission on the Humanities wherein the Commission determined that:

> It is an axiom of our intellectual life that scholarship and art are free and must remain free. Like science, they must judge their ends and means according to their own criteria.
>
> Yet there are special problems with studies involving value judgment. These are at once the aspect of our culture most in need of help and yet most danger-

> ous to entrust to any single authority, whether of church or party or state.
>
> We must unquestionably increase the prestige of the humanities and the flow of funds to them. At the same time, however grave the need, we must safeguard the independence, the originality, and the freedom of expression of all who are concerned with liberal learning.[41]

The Commission then expressed its conviction that this commitment to freedom can be fulfilled, and its independence safeguarded, only if its financial support comes from the wide range of sources; such a plurality of support, we were told, "will generally strengthen the freedom and variety of scholarship in a democratic society."

Correspondingly, the kind of research which we envisage for the accounting profession also involves "value judgment" and must, accordingly, be insulated from the unwarranted and inimical influence and control of government, labor, industry, the profession, per se. In brief, the Foundation for Accounting Research which we propose would give to the scholars the maximum assurance of freedom of intellectual pursuit, the *sine qua non* of creative research.

Is There Any Guarantee of Success for Such a Program?

This leads to the final question as to what assurances might be given that the results of such a new research program would be more effective than that which flows from our present programs; this was the question raised by Professor Mautz as follows:

> [W]e must still face the problem of establishing the results authoritatively. The results of accounting research do not commend themselves for acceptance in the same way that research in the physical sciences does. In the physical sciences research results are profitable to those who have access to them. The ac-

> counting profession visualizes just the opposite effect. You and I can see this is a short-term point of view; yet I think it remains the dominant one. How then do we get research results adopted? If the research were sponsored by an organization as powerful as the SEC, authoritative establishment might be no problem at all. The danger here, of course, is that invalid research results are as likely or even more likely than valid results.[42]

Of course, no categoric assurance can be given that such a pluralistically supported and structured research program will succeed, even if launched and implemented under optimum circumstances. However, the hope that it may stand a better chance than the present program centered in the Institute stems from the same source as that described in connection with our recommendation in Chapter 3 for an Accounting Principles Commission. In brief, it is our hope that the very circumstances of the founding of such a Foundation for Accounting Research, the pluralism of its support and the manner in which the research programs are then launched, should have a dramatic and positive impact on the ultimate acceptance of the results from such research. The giants will be expected to labor at the summit and to bring forth the good doctrine.

Success cannot be asured; a major effort has to be made if accountancy is to make the breakthroughs in its discipline which are so essential to its retaining the encomium and prerogatives of a profession; we must advance with courage, and accept the risk of failure because the goal we seek is so essential to the development of "foresight." Failing such foresight, accountancy is destined to become, in Whitehead's terms, a craft.

Walter Lippmann warned against the paralysis which comes from fear of failure on the part of he who picks his way "through the world as if he were walking on eggs." Those "who are forever preoccupied with their immediate reputation, always counting the costs, are buying rubbish for a fortune." Lippmann then states his position affirmatively: "A mistake matters far less than most of us imagine; the world is not brittle, but elastic."[43]

And a half-century after the foregoing was written Gardner observed that: "One of the reasons why mature people are apt to learn less than young people is that they are willing to risk less." And so it is that we end up by paying "a heavy price for our fear of failure." He then quotes a statement made by Max Planck when accepting the Nobel Prize for his discovery of the quantum theory: "Looking back . . . over the long and labyrinthine path which finally led to the discovery [of the quantum theory], I am vividly reminded of Goethe's saying that men will always be making mistakes as long as they are striving after something."[44]

Conclusion

And the accounting profession does have something worth striving for. In material terms, Spacek described the price paid for the services of the profession most dramatically: "While this can only be an estimate, the cost to investors through fees charged to business by the accounting profession probably aggregates between one and two billion dollars."[45]

But more important, if in a less materialistic vein, this striving is toward a most important prize because in our economic society, which has shifted from an economic democracy to an economic republic with the resultant delegation of responsibility, some profession existing within the society must be charged with the function of keeping the decision makers informed. Because the accountants are the ones who are now presumed to have this responsibility, and because we are given access to the intimacies of the corporate society on a freer basis than any other profession, we must come to recognize the magnitude of this undertaking, to learn and accept the implications of this surrogatory role, and to learn how to discharge it in an economic society which is itself evolving. This striving, learning, and accepting are essential; if the accounting profession does not lend itself to such a pursuit we will find some other profession or agency usurping our prerogatives.

Such a striving, with its risks of failure, is worthwhile if for no other reason than to achieve the foresight which Whitehead has described as being a condition precedent to a professional pursuit. Finally, this anticipation of the future would be proceeding with the counsel given by Thucydides two and a half millenia ago: "For we that must be thought the causers of all events, good or bad, have reason also to take some leisure in part to foresee them."

What might be the areas of this research, of this striving? The preceding chapters furnish some clues: how to come to grips with the defining of the special body of knowledge which the profession professes to know better than anyone else. Then, on the determination of this good doctrine, how are the receptors and communicators (i.e, the financial community and the profession) to be made aware thereof; how is the effective dialogue to be established?

In the ensuing chapters certain additional major areas for inquiry will also be defined. Thus, we will consider such questions as: Who are the parties to the dialogue? Who is speaking with whom? To whom should the profession be speaking and on whose behalf? Is the proliferation of accounting services, and particularly in the realm of management services, consistent with the recognized objectives of the accounting profession? To what extent is this proliferation known to the financial community and accepted by them? How can the profession of accountancy be made to anticipate the forward thrusts and not merely be carried along by pressures from the outside or by a misguided "pragmatism"? How can the profession be made continuously aware of the implications for its pursuit of the advances of knowledge in other learned disciplines?

For our purposes only the broad dimensions of some of these questions will be set forth; it is, however, recognized that each of the aforementioned questions and, in turn, the additional questions which will inevitably arise in the pursuit of significant answers to these questions, are deserving of extensive and intensive research—and with a correspondingly high level of commitment of our material and intellectual resources.

5

The [term] I–Thou points to a relation of person to person, of subject to subject, a relation of reciprocity involving meeting or encounter, . . . The I–Thou relation, which Buber usually designates as "relation" *par excellence,* is one which man can enter only with the whole of his being, as a genuine person.

Herberg, *The Writings of Martin Buber* [1]

The Failure to Define the Parties

Having demonstrated the inability of the accounting profession to define its special idiom, "generally accepted accounting principles," and the ways in which this failure has confounded accounting communication, we turn to another aspect of the breakdown in communications namely, the failure to define the parties to the dialogue.

Leonard Spacek has dramatically described this confusion regarding the presumed subjects and objects of this accounting colloquy as follows:

> Let us first ask the question: "Where does the responsibility lie for providing adequate and reliable information for investors?" Everyone seems to agree that corporate management has primary responsibility for the financial statements, but let's look at the question a little more deeply.[2]

When Spacek does look at this rhetorical question "a little more deeply" he first inquires of his audience of financial analysts whether *they* have this responsibility and finds that they rely on the accountants. Similarly, the stock exchanges, the Securities and Exchange Commission, corporate management, all point their fingers to the accountant as the one who is presumed to be charged with this responsibility. Does the accountant accept this responsibility for "providing adequate and reliable information for investors," and if this responsibility is accepted, is his profession discharging it fairly? Spacek answers these questions in no uncertain terms: "As a professional accountant, I find it hard to take any pride in the knowledge that our profession provides such low quality accounting to the investor at such a high cost. . . ."[3]

Whether this indictment by Spacek is fairly leveled is yet to be determined; it can, however, be demonstrated that the profession has not reached a consensus regarding the presumed audience for its attest function nor, for the other end of the dialogue, regarding the degree of responsibility which the attesting accountant assumes. Further, to the extent that the profession may be said to have reached such a consensus the understanding so reached can be shown to be diametrically opposed to the understanding thereof in the minds of the users of the statements.

In an important sense this failure to determine "who's talking to whom?" and "who's responsible for what?" in accountancy can be seen to parallel the C. P. Snow argument regarding the breakdown in communications between the "two cultures." For him, the great communications gulf that separates the men of the arts (the "intellectuals") from the scientists could be fatal to the Western world; this is because: "There seems . . . to be no place where the cultures meet . . . the two cultures can't talk to each other."[4] So it is that Snow in the macrocosm, and Spacek in the (relatively speaking) microcosm, are despairing over the failure in communication between the parties who should be vitally involved in the outcome of an effective dialogue.

This gulf between the "cultures" in the accounting context will be considered, first, in terms of the audience to which the communication is presumed to be directed, and second by a consideration of the identity of the presumptive communicator; finally, the communications gulf existing within the profession itself will be described.

The First Critical Question: Who Is the "Thou"?

The first of the dilemmas, as to who is presumed to be the

audience for the accountant's communication, is considered to be a manifestation of the split which pervades the American grain, to use Max Lerner's phraseology. Thus: "Throughout the history of the American experience there has been a planetary struggle between the two aspects of the democratic idea." This struggle has been between the opposing concepts of "aristocracy," "republic," and "minority rights" on the one hand and "people," "democracy," and "majority rule" on the other.[5]

And so it is with accountancy. At times, like with Fourth of July oratory, the central interest, or the "vital center" (to adopt Walter Lippmann's phrase) is stated to be in terms of the "people," the "democracy," the "majority rule." But then in the actual implementation of the attest function, it would appear that it is the "aristocracy" who become the object of the communication in the economic republic.

The Case for the "People" as the "Vital Center"

Evidence of a commitment to the people or the democratic ideal is not hard to find; it is implicit in the much-heralded reference to the more than 20 million shareholders in our "corporate democracy." This determination to make the citizenry generally even more extensively committed to our corporate society is part of the American creed. Within the accounting profession this commitment to the "people" was effectively articulated by the Long-Range Objectives Committee of the American Institute of CPAs when it rooted the very existence of the capitalist engine in a widespread system of effective communication of reliable economic data; such a system, we were told, is an essential precondition to the accumulation of capital in a single enterprise.[6]

This need to make the stockholder feel vital, a continuing, integral part of his corporate enterprise, and therefore entitled to have the information required for the making of intelligent investment decisions, was also asserted (in varying contexts) by Graham, Dodd and Cottle,[7] by George O. May,[8] and by Cox.[9] Probably the most sweeping statement of this commitment to the "people" was by Montgomery who said: "It is [the accountant's] duty, after fighting the figures and finding the facts, to assemble the figures and to tell the truth about them, with clarity, conciseness and intelligence so that he who runs may read. . . ."[10]

This democratic-based commitment of the accountant's attest function was also described in a memorandum prepared by The Office of the Chief Accountant of the Securities and Exchange Commission which reiterated with approval the views theretofore articulated by the AICPA:

> The purpose of furnishing accounts to shareholders must be not only to afford them information in regard to the results being achieved by those to whom they have entrusted the management of the business, but to aid them in taking appropriate action to give effect to the conclusions which they reach regarding such accomplishments. . . . The only practical way in which an investor can today give expression to his conclusions in regard to the management of a corporation in which he is interested is by retaining, increasing, or disposing of his investment, and accounts are mainly valuable to him insofar as they afford guidance in determining which of these courses he shall pursue.[11]

That there may be a touch of cynicism in this broad-based commitment for financial communication is evident from the observation by Gaddis that the common shareholder is necessary to establish the legitimacy of management, and that "as such he is deserving of deferential treatment." He then continues: "Along with legitimacy in the eyes of the law and the public, the shareholder gives to the large business corporation the priceless mantle of the *private institutions.*" This "priceless mantle" may well be modern management's most valuable possession because "it retains for it entrepreneurial latitude and freedom." So it is that while ownership in the modern corporation "is now a simulated quality," it should be fostered because of the important benefits it brings to management.[12]

The foregoing counsel to management, to demonstrate a *noblesse oblige,* does have something of a Machiavellian quality to it. (And no pejorative inference should be drawn from the use of the term; instead, it is meant only to imply an objectivity of the kind demonstrated by the medieval philosopher in his counsel to the Prince.)

A corresponding view of the need for involving the masses of shareholders (in order to assure the legitimacy of the corporate function) is expressed by Adolf Berle: "Unlike medieval princes, modern holders of economic power cannot claim God as their source. . . ." They must look to mortals for the source of their legitimacy and authority, namely, to the "body of shareholders having votes."[13]

Berle is, of course, much too sophisticated a commentator on the American economic scene to be beguiled by the periodic appeal to the masses; on the contrary, he sees in this a mere ceremonial rite. Thus, Berle asserts that the conventional assumptions regarding the democratic process are not particularly useful in dealing with the corporation; this is because modern economic decisions "increasingly turn on technical considerations and must be made by men expert in dealing with technical data." In fact he finds that where a democratic consensus is called for (e.g., in a proxy fight), "one is struck with the fact that the campaigners rarely discuss the real issues, probably because they are too complex for easy understanding."[14] (One cannot help but sense an analogy between what Berle describes as a determination of the campaigners in the corporate context to disengage themselves from the real issues, with the corresponding campaign in the political society generally. And it may very well be for the very same reason cited by Berle—the real issues may be too complex for easy understanding.)

This low state of corporate democracy was the subject of a *New Yorker* column; there the "Reporter at Large" reported on his round of 1966 stockholder meetings. In addition to observing that managements are tending toward shifting their meetings from New York City to remote areas where there may be fewer and less hostile constituents, the reporter comments sardonically on the new science of the care and feeding of shareholders. He then describes the chairman's reactions when a badgering shareholder (generally one of the few "professional shareholders") persists in "biting the hand that feeds her."[15]

The Shifting of the "Vital Center" to an "Elite"

So it is that while substantial authority can be introduced to demonstrate that at various times and in a variety of contexts it has been the "people" and the "economic democracy" that have been considered to be "the vital center," it can also be shown that this center may be shifting toward an "aristocratic," "republican," or "elitist" orientation. This is discernible from views such as those of Mautz and Sharaf, who expressed the assumption that the communication should be directed essentially to the informed elite of our economic society; under the caption "An Audit Attitude Toward Adequacy of Disclosure," they maintain that:

> Auditing can no longer base its ideas of fair presentation on the concept of a reasonably informed investor who reads the published financial statements and makes his investment decisions accordingly. Today the investment market is a controlled market; further, it is one in which a number of skilled professionals all play highly integrated and highly important roles.[16]

These views are consistent with those of Berle that the insurance companies and investment trust or mutual fund managers "now fulfill the ritual prerogatives of the stockholders."[17]

In the same vein, in introducing his monograph on *Corporate Reporting for the Professional Investor,* Corliss D. Anderson asserts: "It has often been argued that most shareholders neither understand nor are interested in long detailed Annual Reports. . . . That is true. To an increasing extent security transactions are guided by some sort of professional advice."[18]

So it is that we see the conflicting views regarding the presumed audience for the accountant's communication: On the one hand there is the obeisance to the "people" and "majority rule," and then we are confronted with the contrasting commitment to the professionals, the aristocracy, the elite—all evidencing Lerner's "planetary struggle between the two aspects of the democratic idea."

The Results From the Research Bearing on the "Thou"

To what extent, and in what manner, can this shift in the vital center (and the problems created thereby) be demonstrated by the results of our research? In this connection, the responses to Questions A-3, A-4, A-10, and B-1 are especially significant.

Question A-3 first asked the respondents to state their views regarding "the present-day corporate society, and particularly the relative roles of the publicly owned corporations and their shareholders." The response was overwhelmingly to the effect that this society constitutes an "economic republic." Thus, 89 per cent of the respondents from the financial community and 97 per cent from the accounting profession indicated that the society is "one wherein the shareholders have delegated all essential responsibility to the corporate management and where the shareholders then look to it for results."

This predominant response is confirmed by the responses to Question A-4 wherein the respondents were asked to indicate their opinion as to the relationship "which prevails between the management and the shareholders of a major American publicly owned corporation." The responses from 76 per cent of the financial community and 86 per cent of the accounting profession were that the relationship is one of "Independent manager of property vis-à-vis persons entitled to the fruits of their investments in the property." These responses were to the exclusion of alternatives like "Employee vis-à-vis Employer," "Agent vis-à-vis Principal," and "Borrower . . . vis-à-vis Lender . . ."

Questions A-3 (b) and (c) called for the respondents to give their value judgments regarding the effectiveness of communication to the shareholders in our economic society; A-10 called for such judgments relating to the effectiveness of accounting communication to the various segments of the economic society. These questions and the related responses were:

> *Re A-3 (b):* Is the shareholder getting the information essential for his effective performance in our corporate society?
>
> > The responses: 21 per cent of the financial community and 47 per cent of the profession asserted that the *shareholders were not getting* the information.
>
> *Re A-3 (c):* As to whether the shareholder generally is capable of comprehending and utilizing the information which he is getting for investment decision making.
>
> > The responses: 61 per cent of the community and 66 per cent of the profession stated that the *shareholders were not thus capable* of comprehending and utilizing whatever they were getting.

Question A-10 then asked the respondent to state his opinion regarding the extent to which published financial statements were responsive to the needs and requirements of several "user-groups" in our economic society, including shareholders owning substantial interests and minor interests respectively, financial analysts, and finally "anyone who is willing and competent to read the statements carefully and with discrimination." The results culled from the data included in Appendix C are set forth in Table 6 which appears on the succeeding page.

The foregoing responses, whether they be from the financial community or the accounting profession, cast doubt on the validity of the euphoric conclusion by the Long-Range Objectives Committee of the AICPA referred to heretofore that the standards for the promulgation and communication "are being satisfied" and that "the attest function is being discharged, on a constantly widening scale."[19]

TABLE 6

Opinions of Respondents as to Extent to Which
Financial Statements Are Responsive to the Needs of
Selected "User" Groups in the Economic Society

	Percentages of Respondents Responding Re: Extent Statements Were Responsive to Respective Groups					
	Fully Responsive Col. 1	Substantially Responsive Col. 2	At Least Substantially (Cols. 1+2) Col. 3	Adequately Responsive Col. 4	At Least Adequately (Cols. 3+4) Col. 5	Inadequately Responsive Col. 6
	Responses from the Financial Community					
To "User-Groups":						
b) Substantial Shareholders	5.6%	22.2%	27.8%	22.2%	50.0%	45.8%
c) Minor Shareholders	16.7	30.6	47.3	34.7	82.0	16.7
d) Financial Analysts	0	12.5	12.5	30.6	43.1	52.8
h) Anyone willing and competent to read the statements carefully, etc.	8.3	23.6	31.9	36.1	68.0	20.8
	Responses from the Accounting Profession					
b) Substantial Shareholders	1.6%	18.8%	20.4%	32.8%	53.2%	46.9%
c) Minor Shareholders	10.9	31.3	42.2	34.4	76.6	23.4
d) Financial Analysts	0	10.9	10.9	26.6	37.5	62.5
h) Anyone willing and competent to read the statements carefully, etc.	6.3	18.8	25.1	34.4	59.5	31.3

Source: Responses to Question A-10

Conceivably, a case might be made that this function is being fulfilled in so far as the "shareholders with a minor interest" are concerned. This could follow from the fact that 82 per cent of the financial community and 77 per cent of the accounting profession believed that the statements were adequate (or better) in responding to the needs of this "man in the street." Conceivably, also, but to a lesser degree, this sense of fulfillment might be appropriate for the broad spectrum of users, i.e., "anyone who is willing and competent to read the statements carefully and with discrimination," those persons whom the American Accounting Association presumed to be the "vital center." This sense of satisfaction might follow from accepting with sanguinity the fact that 68 per cent of the community and 60 per cent of the profession asserted that the statements resulting from the attest function are at least adequate to the needs of these "willing and competent" readers. But then there will be those who hold the view that a fulfillment only to such a limited degree is not cause for the aforementioned exhilaration evidenced by the Long-Range Objectives Committee.

It should, nevertheless, be patently self-evident that the conditions so cogently set down by the committee for the performance of the attest function are not being discharged, and surely not on the "constantly widening scale," for the shareholders owning a substantial interest or for the financial analysts who are among the users of the statements. So it is that only 50 per cent of the community and 53 per cent of the profession believed the statements to be *at least adequately* (i.e., adequately, substantially or fully) responsive to the needs of these important shareholders; only 43 per cent and 38 per cent of the two categories of respondents, respectively, believed the statements to be at least adequately responsive to the needs of the financial analysts in our midst.

It must therefore follow that if Mautz, Sharaf, and Anderson are correct in their observations regarding the shift in the "vital center," the attest function is *not* now being discharged.

The responses to Question B-1 (h) cast a most interesting, if not sardonic, light on the responses to this Question A-10 (b); both of these questions relate to the adequacy of the financial statements for shareholders owning a minor interest. As was noted above, in responding to A-10 (b) about 80 per cent of both categories of respondents felt that this "salt of the earth" was at least adequately being taken care of by published financial statements. Presumably they have been thus taken care of consistent with the aforementioned standards of communication, including "readiness by [the preparer] to accept a format for the communication which is comprehensible to the reasonably knowledgeable among the users." Based on the responses to Question B-1, it must follow that this democratic "vital center" is being satisfied on faith rather than through their comprehending the communication. So it is that B-1 (h) inquired whether the respondent believed the body of generally accepted accounting principles to be reasonably well known to "individual investors generally." Both the financial community and the accounting profession categories responded emphatically (89 per cent and 95 per cent respectively) that these principles were *not* reasonably well known to this public. And what about the "customers' men with stock brokerage firms," those who are presumed to be the advisers to this public? Are these principles better known to these guides who are counselors to the hordes? The responses were correspondingly negative; 83 per cent of the financial community and 89 per cent of the profession asserted that these customers' men were *not* reasonably knowledgeable regarding the body of generally accepted accounting principles. It might fairly be inferred that the reason why financial statements are so adequate for the individual investor generally, in view of the fact that he does not comprehend the idiom with which the statements are developed, is that he doesn't really matter very much. And in so far as his advisers are concerned, it is probably another case of the halt leading the blind.*

* After viewing the foregoing data one may well wonder as to who heeded the counsel offered by Mr. Justice Douglas in 1936 when he was the Chairman of the Securities and Exchange Commission. Speaking to a group of neophytes in the securities profession he observed that if the institution of customers' men is to survive they must: "become serious students of corporations; let them be in a position intelligently to advise clients on reorganization plans; . . . let them be competent to advise on mergers, consolidations, recapitalization and the like; . . . let them become studiously concerned with the fundamentals of business and of finance. The only social vindication of that institution is to be found in such a course."[20]

Our Response to the Question Regarding the "Thou"

In the light of the foregoing it appears essential, urgently so, for the accounting profession to determine first for itself and then to make clear to the community, just who does comprise the audience to which it is presumed to be communicating. To be speaking in terms of a "public," "democratic," "mass consensus" responsibility, but yet proceed with an "elitist," "aristocratic," or "republican" body of assumptions and procedures is to perpetrate a hoax—an undertaking unworthy of any important calling, and surely not of a profession. Unquestionably, further research needs to be undertaken in this important respect to avoid further expressions of euphoria from responsible leaders of our profession; expressions which are based in the first instance on hope and presumption but which might then be shown to be mere rhetoric or even hyperbole.

This may very well be the kind of research contemplated by the AAA *Statement;* i.e., research which would re-examine the "reactions of the recipients of the information need[s] to be explored." To this end, we are told, the systematic research would utilize "recent developments in the behavioral sciences."[21] The possible implications of this open question on the auditor's legal liability to members of the financial community who feel that they have been disadvantaged by unfair financial reporting will be considered subsequently in this chapter.

The Second Critical Question: Who Is the "I"?

Having thus considered the identity of the presumed audience for the financial statements resulting from the attest function, we turn to the other end of this communications process to consider the identity of the communicator. This was essentially the question raised by Spacek in the speech referred to at the outset of this chaper. That there is real merit in his indictment to the effect that the accounting profession has not determined the responsibiliy which it is willing to accept for the absolute fairness of the financial statements (as distinguished from merely being fair in accordance with generally accepted accounting principles) can be demonstrated by the literature in accountancy. That this confusion exists at least on the part of the users, if not the producers, of the statements can be evidenced by the results obtained from the questionnaire used for this research; the basis for this conclusion will be described below.

The literature of accountancy makes clear that the responsibility for the financial statements, and the selection of the generally accepted accounting principles on which the statements are predicated, rests with the entity's management. Thus, from the AICPA's Committee on Accounting Procedure:

> *The Company and Its Auditors:*
>
> Underlying all committee opinions is the fact that the accounts of a company are primarily the responsibility of management. The responsibility of the auditor is to express his opinion concerning the financial statements and to state clearly such explanations, amplifications, disagreement, or disapproval, as he deems appropriate.[22]

That this is also the view of the Securities and Exchange Commission is evidenced by the statement of its Chief Accountant[23] and a leading writer on SEC accounting practice.[24]

Dwight Ladd saw the problem in terms of the power vs. property dichotomy, observing that:

> Given the profusion and confusion of professionals . . . it is not surprising that the real authority over accounting for corporations rests primarily with those who have the ultimate power—the managements of the corporations whose status and progress are being accounted for.
>
> . . . .
>
> This is not intended to impute wrong motives to corporation managers. The fact is that . . . corporation managers hold the balance of power. When their best interests, as they see them, are involved it is not surprising that they use the power to protect them.[25]

This condition was the subject of critical comment by John L. Hennessy in his paper delivered to the University of Colorado Symposium, thus:

> It might be well to point out . . . that the auditor is not required to state that the principles followed were proper or that, in his opinion, the financial statements give a fair presentation. Thus it is possible that the individual auditor may actually believe that the statements are not fairly presented. Nevertheless, as long as the accounting practices followed by the company fall within the so-called "generally accepted accounting principles" an unqualified opinion may be rendered.[26]

A corresponding view of the accountant's role (and a corresponding degree of concern) was expressed by Patrick Kemp; in his opinion our rules of professional conduct should be restated so that a CPA who "renders an unqualified opinion where fair presentation does not exist . . . shirks his duty." The present state of affairs, in his view, could undermine public trust in the profession—an intolerable consequence.[27]

And in his article devoted to this subject of the center of the responsibility for the audited financial statements, Herbert E. Miller begins with the aphorism about "too many cooks spoiling the broth" and concludes with the following note of concern:

> Of course . . . audited statements aren't really management's but neither are they the CPA's or the SEC's. They are the product of mixed responsibility, of compromise, of successful and unsuccessful persuasion by the CPA and of chain-reaction imitation of what has been done in some other set of financial statements. This arrangement leaves much to be desired.[28]

In the course of developing his thesis, Professor Miller asks the following questions: "Who is really happy with the present arrangement of mixed responsibility? Are audited statements really management's? Can we expect much improvement in the rate of progress in the area of accounting principles until the statement-jurisdictional problem has been resolved?"[29]

The Results From the Research Bearing on the "I"

Wherein, and to what extent, might the data from our questionnaire be responsive to the questions raised by Miller as well as to the questions generally regarding the ultimate center of responsibility for the financial statements to which the auditor has appended his certificate? Questions A-5, B-3, and B-4 are informative in this context.

Question A-5 asked the respondents to indicate whether, in their evaluation of published financial statements, they assume that they have been prepared by management, or by the independent auditor, or whether it was a joint undertaking. The question then asked those responding with the third alternative (i.e., the "joint undertaking") to indicate whether management or the auditor would make the ultimate determination in the event that there is a dispute between them. The responses to this question are summarized in the following Table 7. (The data in this table are consistent with those included in Appendix C; in addition the responses from the practitioners of accountancy are shown separately from those received from the professors.)

TABLE 7

Opinions of Respondents Regarding Their Assumption As to the "Preparer" of the Financial Statement

	PERCENTAGE DISTRIBUTION OF RESPONSES			
	Accounting Profession Category			
	Practitioners	Professors	Entire Category	Financial Community Category
Assumed They Were:				
a) Prepared by Management and Examined by Auditor	74.2%	52.4%	65.6%	48.6%

PERCENTAGE DISTRIBUTION OF RESPONSES

	Accounting Profession Category			
	Practi-tioners	**Pro-fessors**	**Entire Category**	**Financial Community Category**
b) Prepared by the Auditor	0	0	1.6	4.2
c) Prepared Jointly	25.8	47.6	32.8	43.1
Those Responding "Prepared Jointly," when asked to indicate who would resolve disagreement, responded:	*(Number of Respondents)*			
As Prevails Presently:				
Management	4	8	13	13
Auditor	3	2	5	5
As Should Prevail:*				
Management	3	6	9	3
Auditor	2	4	7	18

Source: Responses to Question A-5

The results summarized in the preceding table indicate that with only insignificant exceptions the respondents recognized that the statements are not prepared by the auditor. But as to the question asked by Miller, "Are audited statements really management's?" there was a significant disparity between the major categories, and also between the several groups within the accounting profession. Thus, while 43 per cent of the user category saw the statements as a joint undertaking, only 33 per cent of the profession so viewed it; correspondingly, while 49 per cent of the financial community recognized the statements as having been prepared by management, 66 per cent of the profession as a whole so responded. As to the divergence within the profession itself: While 74 per cent of the practitioners responded that the statements were prepared by management, and 26 per cent that they were a joint undertaking, the professors' responses were divided 52 per cent and 48 per cent respectively.

Those who view the promulgation as such a joint expedition are generally also able to recognize that management is now given the responsibility for resolving any disagreement which

* Certain respondents indicated definite responses to this sub-question but entered an indefinite response to the question preceding; as a result totals will not necessarily correspond.

they may have with the auditors. What may be particularly significant is the contrast between the way in which the two principal categories of respondents would *like* to see a deadlock broken. Analysis of these data discloses that eighteen respondents from each major category indicated the way in which a disagreement would *now* be resolved; of these respondents, thirteen from each category responded by "management" and five responded by "the auditor." However, when the same respondents were asked who *should* resolve this disagreement, the accounting profession still preferred management (nine to seven) as the ultimate arbiters, whereas the users of the statements asserted (eighteen to three) that it was the auditors to whom they would like to look for the ultimate solution.

The foregoing related to Question A-5 which asked for the respondent's evaluation regarding the statements generally; more specifically Question B-3 requested the respondents to indicate whether they presumed the responsibility to rest with management or the auditor for the determination of the particular situation. These responses are summarized in Table 8; here again, because of what was considered to be a significant divergence in the responses from the several accounting segments, their responses have been grouped so as to show them separately for the practitioners with the major ("Big-Eight") accounting firms, for those with other firms, and for professors of accountancy. This Table 8 follows:

TABLE 8

Opinions of Respondents Regarding
Their Assumptions As to the Party Responsible
for Selecting the Particular Principle to Apply

	PERCENTAGE DISTRIBUTION OF RESPONSES				
	Accounting Profession Category				
	Practitioners				
	"Big-Eight" Firms	Other Firms	Pro-fessors	Entire Category	Financial Community Category
Principle "Would Be" Selected by:					
Management	82.5%	71.5%	90.4%	82.8%	50.0%
Independent Public Accountant	5.9	28.6	4.8	10.9	34.7

PERCENTAGE DISTRIBUTION OF RESPONSES

	Accounting Profession Category				
	Practitioners "Big-Eight" Firms	Practitioners Other Firms	Professors	Entire Category	Financial Community Category
Principle "Should Be" Selected by:					
Management	70.7	50.0	57.1	57.8	36.1
Independent Public Accountant	5.9	50.0	19.0	25.0	55.6

Source: Responses to Question B-3

The foregoing data make it clear that the financial community is confused regarding the implications of management's responsibility for the preparation of the financial statements. This follows from the fact that while only 4 per cent of this category responded that the statements were "prepared by the independent auditor" (Table 7), 35 per cent responded (Table 8) that they believed that it was the independent public accountant who would select the particular principles to be applied in a particular situation. A corresponding divergence might be attributed to the "non-Big-Eight" practitioners; whereas none of these auditors held the auditor responsible for the statements as a whole, 29 per cent entered their view that it was the independent accountant who selected the principles to be made applicable.

What may be even more significant is that the answer to be supplied to Professor Miller's rhetorical question, "Who is really happy with the present arrangement of mixed responsibility through which management holds some degree of influence on financial statements?" might well be that "no one is really happy about it excepting possibly the auditors from the 'Big-Eight' firms." This last inference stems from the fact that while each of the other sectors showed a major shift toward putting the central burden on to the independent public accountant, there was no such shift for the respondents from these major firms. Thus, the financial community shift was from 35 per cent who saw the principle selection responsibility now to be with the auditors, to 56 per cent who would like to see it so; a corresponding shift was evidenced for the practitioners with the "other" firms—from 29 per cent who saw it as the auditor's responsibility in the present, to 50 per cent who would like to see the responsibility vested in the auditor. Not so for the major-firm respondents. They held at a mere 6 per cent of the respondents who saw it now, and who would like to see it, as the auditor's burden.

Question B-4 brought the respondents' views regarding the ultimate responsibility for the selection of the accounting principles to be applied in a particular situation into even sharper focus. This question asked the respondents to indicate the way in which the auditor would and should respond in the event that "management has selected a particular principle to apply but the independent auditor considers another such principle to be preferable." The responses obtained from this question are summarized below as Table 9, which again sets forth separately the responses from the several groups comprising the accounting profession category. This Table 9 follows:

TABLE 9

Opinions of Respondents Regarding
Presumed Action of Independent Auditor
in the Event Alternative Principles May Apply

	PERCENTAGE DISTRIBUTION OF RESPONSES				
	Accounting Profession Category				
	Practitioners				
	"Big-Eight" Firms	Other Firms	Pro-fessors	Entire Category	Financial Community Category
The Auditor "Will Presumably":					
a) Take Exception	5.9%	7.2%	23.8%	17.2%	22.2%
b) Qualify Opinion	17.7	42.9	23.8	23.4	45.8
c) Apply His Selections	0	0	0	0	1.4
d) Subtotal	23.6	50.1	47.6	40.6	69.4
e) Describe the Alternative but Permit Management's Determination to Prevail	23.6	14.3	14.3	21.9	25.0
Total	47.2	64.4	61.9	62.5	94.4

PERCENTAGE DISTRIBUTION OF RESPONSES

Accounting Profession Category

The Auditor "Should":	Practitioners "Big-Eight" Firms	Practitioners Other Firms	Professors	Entire Category	Financial Community Category
a) Take Exception	11.8	14.3	23.8	21.9	34.9
b) Qualify Opinion	23.6	35.8	42.8	28.1	37.5
c) Apply His Selection	0	0	4.8	4.7	11.1
d) Subtotal	35.4	50.1	71.4	54.7	83.5
e) Describe Alternative but Permit Management's Determination to Prevail	17.7	28.6	9.5	18.8	12.5
Total	53.1	78.7	80.9	73.5	96.0

Source: Responses to Question B-4

The foregoing table makes especially clear the major confusion which prevails on the part of the statement users and even on the part of many within the profession regarding the role of the independent auditor in determining the fairness of the statements as he sees the "fair." Thus, we find that fully 69 per cent of the users presumed that the auditor would either take an exception or qualify his opinion; add to these another 25 per cent of the community which presumed that the auditor would describe the alternative but otherwise permit management's determination to prevail. So it is that 94 per cent of these respondents believed that the auditor would do something overt where he believed some other principle to be preferable.

As to the profession itself: 24 per cent of the respondents from the major firms would presume the exception-qualify alternatives; a corresponding number believed that a description of the alternative would suffice; in brief, almost half presumed some overt action on the auditor's part to make his own views known. Practitioners with other firms and professors could be shown to have been deluded in even greater proportions than their "Big-Eight" brethren; thus, about half of the other practitioners and the professors opted for the exception-qualify choices with another 14 per cent in each group presuming the mere description—in brief almost two-thirds of each of these groups within the profession were of the view that something overt would be done by the auditor.

We can show that each of these 94 per cent of the users, and the almost half of the "Big-Eight" respondents, and almost two-thirds of the remaining correspondents from the profession were indulging themselves in an illusion. We know, or should know, that the most appropriate, if not the only appropriate, practice under these circumstances, at least at the time when the research was in progress in 1964, would be to give the client a "clean certificate." It is likely that such a "clean certificate" would still be the common practice even today; the reasons for believing that there might be some change for the better in the past two or three years will be considered presently.

In connection with the second phase of this question (i.e., relating to the action the auditor *should* take), the respondents selecting the last response (i.e., none of the identified alternatives) were also asked to describe the alternative they would prefer. While one such respondent remarked that the auditor should resign the account, another who described himself as a "partner in a national CPA firm specializing in SEC matters" commented: "The auditor should of course use his strong persuasion for adoption of the preferred treatment. However, so long as management's selection is generally accepted for reporting purposes, the auditor should not confuse the situation by reporting an alternative method." The consensual response from these respondents (all of whom, it should be noted, were from the accounting profession) was that a "clean opinion" was warranted as long as the principle selected by management is in accordance with generally accepted accounting principles.

Apparent from the data summarized by the foregoing table is the fact that the professors of accountancy and the financial community are most desirous of seeing an extension of this presumed critical and autonomous response on the part of the auditor. Thus, while 48 per cent of the professors *would now presume* an exception or a qualification, or similar overt expression from the auditor, 71 per cent *would desire* such action to become the standard. Similarly, 69 per cent of the financial community category *would expect* the exception or qualification at present, while 84 per cent *would like* to see this become the standard.

What is undoubtedly of paramount significance within the context of this analysis of the "effectiveness of communication" is that not a single respondent from the financial community recognized the prevalence of the condition which is now entirely appropriate, and which is (as noted above) undoubtedly an entirely respected generally accepted practice, i.e., the giving of a "clean certificate" and saying nothing regarding the divergence. Ironically, it is precisely this desire of many within the accounting profession, to see a departure from this "clean certificate," that was at the heart of the controversy at Philadelphia in 1960 and Boca Raton and Miami in 1964, and is at the root of the "uniformity controversy" today. It was only after much heat, cooled somewhat by a special committee, with reports and dissents, and a hammered-out compromise, that the Council of the Institute at its October, 1964, meeting finally recommended that:

> 5. If an accounting principle that differs materially in its effect from one accepted in an Opinion of the Accounting Principles Board is applied in financial statements, the reporting member must decide whether the principle has substantial authoritative support and is applicable in the circumstances.
>
> b. If he concludes that it does have substantial authoritative support:
>
> 1) he would give an unqualified opinion and
> 2) disclose the fact of departure from the Opinion . . .[30]

This action of the Council was made applicable only to "financial statements for fiscal years beginning after December 31, 1965." Clearly, the financial community has been permitted to live an illusion, since in mid-1964 (when the research was in process) fully 69 per cent of their respondents presumed a standard of disclosure *transcending* the standard which the Council directed to be made effective a year and a half thereafter (and for calendar year corporations this new standard would be reflected in reports promulgated only after another year beyond this year and a half). In fact, the results summarized above indicate that over 94 per cent of the financial community believed that a standard at least as high prevailed at the time when the research was in progress as that which was first only recommended by the Council in October, 1964 (i.e., six months later), and even then was made effective only prospectively for 1966.

As a matter of fact the contrast between the reality and the appearance can be seen even more dramatically by the realization that the Council's action relates to situations where there has, in fact, been an actual departure from a principle promulgated as an Opinion of the Accounting Principles Board (or at least subsumed therein). Since these opinions themselves are frequently ambivalent (e.g., regarding long-term leases), or do not exist in many areas of conflict (e.g., research and development), the need to disclose will, even in 1967, be far more restricted than that which the financial community almost unanimously believed to be the prevalent standard in 1964.

While the financial community has been thus shown to have been deluded, a very significant segment of the accounting profession also has been indulging itself in old myths, while ignoring the stark new realities. So it is that 63 per cent of the profession as a whole, and over 60 per cent of the professors of accountancy, and the respondents from the "non-Big-Eight" firms, similarly presumed (in mid-1964) a standard of disclosure which can be considered to be at least as strict as that which becomes generally operative only in 1967.

Our Response to the Question Regarding the "I"

To sum up this phase of the discussions regarding the parties to the dialogue: It is abundantly clear that serious confusion prevails regarding the center of responsibility for published financial statements; there is even greater confusion regarding the responsibility for the selection of the principles which are to apply in a particular circumstance; this confusion becomes especially aggravated where there are divergent accounting principles, several of which might be deemed applicable in a particular situation. From the foregoing it becomes apparent that Spacek's indictment regarding present practices is entirely justified by the results obtained from the responses to our questionnaire.

How shall we cut this Gordian knot? It is of course expected that the October, 1964, Resolution of the AICPA Council will have a salutary effect. Nevertheless, it is believed that the principal recommendation made in Chapter 3 is more forthright and direct and accordingly will be more effective in the fulfillment of the attest function. By our making explicity known, and in no uncertain terms, that it is the auditor who is to be made responsible for the selection of the particular principles to apply for a particular corporation, and that the selection is based upon *his* views of fairness (after, of course, seeking management's advice but not necessarily its consent), the question regarding the "I" would be resolved. By so doing the profession would be supplying a positive and, in our view, appropriate answer to the question posed by Spacek: "Where does the responsibility lie for adequate and reliable information for investors?" Such a categoric and positive answer from the profession, whereby we accept this responsibility, would end the pointing finger going round full circle.

We can see recent demonstrations of support from many important sectors of our economic society for just such a shift in the center of responsibility for the determination of the fairness of the financial statements. Illustrative of this mounting support are the following:

From a leading bank executive:

> Discussions with corporate executives, accountants, bankers, and investors generally reveal a wide diversity of opinion. Bankers, investors and the general public view the auditors' responsibilities in a far broader context than does the accounting profession. The corporate executive, however, puts an accountant's role in a narrow, reporting perspective. Some auditors seem to see themselves as non-questioning reporters working within the confines of "generally accepted principles."
>
> The fact is, of course, that the auditor is actually working for the investor. . . . I have heard corporate executives say that those who advocate more precise, informative accounting procedures are in effect questioning management. Of course they are, for that is precisely what an audit is supposed to do.[31]

From a Professor of Law:

> Changing the relationship between auditor and corporate management might offer some hope for improving the ability of the individual accounting firm to resist management's preference for a practice deemed objectionable, but little attention has been given to reform in this area.[32]

From a Professor of Accounting and Dean: After observing that "perhaps we should take a hard look at the traditional premise that published financial statements are managerial representations on which the auditor's opinion is sought," Dean Johnson concludes:

> Management is primarily responsible for the choice among alternative accounting principles used in compiling financial reports. Yet accounting statements are essentially reports on managerial performance. Apart from the obvious conflict of interest in such a situation, there is little assurance that management, beset by a variety of pressures to mould accounting results purposively, uses the best measurement criteria in reaching its accounting policy decisions.
>
> If management's control over corporate accounting policies were restricted, the independent accountant's ability to narrow the range of accepted alternatives would be strengthened. More important, where alternative accounting measurement procedures are available, the independent accountant would be encouraged to make his choice on grounds more consistent with the basic objectives of performance measurement. . . .[33]

From a Professor of Finance:

> Management's freedom of action in choosing alternative accounting procedures that have a material effect on the reported results should be strictly limited, if not eliminated, as there is a natural inclination

> for management to select the alternative that will make its position appear most favorable.
>
> The outside auditor and *not* management should be in full control of the "ground rules" for the preparation of financial statements.[34] [Emphasis in original.]

From another Professor of Law:

> Accountants invite judicial disfavor and adverse case holdings when they worship the false idol of managerial privilege and when they prostitute their professional skills in applying a rubber stamp to whatever management chooses to do instead of performing as independent arbiters of the soundness and fairness of what management proposes. If financial statements are in some respects misleading, accountants should not be surprised if the courts lay a large part of the blame at their door.[35]

It is significant that all of these evidences of a demand for the shift in the "center of gravity" are of recent vintage; a fair inference if not prophecy is that the pressures for such a shift will increase, probably at an accelerating rate as the shortcomings in published financial statements become even more evident. In our view these mounting pressures should have an entirely salutary effect on both the manner in which our principles are determined and what may be of greater import for our purposes, their mode of application.

Undoubtedly such a forthright revolution in responsibility could not be achieved speedily, despite the pressures described above; this is not a cynical prognosis but follows logically from the study of the Philadelphia-Boca Raton-Miami saga. It is therefore recommended, by way of an interim procedure, that the profession move to amend the wording in the standard form of the auditor's certificate in order to:

1. Re-emphasize the initial phrase "we have examined," and thereby to make abundantly clear that

"we have not prepared," and

2. Have the opinion clause read that the fairness was determined "in conformity with the generally accepted accounting principles adopted by the corporation's management, which principles were applied on a basis consistent with that of the preceding year."

While this interim measure would not, of itself, affect the fairness of the statements, it should go a long way toward clearing up certain of the semantic problems surrounding the meaning of the auditor's certificate and the nature and extent of his undertaking.

A Digression to Consider the Question of the Auditor's Liability

It is readily apparent from a reading of the professional publications, and even those for general dissemination, that our profession is experiencing at least its share of professional liability actions; in our view much of this litigation can be traced to the confusion regarding the parties to the dialogue. We are not here alluding to the narrow question regarding the standards of third-party liability so well reasoned by Judge Cardozo in the oft-cited *Ultramares* case;[36] instead we have in mind the proliferating cases wherein an aggrieved shareholder or creditor pursues the auditor to effect restitution on losses sustained from an investment or a loan and where the auditor resists the claim on the ground that the claimant doesn't really comprehend the limits on the auditor's function. In brief, the complainant is shown to have been deluded by the pervasive myth demonstrated by our research; the auditor in his own defense seeks to point up the realities as these are documented in our professional literature.

In this connection a recent *Fortune* article summarized a series of "spectacular lawsuits, revolving around auditing engagements" which has brought one of our principal accounting firms "into the headlines in not an entirely welcome way." The article then catalogues these cases: (1) On the West Coast the world's two largest banks, Bank of America and Chase Manhattan, have joined with two others to file a $6 million lawsuit alleging that the auditor failed to notify them that Otis, McAllister & Company, a major coffee importer, was using money from the sale of specifically designated coffee shipments for general corporate purposes instead of paying off the banks' loans as agreed upon in the loan arrangement. (2) In the Midwest management of Thor Power Tool Company was ousted when a merger with Stewart-Warner was aborted because Thor's inventory was actually $8.5 million less than the amount attested to by the auditors. Some Thor shareholders sued the management claiming damages; the new management sued the auditors. (3) In New York "the firm has been hit with eighteen lawsuits stemming from its role as auditor of the Yale Express System, Inc." (a fiasco described euphemistically as "The Big Skid at Yale Express"). (4) And also on the East Coast an investor in the Schrafft candy complex is suing the auditor for their failure to discern a conspiracy on the part of a number of executives to "candy-coat" the profit picture of a subsidiary.

The article then goes on to put all this litigation into better perspective, thus:

> Such notoriety has made Peat, Marwick management somewhat nervous and sensitive. Actually, however, P.M. has plenty of company in its legal headaches. Haskins & Sells, for example, is involved in a stockholder derivative lawsuit stemming from the great salad-oil scandal involving an American Express warehousing subsidiary. Lybrand, Ross Bros. & Montgomery is faced with a $41 million lawsuit involving Continental Vending Machines Corp. Arthur Andersen, Price Waterhouse, and Touche, Ross, Bailey & Smart all are involved in legal disputes over their accounting practices. In none of these cases is there any suggestion that the auditing firms or partners profited as a result of the troublesome audits. Instead, the plaintiffs are, in most cases, seeking to demonstrate that the accountants did not do an adequate job in auditing the corporation; as a result the audit failed to uncover an irregularity and allegedly caused

> a loss to the plaintiffs. Since auditors, especially the major ones, carry large liability policies, the plaintiffs are obviously hoping to recover some of the losses from the issuers.
>
> While the issues are serious and the details fascinating, the cases are, individually and collectively, almost totally misleading as any sort of guide or reflection of the scope, range, and depth of today's accounting firms. Instead, they tend to reflect the growing responsibilities and hazards of the accounting profession in an age of increasingly complex international business.[37]

This question of the auditor's responsibility for the financial statements is undoubtedly crucial in the colloquy before the United States District Court, Southern District of New York, in the litigation resulting from the Yale Express System, Inc. fiasco. On the one hand, we have the auditors asserting in their defense that: "No legal or ethical duty exists which imposes on an auditor the obligation to voluntarily reveal (other than to his client) information which he receives after he has certified financial statements which contradicts these statements. . . ." The Securities and Exchange Commission sees it differently. The Commission, which interposed itself *amicus curiae* between the plaintiffs (the shareholders, *et al.*) and the auditors (PMM), described the controversy as follows:

> Plaintiffs have alleged that shortly after PMM's certification of the financial statements of . . . Yale on March 31, 1964, for the fiscal year ending December 31, 1963, PMM discovered that these statements were materially incorrect in that they substantially overstated Yale's reported net worth and reported a substantial net income for Yale for 1963, when in fact Yale had incurred a large operating loss for that year. It is further alleged that PMM remained silent regarding the falsity of these financial statements until May 4, 1965, over a year later, when it restated Yale's

> 1963 financial statements as part of a report issued on that date.[38]

Then, on the basis of these allegations the SEC refutes the auditor's aforementioned assertions, thus:

> The Commission respectfully submits that this proposition represents neither good law nor sound accounting practice; that an accountant may not be silent if he knows that financial statements filed with the Commission and the Exchange, which bear his certificate, are false; and that public investors in evaluating such securities, have a right to rely on the accountant's certificate, as a continuing representation on the part of the accountant, that the statements which bear his certificate present fairly the financial position of the registrant as of the date of the financial statements.[39]

The auditors rejoin by stating that if the SEC's view were to prevail, it would impose "an overwhelming and onerous obligation on independent auditors" and would require answers to "certain relevant questions such as the following":

> For how long a period of time would the purported duty to disclose exist?
> To whom would the duty run?
> Assuming a definable group to whom the purported duty would run, in what manner should the notification be accomplished?
> Does liability exist if the after-acquired knowledge is obtained from a different client?
> Does liability exist if the after-acquired knowledge is obtained by a different auditor?[40]

It is most significant that the SEC has determined to pursue the "hard line" indicated by its memorandum in this matter; if its views are upheld, it would certainly require the auditors to re-evaluate their lines of relationship and responsibility. Further, if the Commission's views were to be sustained, it might well direct the auditing firm to detach itself from "special studies" and other "management services," since any information garnered by the accountant which might cast a cloud on the "continuing truthfulness" of the previously published financial statements would thereupon have to be disclosed to those who may be relying on such statements. In fact, such "special studies" appear to be at least one of the circumstances under which the accounting firm was presumed to have come into possession of information indicative of the serious fiscal and operational problems of the express company.

It would, of course, be entirely presumptuous to indulge in predictions as to how the pending litigation will be decided. It may very well be determined that the auditors did, in fact, proceed in accordance with the book of rules then (and possibly even now) in effect for our profession and that the statement users accepted the statements at their peril if they didn't first determine the limited responsibilities which we, in fact, assume. Without reference to any of the cases then or now pending (since we did not undertake a specific study thereof) we had occasion recently to comment as follows:

> One might react to this disparity between myth and reality by asserting that this is indeed a regrettable state of affairs, but that it is not our doing. In my view we cannot exculpate ourselves in this fashion; a profession with our third-party responsibility should be required to make abundantly clear, and in no uncertain terms, just what we are doing so that users would not experience the shock of recognition when they become aware of the facts of life as we really know them to be. Instead, it is principally when we are called to account in a court proceeding growing out of some *cause célèbre* that we are desirous of "setting the record straight." At other times we are pleased to run with the hare and hunt with the hounds; to accept our fees as the searchers for truth regarding the corporate entity and yet to act on the assumption (to switch metaphors) that we can lay the basket on management's doorstep if we get into difficulties.
>
> If now Jeremiah might become a Cassandra, it may yet come to pass that our profession will be severely

> jolted by one or another of the controversies which are presently in the courts. It is not inconceivable that some court may brush aside the niceties to be found in the established catechism and determine that the process of protecting the unsophisticated shareholder requires that the popular view of "who's responsible for financial statements" be deemed to be the standard of performance and accountability, especially where it could be demonstrated that the profession recognized the prevalence of such a pervasive myth. Cassandra is emboldened in this prophecy by the overtones and buzzing in the recent decision of the Supreme Court in the case of the illiterate seamstress, Dora Surowitz. It will be interesting to observe whether the unlettered seamstress has, in fact, introduced something of an unraveling thread for Conrad Hilton, *et al.*[41]

A corresponding prophecy has been made by Professor Bradley on the basis of his special expertise and study; in the course of his paper on "Auditor's Liability" he makes the following points here deemed relevant:

> Any assertion that the work of independent public accountants is riddled with intentional or negligent misrepresentation would be unwarranted and extremely unfair. And there is no basis for a prophecy that accountants are about to be inundated by a flood of actions for misrepresentation arising out of their performance of their auditing function. But the increasing importance of financial statements to more and more people will necessarily cause expectations with respect to the work of accountants to rise. There is already some evidence of a growing impatience in the market place with what is thought to be slipshod or management-biased work.
>
> . . . .
>
> It would not tax the ingenuity of counsel or the courts to locate the elements of an action for deceit

in cases involving deficient financial reports. If this proved awkward in a given case, the great body of negligence law could be pressed into service in validating recoveries against auditors for their role in the issuance of false or misleading financial reports.

Accountants should not take too much comfort in the fact that they have so far escaped liability for their approval of misleading financial statements. Attitudes change, and judges can be educated.

In the past the courts have been remarkably solicitous for the accountant's legal fate. Chief among the reasons has been the fear of ruinous liability. This is best illustrated by the classic *Ultramares* case. But in the light of the economic maturation of the independent accounting profession, further dependence on such judicial solicitude seems ill-advised.[42]

Conclusion

It might very well be that the epigram which introduced Chapter 3 should be reiterated here; in brief, until we know where it is that we are determined to go it matters little which way we do go. We bring this chapter to a close by responding along the following lines to one of the rhetorical questions raised by Professor Miller: We cannot expect much improvement in the rate of progress in the area of accounting principles until the statement-jurisdictional questions, as well as the question of the putative users of the statements, have been determined.

From this it follows that the reoriented research program urged in the preceding chapter should move at least concurrently to the critical reappraisal of these pervasive questions, extending as they do to all financial statements, and to all accounting practice. It is recognized that the ultimate recommendation, that the attesting auditor be responsible for determining the accounting principles, will produce the very displeasure from our clients which Savoie and Powell foresaw as flowing from the adoption of a definitive body of principles, and the extension of the auditor's responsibility for their application. It is accepted that these recommendations could meet with managerial resistance since their "managerial rights actually are at stake,"[43] and they might be expected "to cause controversies between accountants and their clients."[44] Nevertheless, even at the risk of courting such disfavor, it is believed to be good counsel because only then would the auditor be fulfilling the role defined by Montgomery who wanted him to fight the figures, find the facts, assemble the figures and "tell the truth about them, with clarity, conciseness and intelligence so that he who runs may read. . . ."[45]

Also, as was noted in concluding Chapter 3, it is granted that the burdens which we are placing on the auditor are herculean indeed; but then the rewards, in material and psychic terms, can be shown to be commensurate with this responsibility. That this responsibility may, in fact, be deemed to be a duty can be demonstrated by reference to the Encyclical Letter of Pope John XXIII, *Pacem in Terris,* wherein he described "An Attitude of Responsibility" in the following terms:

> The dignity of the human person also requires that every man enjoy the right to act freely and responsibly. For this reason, in social relations especially man should exercise his rights, fulfill his obligations and, in the countless forms of collaboration with others, act chiefly on his own responsibility and initiative. This is to be done in such a way that each one acts on his own decision, of set purpose and from a consciousness of his obligation, without being moved by force or pressure brought to bear on him externally.[46]

It is this exalted standard, so eloquently and forcefully articulated, which serves to close this discussion of the parties to the dialogue in accountancy. Beyond that, this emphasis in the Encyclical on the discharge of responsibility under circumstances which are freed from "force or pressure brought to bear . . . externally" serves to introduce the subject to which we next turn, i.e., a consideration of the problems arising from the attesting auditor's concurrent involvement in management services.

6

> There was a young lady from Kent
> Who said that she knew what it meant
> When men took her to dine,
> Gave her cocktails and wine,
> She knew what it meant—but she
> went.
>
> *Classic limerick*

The Proliferation of Services to Management

A major force identified by our research to be inimical to accounting communication is the auditor's increasing involvement in the rendition of management services for the corporation whose accounts are concurrently the subject of the audit by the same firm which had rendered these management services.

This adverse effect on communication will be seen to extend to:

1. An inability to define (or at least a failure to so define) the nature of the services coming within the ambit of "management services."
2. A failure on the part of the auditor to communicate to the financial community the nature of the services which he has rendered in a situation wherein he is also performing the audit or attest function.
3. A failure on the part of the accounting profession to determine the views of those particularly responsible for comprehending the nature of the audit function, and the implications thereof regarding the compatibility of these extended services with the auditor's independence, in appearance and also in fact.

That the foregoing is not the consensual view is readily apparent from the fact that the American Institute of CPAs, through a formal resolution of its Council, has taken a position diametrically opposed to the indictment here being leveled. The council, undoubtedly acting on the assumption that it was thereby advancing the interests of the profession, and of the users of the financial statements, determined that:

> It is an objective of the Institute, recognizing that management service activities are a proper function of CPAs, to encourage all CPAs to perform the entire range of management services consistent with their professional competence, ethical standards, and responsibility.[1]

Thereafter, the Committee on Professional Ethics of the Institute promulgated a formal statement, Opinion No. 12, which related to the subject of "independence" and specifically addressed itself to the need for the auditor's avoiding any "relationships which to a reasonable observer might suggest a conflict of interest." The statement then concluded that in the opinion of the committee "there is no ethical reason why a member or associate may not properly perform professional services . . . in the [area of] management advisory services, and at the same time serve the same client as independent auditor. . . ." This followed from the fact that the committee had determined that the rendering of these peripheral services would not "suggest to a reasonable observer a conflict of interest."[2]

It is to be added that the committee's conclusion that there was "no likelihood of a conflict of interest arising" was predicated on the assumption that in this area the CPA's services would consist of advice and technical assistance. Only rarely, the committee observed, would management "surrender its responsibility to make management decisions." And, of course, where the auditor-management adviser finds that he is making "such decisions on matters affecting the company's financial position or results of operations, it would appear that his objectivity . . . might well be impaired." Consequently, the auditor is directed to avoid such situations.

And to expedite the performance of these management services by CPA firms the Institute's Committee on Professional Ethics promulgated its Numbered Opinion 17 introduced by the headnote: "A member firm may form a separate partnership with non-CPA specialists in management services, provided such partnership observes the profession's Code." The objective of this opinion was to find some way of accommodating the present rule of the Institute, as well as the accreditation or regulatory statutes of the States, which demand that firms which practice as "Certified Public Accountants" be comprised entirely of CPAs. The problem, as the AICPA committee presented it, was that "CPA firms frequently find it necessary to . . . associate with technical experts who may not be certified public accountants. This creates the problem of providing these specialists with adequate recognition within the framework of the profession's ethical standards." The committee then gave its blessing to two alternative practices for resolving the problem, i.e., "(1) elevating non-CPA specialists to the rank of 'principals,' and allowing them to participate in the profits of the firm; [and] (2) establishing a separate partnership which does not hold itself out as practicing public accounting and therefore may have non-CPA partners."[3]

The former procedure is justified on the ground that the "principals" do not make a capital contribution, do not share in losses, and do not participate in "partnership decisions." Undoubtedly there are many partners, especially junior partners in large firms, who might well say that as far as they are concerned the committee has hit upon a distinction without a difference.

As to the subsidiary partnership procedure, this was approved because they are presumed not to hold themselves out as practicing public accounting. Unanswered, in our view, is the question regarding the possibility that the subsidiary partnership might well be deemed to be a "feeder organization" for the CPA firm, and vice versa. Surely such a posture should be held to be inconsistent with a professional code.

Be that as it may, Numbered Opinion 17 is now officially promulgated by the Ethics Committee as a standard by which to judge ethical conduct.

So it might be said that the rendering of these management services has received the *nihil obstat* and the imprimatur from the Institute. That any opposing view might be anathematized is indicated by a colloquy appearing in the Letters to the Editor section of *The Journal*. Thus, a letter from Professor Joseph

E. Lane, CPA, included the following expression of concern flowing from an editorial which had previously appeared in that magazine:

> The accounting profession must not try to whitewash itself in respect to a problem which concerns responsible members of the business community and the public. It must consider carefully the fact that some reasonable persons having knowledge of the facts do believe that an auditor's independence could be impaired by his rendering certain "management services." This problem deserves further attention.[4]

This was followed immediately, if not peremptorily, by an Editor's Note asserting that Professor Lane failed to refer to an April, 1963, article and the opinion of the Committee on Professional Ethics, all of which demonstrated that the subject had been given "further attention."[5]

And yet the controversy will not be laid aside. To the contrary, it may well be demonstrated that by its own terms the determination of the Committee on Professional Ethics was unwarranted. Thus, the committee rooted its conclusion in the determinations which might be reached by a "reasonable observer" regarding the compatibility of these management services with the independent audit function. If, then, it could be demonstrated that reasonable observers do, in fact, believe that there is or may be a conflict of interest, then it must follow that the committee would be constrained to proscribe the member or associate performing the independent audit function from the rendering of management advisory services. The committee does not indicate whether they had made any inquiry to determine the views of "reasonable observers," nor does the opinion define who these reasonable observers might be. It may be that the committee was therefore relying on its presumptions as to what might be these views; conceivably, the committee was relying on the same data as those which led John L. Carey to assert that: "Far from impairing the reputation of the CPA, entry into the management services field, in the view of public opinion experts, tends to enhance his reputation. . . ."[6]

The foregoing notwithstanding, there are signs that even the Institute has its moments of doubt, if not misgivings. So it is that President Trueblood's Remarks to Council in May, 1966, described as "a further cause of criticism" of our profession the "subtle, underlying doubt of the CPA's independence" as follows:

> And I think I must warn you that the question of independence is being raised not only in the press. You will hear something later in this meeting about questions as to the relation of management services to audit independence. And we cannot brush these queries away. Our rules of independence—no matter how meticulously worked out by our committees—will be acceptable to the public, only if the public understands our position and believes in our integrity. In the final analysis, our rules and attitudes about independence must satisfy society, rather than only ourselves.[7]

The very questions to which Trueblood referred were also to be asked at the Institute's annual meeting in October, 1966; this time by SEC Chairman Cohen who introduced the following "word of caution" with respect to "consulting services . . . such as market surveys, factory layout, psychological testing . . . public opinion polls . . . [and] executive recruitment for a fee":

> An accountant who directs or assists in programs of this kind raises serious questions concerning his independence when it comes time to render to creditors, to investors and to the public his opinion on the results of the programs. Public accountants should carefully reconsider their participation in these activities lest their continuation and extension undermine the main function of the independent accountant—auditing and the rendering of opinions on financial statements.[8]

The Results from Our Research Bearing on This Problem

As had been indicated heretofore our questionnaire was directed to a "financial community" believed to be comprised of "reasonable observers"; the results of our inquiry lead unequivocally to the conclusion that they would consider the complex of management services to be incompatible with the independent audit function. That the seventy-two respondents from the financial community probed herein are at the least "reasonable observers" might be demonstrated by the fact that they were drawn from the following fields of activity:

Investment analysts with advisory services and financial writers	15
Investment analysts with brokerage firms	11
Investment analysts with banks	13
Investment analysts with mutual funds, insurance companies, and associations	18
Others—including officials with governmental agencies, lawyers extensively engaged in securities underwriting	15

The "quality" and "reasonableness" of these respondents are further evidenced by the fact that forty-nine of them (68 per cent) are members of a financial analysts organization; ten (14 per cent) are chartered financial analysts. A review of the roster of respondents included as Appendix D will undoubtedly confirm this value judgment.

So it is that we turn to the results of this research which, in our view, would not support and in fact negate the optimistic conclusions of the Institute's Committee on Professional Ethics.

The roadblock to communication alluded to at the outset of this chapter can, in the first instance, be readily demonstrated by considering the data disclosed by the following Table 10, which summarizes the responses to Questions A-11, 12, 13, and 14 of our questionnaire. Summarized in this table are the responses from the accounting profession and financial community categories, which data are consistent with those reflected by Appendix C. In addition, this table classifies the responses from the accounting profession to disclose separately those received from practitioners with the "Big-Eight" firms, other practitioners, and professors of accountancy. Again, the accounting category was here subdivided because significant divergencies in the responses were noted within the profession itself. This Table 10 follows:

TABLE 10

Respondents' Views Regarding Management and Tax Advisory Services by CPAs Performing the Independent Audit Function

	PERCENTAGE RESPONDING AFFIRMATIVELY				
	Accounting Profession Category				Financial-Community Category
	Practitioners			Entire Category	
	Big Eight	Other Firms	Professors		
Frequencies:	(17)	(14)	(21)	(64)	(72)
A-11 In your opinion the rendering of management services by CPAs in situations where they will also be fulfilling the independent audit function will:					
Enhance the significance of the auditor's opinion	11.8	7.2	4.8	7.8	16.7
Detract from the significance of this opinion	0	35.8	28.6	21.9	52.8
Have no important effect on the significance of this opinion	88.2	57.2	66.6	68.8	18.1
No definite views thereon	0	0	0	1.6	11.1
A-12 In your opinion the rendering of *management services* by CPAs in situations where they will also be fulfilling the independent audit function is:					
a) Compatible with the traditions of the Auditor	88.4	50.0	66.6	65.6	22.2
Incompatible with these traditions	5.8	28.6	28.6	21.9	48.6
No definite views thereon	5.8	21.4	4.8	12.5	25.0
b) Compatible with the independence of the Auditor	94.2	64.3	61.9	71.9	22.2
Incompatible with such independence	0	28.6	33.3	21.9	58.3
No definite views thereon	5.8	7.2	4.8	4.7	16.7
c) An involvement which should be encouraged and extended	94.2	57.2	47.6	59.4	18.1
An involvement which should be discouraged and restricted	0	35.8	28.6	21.9	54.2
No definite views thereon	0	7.2	23.8	15.6	26.4
A-13 In your view the rendering of *extensive tax consultative services* by CPAs in situations where they will also be fulfilling the independent audit function is:					
a) Compatible with the traditions of the Auditor	94.2	100.0	85.7	87.5	66.7
Incompatible with these traditions	0	0	14.3	9.4	20.8
No definite views thereon	5.8	0	0	3.1	8.3
b) Compatible with the independence of the Auditor	100.0	100.0	71.4	84.4	69.4
Incompatible with such independence	0	0	28.6	14.1	25.0
No definite views thereon	0	0	0	0	4.2
c) An involvement which should be encouraged and extended	100.0	100.0	52.4	76.6	48.6
An involvement which should be discouraged and restricted	0	0	23.8	10.9	27.8
No definite views thereon	0	0	23.8	9.4	23.6

	PERCENTAGE DISTRIBUTION OF RESPONSES				
	Accounting Profession Category				Financial Community Category
	Practitioners			Entire Category	
	Big Eight	Other Firms	Professors		
A-14 In your view, the rendering of *both* management services and tax consultative services by CPAs in circumstances where they are also performing the audit function is:					
a) Compatible with the traditions of the Auditor	94.2	71.5	71.4	75.0	26.4
Incompatible with these traditions	0	14.3	28.6	17.2	45.8
No definite views thereon	5.8	7.2	0	6.3	20.8
b) Compatible with the independence of the Auditor	94.2	78.6	61.9	75.0	26.4
Incompatible with such independence	0	14.4	33.3	18.8	56.9
No definite views thereon	5.8	0	4.8	3.1	11.1
c) An involvement which should be encouraged and extended	94.2	71.5	47.6	62.5	23.6
An involvement which should be discouraged and restricted	0	21.5	28.6	18.8	52.8
No definite views thereon	5.8	0	23.8	15.6	18.1

Source: Responses to Questions A-11, 12, 13, 14 of the Questionnaire.

The Data Regarding the Compatibility of These Services Generally

Study of this Table 10 discloses the following significant contrasts:

> When responding to Question A-11, 53 per cent of the financial community believed that the rendering of management services by CPAs in situations where they will also be fulfilling the audit function would *detract* from the significance of the auditor's opinion, whereas only 22 per cent of the entire accounting profession category believed it would so detract. And while 69 per cent in the profession category were confident that the management services would have no effect on the opinion, only 18 per cent of the user category were similarly sanguine.

Within the profession itself, it is noted that not a single respondent from among the "Big-Eight" practitioners felt that these management services would detract from the opinion, while 53 per cent of the financial community believed that the opinion would suffer if the auditor also performed management services.

Turning next to the response to Question A-12, it is noted that while 66 per cent of the accounting profession category believed that the rendering of these management services by CPAs (in situations where they will also be fulfilling the independent audit function) would be compatible with the traditions of the auditor, only 22 per cent of the financial community so viewed the dual practice. That the profession itself shows significant internal conflict in this regard is demonstrated by the fact that while 88 per cent of the practitioners with the "Big-Eight" firms indicated such a compatibility, only 50 per cent of the other practitioners, and 67 per cent of the professors, were of the same mind.

Also from this Question A-12, when asked whether they believed such services to be compatible with the independence of the auditor, 72 per cent of the profession replied affirmatively, whereas only 22 per cent of the community so believed. Again, there were significant disparities within the profession where affirmative responses were received from 94 per cent of the "Big-Eight" practitioners, but from only 64 per cent of the other practitioners, and 62 per cent of the professors of accountancy.

Question A-12, subdivision (c), then sought to determine whether the aforementioned view of the Council of the Institute (that it should be an objective of the Institute to encourage management services by CPAs) is a view shared by the respondents herein. The responses to this part of the question show that 59 per cent of the profession category as a whole, but only 18 per cent of the user category, would confirm the Council's view. Possibly indicative of the consensus expressed by the Council are the subsidiary data disclosed by this question. Thus, while fully 94 per cent of the practitioners with the "Big-Eight" firms would support this position of the Council, only 57 per cent of the other practitioners, and 48 per cent of the professors,so indicated.

Question A-13 revealed results which are of some interest even though they are less dissensual. When asked whether they believed extensive tax consultative services to be consistent with the auditor's traditions, 88 per cent of the profession and 67 per cent of the financial community responded affirmatively. Similarly, 84 per cent of the profession and 69 per cent of the users believed such services to be consistent with the auditor's independence. (The profession's response would have been even more preponderantly affirmative if it were restricted to the practitioners; excepting for one such respondent who expressed "no definite view" on the traditions aspect, the practitioners uniformly believed that these services were compatible with both the traditions and independence. It was the professors who served to reduce the percentages to the 88 per cent and 84 per cent noted above.)

As to whether even these tax services should be encouraged and extended: While 77 per cent of the profession replied affirmatively, only 49 per cent of the financial community category were of a like mind. Here again, divergence has been shown to exist among the groups comprising the accounting profession category; while 100 per cent of the practitioners believed that tax services by CPAs should be "encouraged and extended," only 52 per cent of the professors held that view.

Question A-14 combined the services which were the subjects of Questions A-12 and A-13, and then asked the respondents to state their views regarding

> the compatibility of the tandem of tax and management services with the traditions, independence, and orientation of the profession. As might be expected, the responses were essentially consistent with those regarding management services; in brief, it was the more restrictive category of service which dictated the response for the nexus of services.

The foregoing conclusions are consistent with those reported by Professor Schulte in the July, 1965, *Accounting Review,* as follows:

> Acting as a management consultant does suggest a conflict of interest to 33 per cent of the reasonable observers answering our questionnaire. Thus, the contention of the AICPA's Committee on Professional Ethics that the rendering of management advisory services would not suggest to a reasonable observer a conflict of interest is challenged by the findings of this study. . . . In the opinion of this investigator, criticism reflected in this survey by the substantial group of third parties who do see a conflict of interest represents a serious factor about which the public accounting profession should be concerned.[9]

This finding of Schulte was distasteful to Messrs. Carey and Doherty; when compiling their 1966 treatise on ethical standards they determined to reject it (even if they could not refute it) thus:

> But nowhere in the questionnaire or the article interpreting it is there a definition of the term "management consulting." This term may well evoke a reaction different from that evoked by "management services," which is commonly used by the profession itself. In any event, it cannot be assumed that all the respondents to the questionnaire were familiar with the specific services offered by CPA firms as aids to management. The respondents may have read into the question types of "consulting" which in fact are not commonly engaged in by CPAs.[10]

Messrs. Carey and Doherty then conclude:

> It is difficult to believe that reasonable observers—stockholders, creditors or other users of financial statements, or the business public generally—would see any conflict of interest in the fact that the auditor, in addition to giving an opinion on the financial statements, also applied his technical knowledge and skill to the improvement of management's planning, control and decision-making processes.[11]

And because it was difficult for them to believe, Carey and Doherty determined to reject Professor Schulte's findings and to reiterate the conclusion of the Ethics Committee's Opinion No. 12—that there is "no basic incompatibility" between management services and the attest function. It might well be emphasized that the Carey-Doherty difficulty in believing did not move them to ask for a research study to be conducted by the AICPA, or anyone else, to develop data empirically in order to substantiate or refute the Schulte indictment; instead their very difficulty in thus believing was presumed to negate his findings.

Entirely fortuitously, our study did not use the emotionally charged term "management consulting" and instead used the phrase approved by Carey-Doherty, namely, "management services." And even though we used the phrase which would meet this Carey-Doherty test, the results obtained by our inquiry also reject their sanguine acceptance of the compatibility of the two functions.

Proceeding further, our questionnaire did do exactly what Carey-Doherty asserted that Schulte should have done, i.e., give the respondents an opportunity to express their views regarding "the specific services offered by CPA firms as aids to management." We turn to this phase of our inquiry.

The Data Relating to Specific Services

The foregoing questions pertained to management services (or tax services) generally; so it is that with respect to such management services each respondent was free to determine for himself just what services might be brought within the frame of such services. Question A-15, however, directed the respondents to specific kinds of services which, based on the professional literature, accounting firms believed that they were ready, willing, and able to render. This question asked the respondents in the first instance whether they were aware of the fact that the specific service was now being offered by accounting firms to corporations for which these firms are performing the audit function; the question then asked whether the respondents felt the particular service should be thus offered. Both aspects of this question were deemed vital to the determinations regarding the effectiveness of communication in this connection; the responses clearly demonstrated the breakdown in communications in all three of the respects set forth in the introduction to this chapter. The justification for this conclusion is contained in the following Table 11, which summarizes the affirmative responses to this Question A-15. These data are again consistent with those set forth in Appendix C. Consistent with the development of the preceding table, this Table 11 subdivides the affirmative responses from the accounting profession category into those from the "Big-Eight" and "Other" practitioners and the professors of accountancy. Table 11 appears on the following page.

The Series of Graphs Developed from These Data

From the data in this Table 11 there was developed a series of graphs (included in Appendix F as Figures 11 through 20) designed to demonstrate the degree of relationship of the responses received to the queries in Question A-15. Figures 11 and 15 each charted the relationship between the responses from two different populations to the first probe of these questions, i.e., whether they believed the particular category of management service was now being offered by the attesting firm. Figures 12 and 16 each charted the relationships between two different populations for their answers to the second probe of these questions, i.e., whether they believed the particular kind of service should be offered by the auditing firm.

Figures numbered 13, 14, 17, 18, and 19 are each for a single population and show the shifts or spreads between that population's responses to the "are now" and "should be" probes.

TABLE 11

Respondents' Views Regarding Specific Kinds of Services by CPAs Performing the Independent Audit Functions

A-15 Listed below are a number of categories of management services which might be required by corporations. For each category indicate:

(A) Whether you believe such services *are now* being offered by public accounting firms to corporations for whom they are already performing the independent audit function.

(B) Whether in your opinion they *should be* so offered.

		PERCENTAGE RESPONDING AFFIRMATIVELY					
		Accounting Profession Category					Financial Community
		Practitioners				Entire	
		Big Eight	Other Firms	Combined	Professors	Entire Category	Financial Community Category
Frequencies:		(17)	(14)	(31)	(21)	(64)	(72)
a) Review all phases of a business in connection with a plan to expand profits	A*	88.4	85.7	87.1	61.9	71.9	36.2
	B*	76.6	78.6	77.4	61.9	64.1	27.8
b) Review all phases of a business in connection with a plan of the accounting firm's client to buy the business	A	82.5	92.9	87.1	80.9	84.4	62.5
	B	82.5	92.9	87.1	66.7	75.0	59.7
c) Review all phases of a business in connection with a plan to reorganize the company	A	82.5	92.9	87.1	76.2	82.9	58.3
	B	82.5	78.6	80.6	66.7	71.9	52.8
d) Appraise the organizational structure of the entity and the preparation of a manual defining responsibilities and lines of authority	A	88.4	71.5	80.6	76.2	76.6	19.4
	B	82.5	50.0	67.7	57.1	60.9	8.3
e) Prepare an executive development program	A	58.9	21.5	41.9	28.6	37.6	8.4
	B	58.9	14.3	38.7	24.6	31.3	2.8
f) Develop a plan of Executive Compensation (including "fringe benefits")	A	94.2	71.5	83.8	66.7	76.6	33.4
	B	88.4	78.6	83.8	52.4	68.7	29.2
g) Develop sales forecasts and budgeting in connection with sales controls	A	94.2	78.6	86.1	38.1	63.1	29.2
	B	94.2	50.0	73.2	28.6	49.1	19.5
h) Determine market potentials and plan profitable sales territories	A	82.5	42.9	64.5	33.3	51.6	8.4
	B	64.8	14.3	41.9	19.0	31.2	2.8
i) Determine sales quotas and salesmen's incentives	A	82.5	42.9	64.5	28.6	48.5	7.0
	B	76.6	14.3	48.4	14.3	29.7	5.6
j) Determine programs for increasing volume and profits through improved pricing methods	A	88.4	85.7	87.1	57.1	74.9	30.6
	B	94.2	71.5	83.8	47.6	67.1	30.6
k) Analyze job functions and responsibilities of the entity's personnel	A	94.2	78.6	87.0	52.4	71.9	22.3
	B	82.5	42.9	64.5	47.6	53.1	5.6
l) Determine the relative contributions of the entity's personnel	A	58.9	64.3	61.3	42.9	54.7	18.0
	B	58.9	42.9	51.7	42.9	45.4	8.3

* Refers to the (A) "are now" and (B) "should be" aspects of the question as set forth above.
Source: Responses to Question A-15 of the Questionnaire.

Figure 20 is a collage, bringing together Figures 13 and 19.

Specifically, and in greater detail, the relationships shown by these ten graphs are the following:

Figure 11: Relationships between affirmative responses received from the financial community and the accounting profession categories to the first probe of the Question A-15 queries: "(A) Whether you believe such [management] services are now being offered by public accounting firms to corporations for whom they are already performing the independent audit function."

Figure 12: Reflects the relationships between the same population categories with respect to the second probe of the Question A-15 queries: "(B) Whether in your opinion they should be so offered."

Figure 13: Relationships between affirmative responses received from the financial community category to the first probe of the Question A-15 queries (whether the services are now being thus offered), with responses received from the same category to the second probe thereof (whether they should be so offered).

Figure 14: Reflects the same relationships as Figure 13, except that they are here shown for the accounting profession category.

Figure 15: Shows the same set of relationships reflected by Figure 11 (i.e., the "are they now being offered" probe) except that the populations here being compared are the accounting practitioner and accounting professor groups (both of which are included in the accounting profession category).

Figure 16: Shows the same relationships reflected by Figure 12 (i.e., the "should they be offered" probe) except that here again (as in Figure 15) the populations being compared are the practitioners and professors of accounting groups.

Figure 17: This graph is consistent with Figures 13

and 14, except that here the relationships between the "are now" and "should be" responses are being shown for the accounting practitioners group.

Figure 18: Correspondingly, this graph reflects the relationships between the "are now" and "should be" affirmative responses from the professors of accounting group.

Figure 19: This figure is consistent with Figure 17, excepting that the relationships between the "are now" and "should be" affirmative responses are here being shown for the practitioners with the national ("Big-Eight") firms. (These respondents are included in the practitioners groups and accordingly their responses are also reflected in Figure 17 above.)

Figure 20: This graph is a collage of Figures 13 and 19 and therefore reflects the relationships between the "are now" and "should be" responses received from the financial community category, as well as the same relationships of responses from the practitioners with the "Big-Eight" firms.

A 45° curve (solid line) has been superimposed on each graph. Any point along this curve would reflect agreement in the affirmative responses received with respect to the particular question from the two populations being measured (or for the two probes from the same population, as the case may be). The extent of departure from this 45° curve would measure the degree of divergence of one population from another (or measure the divergence between the "are now" and "should be" responses from a single population).

In addition, broken lines paralleling this 45° curve have been drawn to measure "20 percentage point" deviations from the aforementioned "identity of agreement" curve. For purposes of this commentary any deviation or divergence in excess of such "20 percentage points" (and therefore causing the relationship to fall outside these "broken lines") was presumed to be a major divergence. A description of the major divergencies disclosed by each graph is included at the bottom thereof.

Again, these various graphs are included herein as Appendix F.

From the foregoing tables and aforementioned graphs it becomes abundantly clear that our financial community, comprised of the kind of reasonable observers whom the Institute's Committee on Professional Ethics presumably had in mind, would undoubtedly frown upon the nexus of management services being offered by public accounting firms, if the firms are also then performing the attest function to the client. That this is not essentially the view of the accounting profession has already been noted. This dissensual view of the financial community is most dramatically demonstrated by Figure 20 wherein the responses of the financial community and those from respondents with the "Big-Eight" firms were compared. Because of its special significance this polarization warrants our special consideration.

The Critical Divergence Evidenced by Figure 20

Because it is the national firms, the so-called "Big-Eight," which are so importantly engaged in the attestation of the financial statements which are then used by the financial community in its decision-making process, a comparison between the "are now" / "should be offered" relationships from these two groups of respondents was deemed to be particularly significant; this is the contrast discerned from Figure 20. In our opinion none of the graphs or tables referred to in this chapter, or probably in any of the other chapters of this study, more dramatically demonstrates the "two-cultures trap" which prevails in accountancy communication. Because of this special interest this graph is being reproduced on the following page also.

Study of this graph shows that the responses from the "Big-Eight" are uniformly in the "northeast (upper right) quadrant," thereby indicating that more than 50 per cent of these respondents asserted that they were aware of the fact that the services are being offered and furthermore that they should be offered. In fact nine out of the twelve categories of services are concentrated in what might here be described as the "northeast

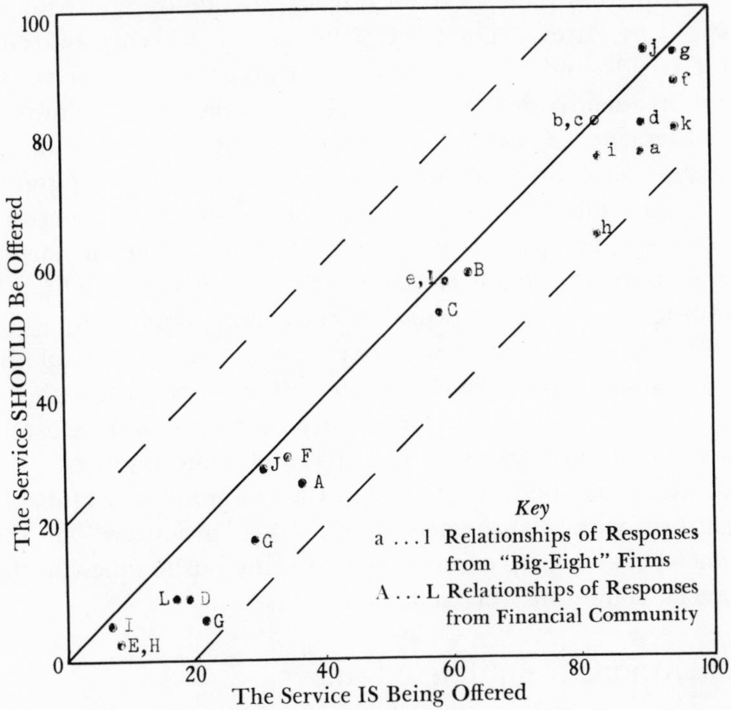

tip" of the chart. This configuration of responses from the "Big-Eight" fully confirms the established view of the Institute described heretofore.

On the other hand with the exceptions only of service categories (b) and (c) (relating to studies regarding an entity acquisition or reorganization, respectively) the responses from the financial community are all in the "southwest (lower left) quadrant." This indicates that fewer than 50 per cent of these respondents asserted that they were aware of the fact that the services are being offered and also that fewer than 50 per cent believed they should be so offered. In fact, six out of the twelve categories of services are concentrated in the "southwest tip" of the chart. The cleavage indicated by the graph is readily apparent through comparing this polarization of the respective concentrations.

So it may very well be (as asserted by John L. Carey) that there is a "rapidly growing demand by management . . . for more and better information as a basis for planning, control and making decisions . . ." and further "that businessmen expect help from their CPAs in meeting this need. . . ." Also, as asserted by Carey, "The larger CPA firms are keenly aware of these trends, and for years have been preparing themselves to meet broadening demands for what have come to be known as 'management services.' "[12] Nevertheless, the dichotomy of responses from the financial community and the "Big-Eight" practitioners demonstrates that this forward thrust, as described by Carey, is being made without the knowledge on the part of the users of the financial statements to which the auditor is attesting. And what is probably even more significant, while this forward thrust may well have the encouragement of the "businessmen" to whom Carey refers, it will not meet with the approval of the financial community probed by our research. This community was also comprised of "businessmen"; the distinction may lie in the fact that Carey's group was probably identified with management (hence the "producers" of the financial statements) as contrasted with the businessmen in the financial community of "statement users."

Conclusions from These Data

Based on the foregoing analyses of Tables 10 and 11, and Figures 11 through 20, it may be fairly concluded that there has been a breakdown in accounting communication regarding the presumed-to-be independent auditing firm's concurrent involvement in management services. This failure in communications has been shown to prevail:

1. Between the respondents from the accounting profession (particularly those with the "Big-Eight" firms) and those within the user category—a serious gap here manifested by the sanguine view expressed by the profession regarding the appropriateness of these services in the circumstances described by the questionnaire; these views are not shared by the financial community. Hence, any determinations on the part of the practitioners to move forward aggressively (and at an accelerated pace even, as recommended by Council of the Institute) must have been made without the sanction or even the

awareness of the financial community.

2. Within the financial community, which is not aware of the proliferation of management services which the accountant is performing concurrently with the audit function.
3. Among the several groups within the accounting profession itself, wherein there are conflicting views regarding the nexus of services which might be fairly presumed to come within the ambit of "management services by public accounting firms."

The Statement of the Case in Favor of Management Services by CPAs

In the light of our indictment, based on the results obtained by our research, how can the advocates of these services justify the position of Council that: "It is an objective of the Institute . . . to encourage all CPAs to perform the entire range of management services . . ."? It is to this general question that we direct our attention.

It is, of course, conceded that the rendering of these services has had an entirely salutary effect on the economic well-being of the profession. This was pointed up by T. A. Wise in *The Insiders;* after noting that some accountants find that these services are a "lucrative extension of what they have been doing in the financial field all along," Wise observes:

> Some of the big auditing firms have committed themselves wholeheartedly to the management-service field. . . .
>
> Ernst & Ernst, for example, will tackle any assignment in labor negotiations, personnel selection (it has its own staff psychologists available for consulting), new-product planning, and factory design and layout.[13]

More recently the same writer had occasion to comment on the CPA's great leap forward into management services as follows:

> It is noteworthy . . . that the Securities and Exchange Commission has been in no great hurry to condemn multifaceted auditing operations. Close students of the situation believe that this hands-off attitude reflects the view of Andrew Barr, chief accountant of the commission, who believes the public is better served by permitting the auditors to advise on a fairly wide range of subjects. This view is based on the conviction that auditors, as professional men bound by strong ethical canons, will be a strong force for more complete disclosure and sounder management methods through business.
>
> . . . .
>
> In fact it is not unlikely that within a short time Peat, Marwick and other auditing firms will have doctors, educators, industrial psychologists, and even advertising analysts on their professional staffs. Seemingly there's no natural limit to the fields in which modern management methods can be applied and therefore no limit to the areas in which accountancy —in its broadest sense—can be employed.[14]

The matter of the professional economics of these services has been the subject of critical comment by George Mead who considered the dilemmas raised by this proliferation of accounting services and relates this tendency to the profession's profit motive, and its commercial (if not acquisitive) instincts generally.[15]

Expressing himself enthusiastically on the salubrious effect these services can have on the well-being of the profession is Kenneth Axelson; when writing in the house organ of the firm with which he had been associated, he observed:

> In recent years advisory services to management have become an important part of the practice to many public accounting firms. In most large firms and many smaller ones as well they have won acceptance as the third major area of practice, along with auditing and tax services.[16]

The economic implications of the CPA firms' involvement in management services were prominently featured in a recent *Forbes* article. After noting that management consulting, excluding strictly technical engineering work, is today big business, grossing close to $900 million a year, and that Peat, Marwick, Mitchell & Co. grossed an estimated $17.5 million in management consulting in 1965 (compared with the $20 million grossed domestically by the largest general management consultant, Booz, Allen & Hamilton), the article continues:

> For the so-called "Big-Eight" national CPA firms, the dollar volume of management consulting operations is expanding at an average annual rate of 15%, as against 4% for the consulting business in general, and 10% for the 45 general management consultants who belong to the elite Association of Consulting Management Engineers. According to an authoritative estimate, the average percentage of gross revenue derived from management consulting by the Big-Eight CPAs rose from 5% ten years ago to 15% last year, and may be expected to reach 40% by the year 1980.[17]

Clearly, then, these services can be demonstrated to have had an entirely positive effect on the material well-being of our profession. But a professional pursuit is presumed to transcend mere material self-interest; to be legitimately pursued by a profession, such an important service involvement must be shown to be consistent with (or at least not inimical to) the thrust of the profession generally; the involvement must be shown to at least sustain (even if it does not advance) the profession's *raison d'être*.

The Summary of the Arguments Advanced by the Proponents of Management Services

Those who advocate the accountant's continued and expanded involvement in management services generally assert that:

1. The history of the auditor's pursuit confirms the

legitimacy of such an involvement.

2. Management services flow directly from the audit function and are complementary thereto.
3. If the auditing firm doesn't perform these services someone else (possibly less knowledgeable and less competent) will fill the void.
4. The CPA can perform both the audit function and management services without impairing his independence because the final decision is made by the management of the entity and not by the consultant. The consultant merely recommends (and may help in the implementation of the recommendations) but the decision is not his.
5. The accountant who becomes involved in the dual capacity of rendering management services and performing the attest function will presumably perform effectively since he is subjected to exposure by a subsequent probe. (This is what John L. Carey refers to as "the test of review.")

We turn, then, to the dialogue between the antagonists revolving about each of the foregoing arguments.

The Argument Regarding the Historical Legitimacy of These Services

Those who advocate the extension of management services by accounting firms assert that their legitimacy is established by the fact that the services have traditionally been rendered by auditors in order to help management do a better job; and that in any event these services flow logically, even if tangentially, from the audit function.

In this connection we have Axelson asserting that while management services may seem to be far removed from accounting, nevertheless "they have been a part of the work of the members of the profession from the beginning." Then, to prove his point, he points to a business development proposal letter sent by a public accounting firm in 1911, which he introduces as evidence:

> The letter describes the firm as "leading Production and Efficiency Engineers and Scientific and Economic Cost Accountants." It lists seven steps the firm would take in the course of devising a cost accounting system. Along with standard costing, expense classification, cost reporting, and departmental cost control, the list includes equipment arrangement, tool standardization, and materials handling standardization. "Our staff," the letter concludes, is composed of "skilled mechanics, engineers, and accountants specially trained in the introduction of modern cost accounting systems and efficiency work."
>
> As this example illustrates, the public accounting profession was in on the ground floor of the American scientific management movement. During the period between the two world wars, however, although the accountants certainly didn't get out of this field altogether, they did lose some of their early identification with it.[18]

One cannot be certain whether the year 1911 would also have found barbers engaged in dentistry and cupping. For present purposes it might very well be that the aforementioned letter should better find its way into some accounting museum with a caption like "An Unprofessional Card," rather than used as a standard for present-day conduct.

Similarly John L. Carey, who, when summarizing the views on the future of the accounting profession as developed by the American Institute of CPA's Committee on Long-Range Objectives, first described the kind of services embraced by the term "management services," and then showed how these services flow directly (possibly, though, tangentially) from the audit function. This last point is made by showing that these services are mere outgrowths of the auditor's "familiarity with the information and control system of a business," his "evaluation of internal control, which includes the systems and procedures" incidental to the system. So it is that: "Budgets, cost systems, inventory control, production control, financial management, and in general all procedures yielding data used as a basis for decision making are within the natural scope of CPA's management services."[19]

The Refutation of This Historical Rationalization

A study of the literature bearing on the history of auditing, and particularly with reference to the auditor's involvement in special services to management, would at least put into question, if not negate, the historical argument advanced by those who espouse the rendering of these services.

Writing under the title "The Independence of the Public Accountant," Darwin J. Casler reviews the literature of the profession of the early part of the century, describing the controversy which was then current regarding the kinds of services which an auditor might render and still be considered to be "independent"; he then notes that "the problem of independence which is involved in these relationships is remarkably similar to some of the problems faced by contemporary accountants."[20]

Also putting into question the historical justification of these services are the views of Pixley in his work on *Auditors: Their Duties and Responsibilities,* which is unquestionably the watershed of auditing history from the vantage point of the late nineteenth century. He there counsels the auditors that their duty is to be "strictly confined" to "ascertaining that the results of . . . management are correctly laid before the shareholders to the best of their knowledge and belief." This is a major responsibility being vested in the auditor because the shareholders of a company thereby acquire "two representatives of their interests, the one administrative, as represented by the Directors, the other critical, in the person of their Auditor."[21]

From the foregoing it should be apparent that the endeavors on the part of the firm to which Axelson referred, and the natural extension from the auditor's familarity with the information and control system described by Carey, were tendencies which were at least involved in controversy in our early evolution. In any event, while the public accounting profession may have been "in on the ground floor of the American scientific management movement," as Axelson asserts, it could be shown that there was sand in the foundation on which this ground floor rested.

The Rejection of the Historical Argument As a Guide to Present Conduct

Even assuming the validity of the historical justification, it would still be deemed to be desirable to preclude (certainly not extend) the involvement of the independent auditor in the complex of management services, at least for those entities for which he is performing the attest function. This conclusion follows from the fact that the environment in which the auditor is presently fulfilling his independent audit function has changed, is changing, and is destined to change at an accelerating rate in the immediate future. This dynamic process was recognized by George O. May[22] and, as emphasized heretofore, has been considered extensively by Adolf A. Berle, Jr., in his many works, especially *Power Without Property*.[23]

This changed economic environment has been clearly recognized by both the financial community and the profession probed herein, as is evident from the responses to Questions A-3 and 4 of the questionnaire.

Thus, Question A-3 invited the respondents' "view of the present day corporate society, and particularly the relative roles of the publicly owned corporations and their shareholders. . . ." The answer was almost unanimous: 89 per cent of the financial community and 97 per cent of the accounting profession asserted that it was "one wherein the shareholders have delegated all essential responsibility to the corporate management and where the shareholders then look to it for results." This was confirmed by the responses to Question A-4 wherein 76 per cent of the statement users and 86 per cent of the profession expressed the opinion that the relationship between the corporate management and the shareholders of a major American publicly owned corporation was best characterized by the statement: "Independent manager of property *vis-à-vis* persons entitled to the fruits of their investments in the property."

Looking somewhat into the future (and the not too distant future at that) it is probable that the alienation of the shareholder from the corporation's activities will become aggravated. This prophecy follows from the fact that the rapid expansion of our computer technology and its multifarious (nefarious?) applications permit communication and logistics to be extended far beyond any limits conceived of even a decade ago. This extension will, in its turn, require even greater capital accumulations, with a concomitant growth in the corporation per se, leading in turn to the aggravated alienation referred to above. This is the jeremiad suggested by Kenneth E. Boulding: "There seem to be some alarming potentialities in the development of information and control systems." This is because there is evidence that "we are once again in a period when the internal limitations on the size of organizations are being pushed back still farther."[24]

In such an environment, to whom should the shareholder look to exercise the "checks and balances" on management which are so vital to any constitutionally structured society? How shall we make clear to the shareholder that the responsibility that he had delegated to management is being utilized effectively, and that management is producing for the shareholders the results and the fruits which are appropriate under the circumstances?

When quoting Pixley reference was made to his observation that: "The Shareholders of a Company may, therefore, be said to have two representatives of their interests . . . the Directors, [and] . . . their Auditor." If, then, the auditor has moved into the ambit of management so as to enter into the decision-making process (to be considered presently), can the shareholders still look to their directors for their protective insulation, as "representatives of their interests"?[25]

Apparently not, if the views of Gaddis are fair. Thus, he finds that while the Board of Directors came to exist originally as "a focal point for the exercise of the power of ownership residing in the stockholder," there is now considerable evidence that the presumed apartness of the directors from management "is a tenet honored more in the breach than in the observance." Gaddis refers, with apparent approbation, to the humorous stereotype of the corporate board as "a club for the wise, successful, and elderly."[26]

Clearly, then, the condition today (as seen by Gaddis) is no different from that described by Mr. Justice Douglas a quarter of a century ago when he observed that when the ordinary citizen, or the ordinary stockholder, thinks of the board of directors, he thinks of them "as distinct from and superior to the management." Such a citizen or shareholder presumes that the directors are of such calibre that management will seek their advice and that they "will exercise independent judgment on corporate problems." Justice Douglas then concluded that "this kind of director is too often nothing more than a myth."[27]

To cure this condition, and restore to the stockholder the protection which he has too frequently lost, Justice Douglas proposed a plan for paid directorships.[28] Tangentially, it might be remarked that the surrogatory function envisaged by Justice Douglas might well be appropriately fulfilled by the independent auditor providing that he acted "with no conflicting interests whatsoever" and that he proceeded with determination to "penetrate the mysteries of the balance sheet and see the realities that lie behind it."[29] As a corollary, if the auditor fails to act in the disinterested manner expected of him, and which is presently presumed, he may be confronted with a revival of the demand for such an effective surrogate, to act in behalf of the alienated shareholder and the public generally.

So it is that the modern corporate hierarchy can be shown to comprise professional management, the directors, and the shareholders, each with its own special interests. Since the directors have, in this process of corporate evolution, moved toward a close identification with management it becomes all the more essential for the auditor to move toward an even sharper cleavage between himself and management (including the directors). It is because the performing of management services moves the accountant toward a closer alliance with management (rather than the dissociation which is believed to be so urgently needed) that the rendering of such services by the attesting auditor is considered to be inimical to the fulfillment of the profession's principal function, i.e., that of attestation.

In brief, even if one were to grant to the advocates of expanded and extended management services by CPA firms that such services were well rooted in the traditions of the accounting profession, such an extension would still be considered to be inconsistent with the effective functioning of the auditor, the attesting accountant, in our present-day corporate society. Further, even if the past had shown a pattern of progressive involvement in management services the recent history of the corporation complex should direct that this pattern be reversed. But what may be of even greater impact in this immediate context is the view demonstrated above that the performance of management services by the auditors had, in fact, been frowned upon traditionally, and existed essentially in the penumbra of the auditor's professional practice.

The Argument Regarding the Implications for Independence

Here again Axelson's evaluation is significant. He recognizes that independence is one of the most widely discussed ethical problems and that there are those who question whether a firm can act in an independent, disinterested manner when auditing a company's financial practices while "at the same time it is becoming involved with the same management by advising it how to run the business." Axelson enters his judgment with the assertion that: "In my opinion, too much has been made of this issue. The same objection applies, with even greater force, to tax work, yet for many years we have managed to audit the financial reports of companies whose tax returns we prepared without any sacrifice of our ethical standards."[30]

In another context in the same issue of the house organ of his erstwhile firm Axelson expanded on this theme that we are all probably "contaminated" even without the rendering of management services, but have nevertheless managed to retain our virtue if not our innocence. This Faustian dialogue is developed by him along the following lines:

> The threats to an auditor's independence are already substantial. After all, the auditor, like the consultant, collects his fees from management, and over the long-run audit fees are bound to be greater than those from

> consulting. The auditor is always subject to the pressures of personal friendship, a natural desire to see the company do well, and his desire to retain it as a client.
>
> Such pressures have not, in practice, destroyed audit independence because there are overriding pressures that work for independence. The auditor is always conscious of his legal, financial, and moral responsibility to third parties, of the possibility of re-audit by another firm, of the strictures of a highly organized profession, and of his own professional standards and training.[31]

Correspondingly presenting the problem in terms of such a dialogue is Morton F. Moss; he also first summarizes the arguments advanced by the opponents of management services by CPAs revolving, generally, about the tarnishing of the CPA's image of independence and the detraction from his *raison d'être,* i.e., the attest function. He too responds by asserting that we have already lost our innocence through our acting as the "income tax consultant." Moss then emphasizes the fact that those who criticize these extended services by CPAs just do not understand the decision-making process and they thereby assume that the accountant is involved therein. This he believes to be erroneous because:

> [T]his point of view tends to confuse management services and managerial decision making. . . . This confusion can be disspelled by dissecting the decision-making or management process into three parts. The parts are (1) finding occasions for making decisions or determining what the problem is; (2) discovering alternative courses of action; (3) selecting that course of action which will lead to the profit objective of the firm.
>
> The independent CPA can and should aid management in the first two phases of the decision process noted above. . . .[32]

(As to whether Moss's dissection of the decision-making process is fair, and whether his conclusion that the accountant is thereby not really making decisions is well-founded, will be the subject of further consideration below.)

There are those who at times are seen to reject the concern over independence rather peremptorily. Indicative of this reaction is Clinton W. Bennett's observation: "I have no patience with those who say that because the CPA performs some services for his client beyond the scope of the normal audit or tax service he loses his independence."[33] And in somewhat more measured terms, but nevertheless reflecting a sense of impatience, we hear Carey telling the University of Colorado Institute on Accounting that:

> Logic has limits, and so has independence. I doubt whether any human being can attain pure, perfect objectivity uninfluenced by any consideration of self-interest. I doubt whether the public expects superhuman independence on the part of auditors. If this were expected, then it would be necessary to have the auditor's fees paid by the state. . . . Obviously, the fee is important to the auditor, and if he is a weak vessel [should it be vassal], the fear of losing the audit fee will influence him more than the fact that he has done tax or management work for the client.[34]

Elsewhere, Carey furnished us with a more dispassionate response to the challenge to the auditor's independence interposed by those criticizing his involvement in management services. When summarizing the views of the Long-Range Objectives Committee of the Institute, Carey observed that the real test of the CPA's independence lies in the environment in which the CPA works; he then proceeds to outline the test of review in the following terms:

> All phases of his audit and tax work and all phases of his management service activity are, if challenged, subject to review, examination, and criticism by his fellow practitioners. If the test of review can be ap-

> plied to the work of any CPA, and if the individual CPA is willing to undergo the critical appraisal of his work by others, then it is difficult to raise serious questions of independence about the propriety of a combined auditing and management service activity.[35]

We can see AICPA President Trueblood allied with the state-of-mind advocates; thus, he recognized that "no CPA can split himself into two persons—one an advocate, the other an attester. But he *can,* I believe, always keep in mind his professional duties in both roles, and he *can* discharge his responsibilities." Who will judge these two "cans" which were emphasized by Trueblood? In his view "the individual himself must decide when and where his dual roles might conflict, and he must sometimes make his choice of one or the other. But specified rules will probably not be of much use."[36]

The Summary of the Independence Argument As Seen by the Proponents of Management Services

The rebuttal, then, to those who are concerned lest the auditor lose his independence by reason of this proliferation of management services, may be summarized as follows:

1. The auditor's independence has already been put into question by the practicalities inherent in the engagement. This follows from the fact that it is the corporation's management which controls the appointment and compensation of the auditor.
2. The wall of independence has already been breached by the fact that the auditor has traditionally involved himself in the tax consultative role.
3. Independence is, after all, a state of mind. So long as the auditor's mind and his conscience are satisfied that he is independent, then independent he is.
4. The management services relationship is purely that of counselling management. The decision making is still that of management and *not* of the auditor-management counsellor.

5. The auditor who is also rendering management services for his client is constrained to perform both these tasks with independence since his work may, "if challenged, [be] subject to review, examination and criticism by his fellow practitioners." This is the "test of review" suggested by Carey as being the ultimate constraining and self-disciplining force.

A Dissensual View Regarding the Auditor's Involvement in Management Services

What judgment shall we enter regarding the issue here under consideration, whether the attesting accountant has compromised his independence, in appearance, at least, if not in fact, when he has permitted himself to render management services to the entity which is the subject of his attest function? Our response will follow the several "lines of defense" suggested by the foregoing.

Independence has already been breached by the circumstances of the engagement. To this argument, that the amenities regarding the engagement and compensation of the auditor have already corroded his independence, there is no ready answer at present excepting to say that: Not inconceivably this very corrosion in the profession's independence, coupled with the dilemmas stemming from its failure to define the underlying body of its knowledge, i.e., its generally accepted accounting principles, may combine to produce a demand that the auditors of our major publicly owned corporations (at least) be engaged by a public commission, and compensated from a pool provided by levies against the corporations. This is a practice which already prevails in some regulated industries; this possibility has already been alluded to in presenting Mr. Justice Douglas's recommendation for the designation of "paid directors." In fact, it might fairly be asserted that it is this very inherent conflict, stemming from the engagement and compensation of the auditor, which should compel the profession to be even more circumspect regarding its image and posture of independence than might otherwise be necessary.

Independence has already been breached by the auditor's

rendering of tax services. To this argument, the response might well be that this service, also, should be declared "off limits" for the attesting accountant. Nor is this a mere capricious, "flip" remark; it is squarely consistent with the way in which Professor Bittker "put it on the line" for us in closing his Ford Distinguished Lectures:

> Much has been said about the independence of the accountant, especially his obligation to prepare financial statements in accord with professional standards, however much this may offend his client, because lenders and other members of the public rely on these statements. This is a noble ambition, but I cannot help but feel that its achievement is jeopardized by the accountant's role as planner and as advocate in tax matters. If the accountant has advised his client on the tax consequences of a contemplated sale of property or a liquidation of a subsidiary, what is he to do when preparing a financial statement if further research or a new administrative ruling or judicial decision casts doubt on the validity of his original views? . . . Similarly, if an accountant represents his client before the Internal Revenue Service in a tax dispute, can he properly claim to be independent in certifying to the client's financial statements? If in the administrative proceeding the legal validity of the accountant's classification of items in the taxpayer's accounts is disputed, can he properly be both a witness to the facts and a representative of the client urging a partisan position? Viewing these issues as a lawyer, I am doubtful that independence can be maintained under the pressure of a competing role, and even more doubtful that the public appearance of independence, which is also of importance to the profession, can be preserved in such cases.[37] [Citations omitted.]

Independence is in all events "a state of mind." Such an argument, which makes the presence or absence of independence depend on the attesting accountant's own viscera, conscience, and consciousness, is undoubtedly fair and appropriate. Unquestionably there are men who are absolutely and unqualifiedly beyond corruption, regardless of the circumstances and the temptations. To the extent that such men exist in the accounting profession and are determined to be involved in management services, the conclusions herein set forth will be unfair and unjust. However, in the real world it is necessary to rely on the "preponderance of probabilities," and this militates against any such presumption of incorruptibility. And if the profession did want to indulge itself in such a presumption of incorruptibility the data developed by the questionnaire disclose beyond any doubt that the users of the financial statements would consider such a self-indulgence to be presumptuous.

That this should be deemed to be presumptuous on our part can best be demonstrated by reference to the general question of "conflict of interest" raised in the public sector of our society. This general problem was the subject of extensive analysis by a Special Committee of the Association of the Bar of the City of New York on the Federal Conflict of Interest Law. Included in its report were discussions of several *causes célèbres* from recent political history; especially noteworthy for present purposes was that involving the confirmation of Charles E. Wilson as Secretary of Defense. The Senate Committee recognized that the economics of Wilson's holdings of General Motors stock was not the central issue; instead it was because of the unacceptable appearance of conflicting interest that the matter took on such major proportions. The report of the Committee of the Bar quotes Wilson's recognition of this fact: "The thing that perhaps I overlooked myself was that not only did I have to operate honestly and fairly without prejudice, but all the people should also think that that was the way I was operating and that part of it I did not quite appraise."[38]

The Bar Association Committee then generalizes on the Wilson proceedings by asserting that: "In some measure the required stock divestment partakes of a ritual public cleansing, an act of forced ablution dedicating the actor to a public role after a private past."[39] For corresponding reasons, the very same detachment, and the avoidance of even the appearance of any entangling alliances, should be expected from the accounting firm performing the attest function; to assert otherwise would be to make an invidious distinction which might, indeed, be fairly interpreted as arrogance on our part.

Proceeding beyond the ritualistic aspects of the public purging, the so-called Talbott Affair (involving Harold E. Talbott, a former Secretary of the Air Force) serves to demonstrate the inherent wisdom in this absolute requirement for the avoidance of conflict of interest (in appearance and also in fact) in order to preserve the democratic process and the confidence of the citizenry in that process. A trenchant analysis of the "Affair" was presented by Walter Lippmann under the title "The Official and the Partner." In that analysis Lippmann effectively demolishes the "state of mind" argument, demonstrating that there are times when the mind does not know what state it's in.[40]

So it is that the "state of mind" argument has been exposed in different contexts in the public sector and rejected when discerned (and where the conflict was not recognized timely the state of the mind has been shown to have produced some unfortunate consequences). If, therefore, those aspiring for public office are to be subjected to the ritualistic public cleansing, an act of forced ablution, as a condition precedent to their undertaking a public role, then so should the auditor. This should follow from the fact that the attesting accountant is within the public sector because of his responsibility to third parties who rely on his determinations and advice, and especially because of the fact that these third parties are generally denied an equal access to the books and records and other underlying data which were made available to the attesting accountant by reason of this public function.

Still another refutation of the "state of mind" argument flows from the fact that the "state of mind" of the auditor must be different from the corresponding state of the accountant engaged in management services. Unless, then, we are willing to acknowledge a schizoid personality the argument of the advocates of extended management services must fail. It might be fairly asserted that the attest function presumes the "disinterested mind" (to adopt another Lippmann phrase), whereas the accountant engaged in management services must develop a management bias in order to fulfill his function fairly. It might even be said that if the management adviser did not develop such a bias or empathy he could not be an effective adviser. This has been commented on in the field of psychoanalysis by Izette de Forrest, (a post-Freudian analyst) asserting: "It is outside the realm of possibility that an analyst who is sincerely determined to cure his patient does not grow to care for him."[41]

A corresponding view was expressed even more sensitively by Martin Buber in a postscript to *I and Thou* where he describes the relation between a "genuine psychotherapist and his patient": "While it's true that the objective analysis might bring to light some unknown factors and be successful in some repair work," yet "the real matter . . . will not be achieved." Instead, Buber asserts:

> This can only be done by one who grasps the buried latent unity of the suffering soul with the great glance of the doctor; and this can only be attained in the person-to-person attitude of a partner, not by the consideration and examination of an object.[42]

In fact, after reflecting on the two preceding citations from Buber and de Forrest, it can be argued that a management consultant, i.e., the analyst in the materialistic world (as contrasted with the psychic), might very well be derelict in his duties if he *did not* develop such an identification, an empathy, with his subject. If he sought to retain an antiseptic air in order to preserve intact his independence and image of independence he might find that this "antisepticity" gave rise to a sterility in his performance of the management consultative tasks. This would mean that while he avoided the Scylla, he came a cropper on the Charybdis.

Proceeding further with the potentially schizoid presumption implicit in the duality of function of the accountant, the question arises regarding the responsibility of the accounting firm which finds that the major, and presumed to be vital, recommendations of its management services division are being blithely ignored by the entity's management. Is the audit sector of the accounting firm to be advised forthwith so that the shareholders will be advised that its management may be incompetent? More specifically, assuming that the management services division of the firm determines that a particular product is patently uneconomic and recommends categorically that it be abandoned, and assuming that there are substantial investments in development expense and other deferred charges shown by the balance sheet as being related to this product, should the auditor then be advised forthwith so that he could effect an immediate write-off of these deferred items?

To sum up this extended rebuttal—while the "state of mind" argument may appear at first blush to be logical and persuasive it soon becomes clear on analysis that it is a concession we do not make to others. Further, even if such a subjective test were feasible, it then becomes evident that to perform effectively in both the attest and management services functions we really require two minds, or at least one mind in two states—separated by a great distance.

The management adviser merely advises; he does not make the decisions for management. This was the argument implicit in the three-tier analysis of management services described by Moss.[43] The quick, possibly even the flip, response might be that neither is it the surgeon who makes the decision regarding surgery since it is the patient who determines it. This ingenuous argument, whereby the adviser assumes the posture of abject humility, is best illustrated by Machiavelli's letter to Lorenzo de Medici, when transmitting *The Prince*. The self-effacing Machiavelli there asserts (with an appropriate humility and detachment corresponding to the role professed by Moss):

> Nor I hope will it be considered presumptuous for a man of low and humble status to dare discuss and lay down the law about how princes should rule; because, just as men who are sketching the landscape put themselves down in the plain to study the nature of the mountains and the highlands, and to study the low-lying land they put themselves high on the mountains, so, to comprehend fully the nature of the people, one must be a prince, and to comprehend

> fully the nature of princes one must be an ordinary citizen.
>
> So, Your Magnificence, take this little gift in the spirit in which I send it; and if you read and consider it diligently, you will discover in it my urgent wish that you reach the eminence that fortune and your own accomplishments promise you. And if, from your lofty peak, Your Magnificence will sometimes glance down to these low-lying regions, you will realize the extent to which, undeservedly, I have to endure the great and unremitting malice of fortune.[44]

There is no doubt but that Machiavelli was sincere in these professions; yet the legend of *The Prince* has been built around Machiavelli and not about Lorenzo de Medici; so would it be with the counsel given to management by those who have performed management services of the kind considered above (and as probed by our questionnaire). It may very well be that in a less complex era when the decisions required to be made by the manager or entrepreneur were well within his own expertise, or at least frame of knowledge, such a dissected view of the decision-making process might have been appropriate. However, in view of the nature and extent of the involvement of our present-day corporate enterprise, those charged with the making of the ultimate decisions are not generally in a position to recapitulate the procedures followed by the consultants; they must therefore rely implicitly on the conclusions and recommendations of those consultants. Frequently, there is no trail left in the fact-finding processes pursued by the consultant firm; in that event there would be no basis for review even if the ultimate decision maker were, in fact, directly knowledgeable regarding the problem being considered.

More recently than *The Prince* the delicate question of decision making in our complex society was made the subject of Theodore C. Sorensen's *Decision-Making in the White House*. As Sorensen makes clear, the ultimate decision is the result of the interaction of the personalities of the advisers and the decision maker, per se. Much depends on the relative strengths of the several advisers and of the advisers vis-à-vis the President.

It is true that a President with the character and qualities of Andrew Jackson could be heard to say: "I have accustomed myself to receive with respect the opinions of others, but always take the responsibility of deciding for myself."[45]

The late President Kennedy and President Jackson might well have taken on the responsibility of deciding for themselves, after gathering strength and insight from their advisers, their counsellors and the nation. And even they, strong as they might have been, were frequently constrained to make their determinations in terms of their reliance on their advisers rather than on the underlying circumstances; nor could they do otherwise in the real world.

The foregoing retelling of the strength of the late President was the way in which it was presented in our dissertation when it was completed early in 1965; it now becomes necessary to introduce a tragic and ironic postscript because there was an episode demonstrating weakness even in our beloved President; an episode which Sorensen could not reveal in his 1963 Columbia University lectures. So it is that when he turned to his retrospective work on the Kennedy years, Sorensen concluded his Chapter on "The Bay of Pigs" quoting our late President's lament: "How could I have been so far off base? . . . All my life I've known better than to depend on the experts. How could I have been so stupid, to let them go ahead?"[46]

All of which confirms our inability, even for the strongest-willed of us, to make our determinations independently of the guidance and counsel of others; and as the problems expand into dilemmas the inability is intensified, probably exponentially.

Briefly, the lines of communication and the nexus of personalities involved in the formulation, giving, and the receiving of counsel are so complex and interrelated, that the giving of counsel at a high level and on difficult matters by trusted counsellors merges indistinguishably into the decision making, per se. As a result, any apartheid approach to the decision-making process must be branded as unrealistic in the real world.

That this conclusion is also fair in the realm of decision making in business is confirmed by Marion B. Folsom. In analyzing this process he observed that the general view of executive decision making is that it is the work of a single person, the president of a company or someone else in the line organization acting alone. There is, however, much more to this process, thus:

> Decisions generally are the result of a long series of discussions by both line and staff people. . . . It is often hard to pinpoint the exact stage at which a decision is reached. More often than not, the decision comes about naturally during discussions, when the consensus seems to be reached among those whose judgment and opinion the executive seeks.[47]

In the course of developing his thesis, Folsom describes the seven aspects of the decision-making process, including:

1. Analyzing the situation to find out if there is a problem,
2. Collecting facts,
3. Analyzing the factors of the problem,
4. Creating new ideas and new ways to tackle the problem,
5. Weighing alternative courses of action,
6. Deciding on a single definite course of action,
7. Following up.[48]

Correspondingly, the AAA *Statement of Basic Accounting Theory* considers the "various phases of the planning and control functions of management." In that connection they set forth diagrammatically the interrelationships among the various aspects of the process in what "may be viewed as an endless loop," as follows:

Phase 1—Planning and Control: Recognizing and defining problems, which leads to
Phase 2—Planning: Searching for alternative solutions, which leads to
Phase 3—Planning: Evaluating alternatives, which leads to

Phase 4—Planning: Selecting among the evaluated alternatives, which leads to
Phase 5—Control: Reporting on actions taken and results achieved in relation to objectives and goals, which leads back to
Phase 1—and then we go round and round, *ad infinitum*.[49]

It may very well be, as Moss would insist, that Item 6 in the Folsom classification and Phase 4 in the AAA *Standards* would be out of bounds for the attesting accountant but he would, presumably, permit us to become involved in the other phases. To such a position the response is that the excluded phase results logically, and in our view inexorably, from the others. And continued persistence in such an illusion might well be countered by the astute observation of Alfred Marshall made some fourscore years ago: "Experiences in controversies . . . teaches that the most reckless and treacherous of all theorists is he who professes to let the facts and figures speak for themselves, who keeps in the background the part he has played, perhaps unconsciously, in selecting and grouping them, and in suggesting the argument, *post hoc ergo propter hoc*."[50]

Independence is assured by the test of review. Finally, we turn to the so-called test of review argument; the argument presented by Carey and described above.[51] This argument too can be shown to be less than ultimately persuasive. But, if this argument is really fair, then it is difficult to see why an invidious distinction should be made between the subjective test which is to be permitted here while an objective, rigid test, both categoric and overt, is imposed on an auditor who happens to have a financial interest in, or is an officer, director, or employee of, an enterprise which is the subject of his audit. Yet it was deemed to be urgently necessary to amend the old Rule 13 (Number 1.01 in the new numbering scheme) of the AICPA Code of Professional Conduct so as to foreclose the rendering of an opinion in the case of any such entangling alliance; this despite the fact that the auditor-director might have been willing to subject himself to the very same test of review, and even a test of his "state of mind"—the kind advanced by Carey for the management adviser-attesting accountant.

Correspondingly, if the test of review is to be applied subjectively and introspectively by the auditor-adviser, then it should have been permitted to Charles Wilson, and all the other undoubtedly dedicated, honest, government officials who sincerely believed that for themselves there just could not be a conflict because they felt the two positions were mutually compatible, and certainly not antithetical.

(It might also be noted in passing that the foregoing rebuttal to Carey's argument might well be introduced against Trueblood's aforementioned assertion that the individual auditor himself must decide the "when and where" of any possible conflict between his dual roles.)

Then, too, as our research demonstrated, the shareholders, and the financial community generally, are not knowledgeable regarding the nexus of services which the leadership of the accounting profession considers to be fairly within its professional armamentarium. If the user does not know of the services which the statement producers thus deem to be fair game, how is anyone to know that a test of review, or any other test, should be administered?

Finally, to emphasize the contradictions inherent in this test of review argument, we have the question as to who would administer the test in an appropriate case. This was especially pointed up by Carey himself in a strongly worded section on "Testimony" by CPAs against defendant CPAs which appeared in his 1965 compendium. While he agrees that no profession should conspire to deprive the public of expert testimony needed in the punishment of wrongdoing, yet: "It may be questioned whether it is proper for a professional man to testify against a colleague when there is real doubt as to whether he failed to conform with professional standards or not."[52]

So strongly does Carey feel about this point that he would consider proposing a rule of ethics which would prohibit testimony against colleagues excepting where the witness could demonstrate that "there were affirmatively dishonest or criminal acts or gross negligence involved in the case." He feels so intensely about this proposal that he is led to suggest that should such a rule be deemed to be unconstitutional (because it is a "restriction of free speech," for example) he would then look for an "admonitory resolution" so that the CPA who is testifying will know "that such conduct is regarded as unprofessional and is disapproved by the membership." And if this weren't enough, Carey urges the Institute to provide expert testimony as *amicus curiae* in behalf of "CPAs who are the object of claims believed to be unjustified."[53]

Irrespective of the merits of Carey's position regarding the responsibility of a professional to testify as to the activities of a colleague (and we have reasons to doubt such merits) it is abundantly clear that to the extent his views are shared by the profession it would be difficult indeed to find persons within the profession to administer his test of review. And if anyone were to involve himself in the administration of such a test it might well be the examiner, rather than the respondent, who finds himself the subject of professional obloquy and even ostracism. So it is that the test of review also is deemed to be a poor ring of defense for the independence of the auditor who embarks on the rendering of management services for the entity which is the subject of his attest function.

Summary and Conclusions

In sum, we believe that the rendering of management services by accounting firms who concurrently are performing the attest function is believed to be a condition which contributes to the communications gap in financial reporting, as is evidenced by the following gaps:

1. The failure to articulate (probably because of an inability or reluctance to define) the nexus of services coming within the ambit of "management services."
2. The failure to make known to the financial community the services which the profession (or at least the Institute) believes might be appropriately rendered by an accounting firm which concurrently performs the attest function.

3. The failure on the part of the leaders of the profession to recognize that the financial community would be adverse to the extension of such management services. This failure is evidenced by the officially promulgated position of the AICPA which would encourage the extension of these services, whereas our research demonstrates that the community is in opposition thereto.

Based on all of the foregoing it is believed that the answer supplied by Professor Delmer P. Hylton to the question "Are consulting and auditing compatible?" is entirely warranted. His view is to the effect that an accounting firm performing the attest function for a particular entity should be proscribed from rendering any management services to that entity. His solution, "is simply the adoption of the practice of referring the audit client to other CPAs. . . . Alternatively, the auditor could accept the management services engagement and explain to his client that he can no longer serve as his auditor."[54]

This conclusion is consistent with the following recommendations heretofore set forth by us:

> Let us establish standards looking to the dissociation of our profession from the taxation and managerial functions in those situations and circumstances where such involvement might jeopardize our attest function. Only such a dissociation will permit our profession to maintain its posture as a surrogate in our economic society—a role which becomes increasingly vital with ". . . the widening gulf which separates ownership and management in our larger business corporations today. . . ."[55] [Citing Gordon Donaldson's article in the May/June, 1963, *Harvard Business Review.*]

This recommendation for a strict dissociation was recently voiced by *The Economist:*

> There have been welcome signs in the past ten years

> that the larger firms of accountants and even some of the more enterprising medium-sized ones have been emphasizing and improving the management consultancy services they offer. This is all to the good. But as this practice develops, one distasteful truth had better be recognized. Increasingly, the auditor will spend part of his time reporting to the directors on the working of parts of the company, and then periodically change his hat to report on the directors to the shareholders, whom he may never see. Already some people regard auditors as being too closely associated with the directors, with whom they have been working over the years, to maintain the independence they ought to have. This danger could be aggravated as accountants move further into the management consultancy field. It will become acute if the dream of a management audit ever starts crystallizing into reality. At some point it may well become necessary for the accountancy profession to make a special rule for those of its members doing work for public companies: that if your firm does a public company audit, it does no other work for that company.[56]

And then we have the counsel to the same effect given to the 1966 annual meeting of the Institute by Chairman Cohen of the Securities and Exchange Commission to which reference was made heretofore.[57] Assuming that we consider the editors of *The Economist,* Chairman Cohen, the respondents to our questionnaire, *et al.,* to be "reasonable observers" we have another dramatic refutation of the premise for the AICPA Committee on Professional Ethics Opinion No. 12, that the rendering of these peripheral services would not "suggest to a reasonable observer a conflict of interest."

We recognize that the foregoing recommendations made by *The Economist,* Professor Hylton, and by us will not be speedily implemented by the AICPA; in the meantime and pending such ultimate dissociation, the following interim procedures should be instituted to correct the communications gap which has been shown by the research to prevail:

1. The American Institute of CPAs and/or the Securities and Exchange Commission should move to accumulate better and more definitive data regarding the kinds of services presently being performed by public accounting firms, and the revenues being derived therefrom.
2. The Institute and/or the SEC should move to require all proxy statements requesting the shareholders' approval of management's engagement of independent auditors to describe in some detail any services performed during the preceding year by such audit firm other than the independent audit, per se, and the amounts paid for such peripheral services.

In concluding the preceding chapter we related this discussion of the proliferation of accounting services to the Papal Encyclical *Pacem in Terris,* wherein a person of responsibility was directed to act with set purpose "without being moved by force or pressure brought to bear on him externally."[58] This present chapter demonstrated the forces and pressures which may be brought to bear on the auditor through his performance of these peripheral services. We turn then to another standard tied by Pope John to the freedom from force or pressures: the person in responsibility must be possessed of a "set purpose" and a "consciousness of his obligation." The succeeding chapter on the special meaning of "What Is History?" for the accountant and his profession may offer some guidance to the professional accountant in his determination of his "set purposes" and the development of his "consciousness of . . . obligation."

7

> My first answer . . . to the question "What is history?" is that it is a continuous process of interaction between the historian and his facts, an unending dialogue between the present and the past.
>
> Carr, *What Is History* 1

> We have called history "the science of men." That is still far too vague. It is necessary to add: "of men in time."
>
> Bloch, *The Historian's Craft* 2

The Special Meaning of "What Is History?"

We have, thus far, described and discussed the forces inhibiting effective communication between the accountant responsible for the performance of the attest or audit function and those entitled to an understanding of the economic circumstances and accomplishments of the corporation. The forces which were considered were those which are probably most pervasive and perverse, namely: (a) the confused and ambivalent vocabulary or idiom with which this communication is being conducted (i.e., our generally accepted accounting principles); (b) the inadequate and misdirected research apparatus and procedures presently in vogue within our profession; (c) the failure to determine the parties involved in this communication process; and finally, (d) the proliferation of management services and the management bias which may result therefrom. Our research has demonstrated that there is a valid basis for the conclusion that this communication between the profession and the financial community is ineffective. At various points this study took on the mood of a jeremiad, asserting that if the accounting profession fails to make vital and dramatic changes in its ways of thinking and practicing, its status as a profession would be rendered seriously vulnerable. Further, accountancy would, probably should, then be denied a place in the councils of the learned groups seeking ways in which their particular expertise could inure to the advancement of the community and the world.

Wherever appropriate we have introduced our recommendations for effecting what we believe to be these vital and dramatic changes. In the course of these deliberations (and particularly when recommending such changes) guidance was sought from other disciplines. So it is that reference was made to such other fields of knowledge as law and philosophy and even the natural sciences to point up the fact that they too are beset with the problems of ascertaining their objectives and goals as a condition precedent to their role-fulfillment. Recourse was also had to them in order to determine the ways in which these other disciplines were seeking or groping for a solution—for some way of reconciling their transcendent objectives (as they discerned them) with their responsibilities and distractions in the real world. In brief, how did these other pursuits effect a reconciliation between the mystique, the charisma, and the need for maintaining day-to-day efficiency and viability?

It might well be asked that if these problems of defining professional identity and meaning are so common, why the expression of a special sense of urgency for accountancy? The response must be that accountancy (rather than, for example, law, philosophy, or science) is the pursuit which is here of central interest. And one might well feel about one's profession in terms corresponding to those used by Mr. Justice Holmes to describe the feeling of the knight of romance for his lady: "It is not enough to agree that his lady is a very nice girl; if you do not admit that she is the best that God ever made or will make, you must fight."

But probably of greater significance is the realization and belief that in each of these other areas of professional endeavor important efforts are being made to pursue these reflections of professional identity and meaning as a formal subject of intensive and high-level study; hence, courses in the history and philosophy of law, and of science, are considered to be important areas of separate study in our leading universities and their professional schools. In the accounting profession, with some notable exceptions, these areas of knowledge are considered only tangentially, if at all. So it is that in accountancy the problems of the historical and philosophic foundation for the special knowledge of the profession are considered almost exclusively as an incident to its technology—and then principally with the objective in mind of improving its performance in that technology rather than of giving it the sense of mission and purpose for which we must strive. For example, the history of auditing and ethics would, in all likelihood, be considered in connection with the better completion of the audit procedures, or to avoid transgressing the bounds of ethics laid down by the national or state professional organizations.

The special sense of urgency which we are here asserting relative to the future of the profession of accountancy, and of its place in the nexus of learned professions, is believed to be real and not mere rhetoric. In short, we believe that there is an urgent need for a reappraisal by the accounting profession to the end that it will recognize the need for sponsoring formal and extensive studies within the universities; studies structured for the development of identity and meaning for the profession. In addition, the leaders within the profession should be urged to speak freely, fully, extensively, autonomously, and independently on these ultimate problems, so that through this extended dialogue these problems might be more effectively resolved.

If the profession should fail in this enterprise (or fail to undertake it) then it is believed that it is destined to become a craft; true it may become a craft with a high level of technical expertise, but a craft nevertheless. Also to be borne in mind are the implications of such a result on the right of accountancy to be a respected discipline or branch of learning in a university complex.

References made heretofore to the disciplines of law, science, and philosophy were presented only as incidental to the particular problem there under consideration. The particular objective of this chapter is to round out the interdisciplinary aspect of this work and complementarily to give to this interdisciplinary process a unitary composition, a *Weltanschauung*. With this objective in mind the subject of the philosophy of history will be shown to have important parallels with the subject matter of accountancy, and shown to have some significant lessons for accountants. In brief, readings in the philosophy of history have demonstrated that the problems of the historian are very much similar to those of the attesting accountant (allowing for the differences of context in which the respective professions function); accordingly, just as the reflections of the philosophers of history have helped to give identity and meaning to working historians they can be shown to be capable of having a similarly salutary effect upon the accountant.

The Common Problems Which Haunt the Historian and the Accountant

In the Introduction to his compendium, *The Philosophy of History in Our Time,*[3] Meyerhoff sets down the ten problems which Dilthey sought to resolve in his "Critique of Historical Reason" and which Meyerhoff shows "still haunt the modern historical consciousness." These haunting problems for the historian are seen to have their parallels for the accountant; an awareness that the haunting problems are consistent for the two professions should lead to a study of the approach which the historian may be taking toward the resolution of these problems (or at least toward their mitigation).

It is with the objective, then, of learning from the historian that we first set forth the ten problems of the historian as envisaged by Meyerhoff; each of his descriptions will be followed by a statement of the parallel problem in accountancy as we see it:

> 1. The *subject matter* of history presents a problem. It is so vast and complex that it can hardly be subsumed under a single concept. What, then, is history? Chronicles or interpretative narratives? . . .

This question of the *subject matter* of history can be shown to have its counterpart in accountancy by asking whether it is the separate corporate entity or a complex of interrelated entities which are to be considered as a *Gestalt,* and thereupon consolidated. Even when we consider the individual entity alone, the question of the subject matter raises its head in the determination of product cost, divisional profit, contribution to margin, and the like. Further, just as Meyerhoff notes that the term "history" can be considered in a highly restricted sense or as embracing a broad spectrum, so can it be with accountancy; this can be readily demonstrated by recognizing that accountancy can be seen to range from mere recordkeeping, through the attest function, to national income (economic or social) accounting.

> 2. The *facts* of history are peculiar, as historicism has insisted all along . . . the inexhaustible multitude of historical facts are unique events of the past that are accessible to us, not through direct experience or experimental repetition (as the facts in the sciences), but only through memory or through the indirect evidence of physical remains, verbal reports, and written documents.

So are the *facts* of accountancy inexhaustible and multitudinous. Most are lost or obliterated in time; many are not immediately or ever recognized as being facts since they are presumed to be outside of the "entity frame"; others are lost because they are not accessible to the senses, or are not recognized by accountants as being of accounting significance. So it is that accountants too deal with the "unique events of the past that are accessible to us . . . only through memory or through the indirect evidence of physical remains, verbal reports, and written documents."

> 3. The *primary aim* of a historical narrative is to reconstruct these events in their unique individuality, not to formulate general laws, to bring out the particular differences rather than the common properties of the events included in the historical portrait. . . .

Just as the *primary aim* of the historical narrator is "to reconstruct these events in their unique individuality . . . ," so it should be the function of the attesting accountant to bring out from the events of the entity a narrative, a literary work reconstructing the pattern of entity events—in short: the financial statements.

> 4. The *language* of history is different. Again, a historical narrative reads much more like a novel than a scientific text—unless it be a dull history which reads like a tract in sociology. . . .

The *language* of history is different; the configurations developed from the vocabulary of history are peculiar to the historian. And so it has been demonstrated (in Chapters 2 and 3 in the discussions revolving about generally accepted accounting principles) that the special language of accountancy requires a special idiom. Correspondingly, the configurations formed from the presumed constant facts of accounting can also be seen to vary depending on the perspective from which the viewer looks at the facts and on the interpretation accorded the idiom.

> 5. *Fact, theory, and interpretation* form a closely knit complex in a historical narrative. The simple facts of history are not simple at all; or insofar as they are simple and elicit universal agreement among historians—dates, names, places, and the innumerable pieces of factual knowledge we learn in school—they seem to be trivial and only reinforce the demand for an interpretation. . . . The facts of history invariably appear in a context of interpretation. There is no narration without interpretation; and there is no interpretation without theory. How, then, do we disentangle this complex web of facts and theory, narration, and interpretation?

Consistent with all of the foregoing: "*Fact, theory, and interpretation* form a closely knit complex" in any accounting narrative, just as they do in the historical. The simple facts of history are not simple at all; insofar as they are simple (dates, names, places) and elicit a universal consensus, among historians or accountants respectively, "they seem to be trivial and only reinforce the demand for an interpretation."

> 6. The *methods* of history are often dubious and suspect. Some, to be sure, follow ordinary scientific

> procedures of evidence and inference; others, however, are quite extraordinary—whether they be called insight, introspection, empathy, imagination, or "understanding" in Dilthey's sense. . . .

Regarding the correspondence of *methods:* Just as the historian is called upon to first follow ordinary scientific procedures of evidence and inference, but then must demonstrate "insight, introspection, empathy, imagination, or understanding," so must the attesting accountant follow ordinary scientific procedure in the ferreting out of the "facts" regarding the entity and the drawing of inferences therefrom. But then the insight, introspection, empathy, imagination, and understanding become as indispensable to him as they are to the historian.

> 7. *Explanations* in history raise extremely puzzling questions. The historian shares the ordinary belief that to know means to know the causes of things. But what are causes in history? . . . How do we distinguish between secondary and primary, proximate and ultimate causes? What determines the order and hierarchy of causes in terms of which a historian constructs his narrative? . . .

Mere knowledge of facts does not provide *explanations,* either for the historian or the accountant. Just as comprehension of "causality" plays such an important role in the narrating of history, so it is in the forming of the configurations in accounting. The mere recital of such accounting dilemmas as "joint costs," "direct costing," "pooling vs. purchase," "long-term leases," should demonstrate that the accountant, very much like the historian, must "distinguish between secondary and primary, proximate and ultimate causes. . . ." Both the accountant and the historian are then constrained to ask: "How far does it [the order and hierarchy of causes] reflect a subjective point of view?"

> 8. *Freedom* is a special problem for history. There may not be any historical neccessity; but, no doubt, there is a necessity of nature, environment,

> heredity, conditioned reflex, social pressure, legal restrictions, and perhaps even unconscious motivations. Yet there must also be a sense of freedom. . .

"Freedom is a special problem for history"; so is *independence* a very special problem for accountancy. Just as Meyerhoff asserts "there is a necessity of nature, environment, heredity, conditioned reflex, social pressure, legal restrictions, and perhaps even unconscious motivations" which reflect themselves in the historical narrative, so these same forces can be shown to impinge on the functioning of the attesting accountant. Clearly, the historian must be possessed of a sense of freedom in order that his behavior might transcend these recognized limits on his objectivity; correspondingly the accountant must dedicate himself to a standard of independence to permit a corresponding transcending.

> 9. *Values,* emotive meanings, and ideological concepts invariably enter into the study of history. They are, in turn, as historicism has shown, subject to change and social climate. . . .

When objectivity is recognized as being illusory, then the historian (and also the accountant) comes face-to-face with his *values.* Then, recognizing this transcendent significance of "freedom" and the inexorable limitations on "objectivity," the historian asks whether he can (or even should) divest himself of "the preconceptions of his age, class, or personal *Weltanschauung.*" Assuming that he determines that he cannot (or should not) so divest himself, then is he not constrained to accord to someone else, either now or at some other time, the privilege of looking at the nexus of facts which led to his narration from a different perspective, and thereby possibly coming up with a different end-result? So should it be with accountants; recognizing that their pursuit similarly calls for a goodly measure of subjective configuration, we must, with a fair humility, permit others with a possibly divergent orientation or perspective to produce a result which may diverge from our narrative.

> 10. *Meaning* has receded, or vanished, from history in the sense of the philosophical theories discussed above. Instead of a single theoretical law or a universal rational principle, the modern historian operates with a plurality of laws and principles, the logical status of which is often very obscure. . . . Instead of a single linear direction, he discovers multiple and incompatible directions in history—or no direction at all.

Finally, *meaning* in history—which presumes a "single theoretical law or a universal rational principle" as contrasted with "a plurality of laws and principles," "a coherent, unified pattern of world history" juxtaposed against "a great variety of different historical forms and patterns of culture," and "a single linear direction" to be distinguished from the "multiple and incompatible directions in history"—can find all its parallels in accountancy. This is evidenced by the controversies referred to in Chapters 2 and 3 regarding accounting principles; by the debates between the relativists and the absolutists, between those urging that "many flowers be permitted to grow" and those who seek a body of derived dogma which they would then establish as the good doctrine.

The foregoing demonstrates the parallels between the haunting pervasive dilemmas of the historian and those which prevail for the accountant. Whether the problems relate to those of "The Object of the Study" (e.g., the subject matter, the facts, the special language or idiom, the nexus formed by fact, theory, and interpretation), or whether they pertain to "The Professional As the Subject" (e.g., his methods, values, forces, and factors which have helped to shape the professional even before he has entered into the dialectic process with the subject matter of his discipline), the problems of the historian can be seen to have their counterpart for the accountant. It might be fairly said that we could substitute any learned pursuit for accountancy in the foregoing parallelism and the relationship would still be fair. Thus, the problems are undoubtedly common for the law, theology, the natural and behavioral sciences, among others; however, it is the historian and the accountant who are here being weighed in the balance and found to correspond in so far as these haunting dilemmas are concerned.

The Parallel Ends

But then the parallel ends and a distinction needs to be made, a distinction which will be shown to be invidious to the accountant. So it is that for the historian, generations of scholars have wrestled with these pervasive and gnawing problems, both in the abstract and in their implications for specific subject matter. Through their scholarship the historian has been made to see the nature and impact of the problems and has been made to answer to his colleagues for his performance by reference to these pervasive currents. This kind of exegesis is essentially absent in accountancy; the practitioners thereof are denied effective standards for measuring performance, and correspondingly are free to pursue their practice relatively unfettered.

Some References to the Reflections of Historians on Their Pursuit

It would, of course, be entirely inappropriate to burden this work with extensive and lengthy citations from the body of writings which have been informative to the historian, and which might be of assistance to the accountant groping for answers to the "haunting questions." However, some brief reference will be made to some of these writings in order to point up the areas of central interest to the historian and the level of the discussion of these problems; these references should give the accounting profession something of a beacon, set a standard, for its deliberations.

While the readings in the philosophy of history and the historian's craft disclose some reference to method, the principal thrust of the writings deemed significant for our purposes is toward the determination of the meaning of history and the determination of the historian's role in the process. Thus, these readings emphasize the fact that the historian is exhorted to understand himself, to comprehend the centripetal forces at work, before he moves outward. The accountant would recognize that the historian is directed first to know himself before he can presume to be in a position to resolve the problems of substance within the special area which he professes to know better than anyone else. And while the historian is urged to reflect centripetally, the accountant is exhorted to move centrifugally (e.g., the directive from the Council to move more extensively and dynamically into the management services sector, discussed in the preceding chapter).

This commitment of the historian to "know thyself" is also evidenced by the writings of Charles Frankel (who is first a philosopher and only then a philosopher of history);[4] corresponding views are contained in the observations of Nagel who directs the historian to understand that "inquiries into human affairs [are] undoubtedly controlled by the character of a given culture, and sometimes by the status of the student in that culture." Also, "no inquiry takes place in an intellectual vacuum." Further, "the standards of validity operative in an inquiry are causally related to other cultural traits, and that social status, class and national bias . . . influence what conclusions a man accepts."[5]

The most extensive exposition of the problems created by the inextricable involvement of the scholar (the historian for present purposes) in the subject matter of his probe is, in our view, contained in Mannheim's *Ideology and Utopia*.[6] This work, devoted to the sociology of knowledge, considers in depth the ways in which knowledge of an object is obtained, with the conclusion that the examination of the object "is not an isolated act"; instead, "it takes place in a context . . . colored by values and collective-unconscious, [and] volitional impulses. . . ."

Most significantly, this recognition that the observer is part of the observation does not produce in Mannheim a sense of despair; quite the contrary. By accepting this inevitable fact, the social scientist can, by first understanding himself, his drives, and impulses, ultimately hope to "control the unconscious motivations and presuppositions which, in the last analysis, have brought these modes of thought into existence."[7]

Such an awareness would bring forth a "new type of objectivity . . . attainable not through the exclusion of evaluations but through the critical awareness and control of them."[8] Such a critical awareness, Mannheim asserts, would produce a more effective control of those forces which may be inimical to the "objectivity" of the study. At least, if anyone who thereafter relies on the study is made aware of these limits on the observer's and commentator's objectivity, he could then reach his own evaluation regarding the degree of reliability which he is willing to accord to the study. The delusion or the hoax is greatest where the communicator pretends to certitude, and the pretense is accepted by his audience, when certitude is known to be an illusion.

This constraint on the historian to first "know thyself" is consistent with E. H. Carr's counsel: "First, . . . you cannot fully understand or appreciate the work of the historian unless you have first grasped the standpoint from which he himself approached it; secondly . . . that standpoint is itself rooted in a social and historical background. . . . The historian before he begins to write history, is the product of history."[9]

The Implications of the Foregoing for Accountancy

What meaning could the foregoing commentaries (which, it is to be emphasized, are merely suggestive of the extensive writing on the subject by historians and philosophers of history) have for accountants? As was emphasized above, these discussions cannot help much in the procedural aspects of our pursuit (though to the extent they inspire within us a sense of dignity, and cause us to recognize our identity and role, there is bound to be a salutary effect on our practice in general, procedures included). Instead, the meaning of the foregoing for accountants might well be that we, like all other social scientists, are studying the activities of man in his environment and (as Bloch emphasizes) in the context of time. For accountants, this study leads to the communication of the results thereof. And, as Mannheim and Carr make clear, the process of study and communications makes unavoidable the involvement of the accountant in the subject of his study.

If, then, it is further recognized that no one is a "free agent" but is instead directly involved and committed through his very being, we must realize that we are no longer involved in an alienated pursuit, one wherein the object of our study exists in an antiseptic chamber capable of being subjected to a sterile measurement. To switch metaphors, the accountant cannot be considered to be a viewer of a performance coming forth from a television tube; instead, he is part of the live audience whose very presence and reactions contribute to the performance and to the quality thereof. (And even the presumed-to-be-detached viewer of television can be shown to be involved through the feedback processes of rating systems and his responses to the message generally.) In brief, the actor and the audience, the entity and the accountant, the event and the historian, are all mutually interrelated and integrated. Each effects changes on the other in the dialectic process.

The implications of such a process of self-analysis by accountants are believed to be of transcendent significance. Thus, it would undoubtedly have an important impact on the theoretical infrastructure of accountancy; further, it should serve as a checkrein on the accountant's involvement in services which detract from his dedication to pursue and communicate "truth" within the limits demonstrated by Mannheim. Such an introspective process can be shown to have an important impact on the CPA's education, his pragmatism, and his involvement in management services; we direct our attention to each of these in turn.

The Implications for the Accountant's Education

This self-analysis would, for example, give added emphasis to the demands for an intensification of the student's exposure to the liberal arts and the humanities in the schools of business. Such an intensification was demanded by all recent studies of the subject. These demands were evident in the Gordon-Howell[10] and Pierson[11] studies; it was one of the high lights of the study promulgated most recently by the Committee for Economic Development. This last high light was the basis of the remarks of special commendation by Senator William Benton applauding the "Committee's emphasis on the importance of liberal education as an integral part of business education." After concurring in the advice given by the report that students should concentrate their undergraduate studies in the liberal arts and sciences if they plan to attend graduate schools of business, the Senator continues:

> Other things being equal, a thoroughgoing undergraduate liberal arts curriculum is more likely to help a student become a better businessman, as well as a better and happier citizen, than is a business curriculum. At the same time, I agree that there are certain business studies which have a solid academic base if properly taught and that there is a place for business education thus conceived at the undergraduate level.[12]

In brief, such a liberalizing education, furnishing the infrastructure for the self-analysis referred to above, would help to balance the technical emphasis of the education of the accountant (and business leaders generally) which was the subject of complaint in all three of these important studies.

It is only through a shift in the central interest of accounting education within the university from the accountant's "doing" to his "being and becoming" that we will develop accountants in good numbers who have "a clear and compelling vision of [their] profession and of its relation to American life" (to adopt Professor Lawrence A. Cremin's phraseology); it is only when we teach accounting with a "liberating and liberalizing effect" (as President Buell Gallagher, of the City College, put it), that we will be able to overcome the crisis in communications, the crisis in integrity, which presently confronts our profession.

The Implications for Our Philosophy of Pragmatism

Another consequence from such study of the unavoidable involvement of the accountant in the subject matter of his pursuit could also help in the formulation of an underlying philosophy for the profession, and in defining our identity and sense of mission. Specifically, such a study might well bring into critical question the present-day approach to accountancy which passes by the euphemism "pragmatic" and then give us a positive, meaningful philosophy.

This pragmatic approach manifests itself in many ways and in many contexts. It is, for example, implicit in the repeated assertions of the Accounting Principles Board (and of its predecessors) that "the authority of its Opinions . . . rests upon their general acceptability." Pragmatism was explicitly set forth by Moonitz in his Basic Postulates study to be "another popular approach . . . to accounting."[13]

Similarly, pragmatism can be shown to be the motivating force behind Grady's *Inventory;* this appraisal is consistent with the following judgment of the late Weldon Powell:

> The . . . approach taken in the study is avowedly a pragmatic one. The "Inventory" deals with the practical aspects of accounting principles. This accords with the essential nature of the art of accounting. We do not account just for the sake of accounting. We require that any given procedure be useful, in fact sufficiently so to justify its cost. At the same time we require that it produce a result that is fair and not misleading. These points need to be borne firmly in mind by those who would contribute to the development of accounting principles.[14]

(We cite the foregoing solely to buttress our evaluation of the Grady study; accordingly, no inference should be drawn that we are necessarily in accord with Powell's standards for "those who would contribute to the development of accounting principles.")

Specifically, pragmatism in accountancy was emphasized by Professors Littleton and Zimmerman when they sought to explain accounting by first pointing up what it is not; in that connection they state: "Accounting is not as strongly oriented toward logical argument as toward utilitarian service, it is less concerned with deductive generalization than with practical accomplishment. Accounting methods are technological, its ideology has not been deeply philosophical."[15]

This conclusion on their part is then rationalized by their observation that "insofar as accounting has a philosophical content it is pragmatic. That is to say, the frame of reference of accounting thought is a practical one." And to buttress their conclusion that if there is a philosophy of accountancy it is pragmatic (which for them is to be equated with practicality) they refer to Will Durant's recollection of a confrontation with William James which, as reported by Durant and repeated by Littleton and Zimmerman, went as follows:

> He spoke . . . in a racy vocabulary and with a force and directness which made his philosophy of "pragmatism" the mental correlate of the "practical." Instead of asking whence an idea is derived, or what are its premises, pragmatism examines its results. . . . Pragmatism asks . . . what are its consequences [of the idea]?—and turns the face of thought to action and to the future. . . . What were these truths [of pragmatism] but formulations of experience, convenient and successful in practice . . .?[16]

So it is that Durant's views of pragmatism as presuming a "racy vocabulary" producing a philosophy which is the "mental correlate of the practical," and a philosophy whose truths are "but formulations of experience, convenient and successful in practice," are adopted as the standards which Littleton and Zimmerman believe may "necessarily be the case for a technology such as accounting."

This equating of pragmatism with experience, if not with expediency, has given rise to the cynical but all too general observation that pragmatism represents an absence of principle. But this is not the pragmatism envisaged by John Dewey who observed that: "It is often said of pragmatism that it subordinates thought and rational activity to particular ends of interest and profit." While this emphasis on action and the relationship between action and ideals is essential to pragmatism, yet "the role of action is that of an intermediary." Action is vital so that there can be a modification of existence. Dewey continues: "Pragmatism is, therefore, far from being that glorification of action for its own sake which is regarded as the peculiar characteristic of American life."[17]

As between the Durant and Dewey versions of pragmatism it is believed that the latter should prevail. That Durant determined that James spoke in "racy" terms which made his "philosophy of pragmatism the mental correlate of the practical" cannot be denied; it is, nevertheless, distinctly at variance with pragmatism as seen by Dewey. The choice of the definition of pragmatism, at least insofar as accountancy is concerned, can be crucial to our professional evaluation.

The racy concept of pragmatism as espoused by Durant, and adopted by Littleton and Zimmerman, is undoubtedly what Professor Abraham Kaplan described as a "vulgar pragmatism." As he sees it, such a philosophy has "nothing of the philosophical pragmatism of Peirce, James and Dewey." Kaplan proceeds to respond to this vulgar pragmatism (which he believes to be "in the saddle" in America) with the following polemic:

> The issue here is not one of philosophical exegesis; what is at stake is not the correctness of a philosophical interpretation, but the morality of a pattern of action. In holding up the ideal of success, vulgar pragmatism does not ground values in existence, but takes as valuable whatever is existent. The test of success is essentially the same as the test of survival applied in "social Darwinism." What survives is the fittest—the fittest, of course, to survive; but competitive success is taken to be at once the sign and the substance of worth.
>
> In America efficiency is the fetish of the business world and the operation of a business the model for politics and personal life. . . .
>
> In personal life this is the morality of double-entry book-keeping. For such a morality, honesty is a matter of policy, generosity is good business, friendship pays off.
>
> What is called the "pragmatic" temper of the American mind is thus very far from pragmatic, however plausibly it is rationalized as the "scientific" treatment of our problems. It is efficient only if we do not count the cost, successful only in attaining the values

> we have fixed upon beforehand, not those in fact implicated in our actions.[18]

Specifically, then, it is our hope that the study of a philosophy of history (and the recognition of the way in which the historian develops a sense of purpose and identity transcending "the practical") could overcome the condition in accountancy which was described by Littleton and Zimmerman as a pursuit which is "not deeply philosophical"; hopefully, such a study should lead to a recognition that what is presumed to be its underlying philosophy of pragmatism was nought but a base and "vulgar pragmatism," and that a "philosophy" which is "strongly oriented toward utilitarian service, practical accomplishment and an ideology which is not deeply philosophical" is not a philosophy worthy of a professional pursuit. Such a recognition, in turn, should lead to the conclusion that unless the profession of accountancy does develop a vital and positive philosophy it is destined to become a craft. Further, should accountancy persist in its strong orientation toward utilitarian service and essentially practical accomplishment, then any right which it may have to be included among the councils of learned professions would rightfully be foreclosed—or at least be brought into serious question.

Further, the development for accountancy of a positive philosophy, going above and beyond the practical and expedient, might cause the profession to reassess its commitment to the present-day environment of accountancy. It could be, for example, that such a probe would disclose that the corporate form of economic enterprise is important to accountancy only because it is so prevalent; and then this attitude of challenging, or at least questioning, should serve to bring the accountant into the dialogue with the disciplines of the law, economics, philosophy, history, the humanities generally, all of which are presently raising serious challenges to the appropriate role to be played by the corporations in our evolving economic society.

Such a study and reappraisal could also lead to some different perspectives on the auditor's involvement in management services. This was, of course, the subject of extensive discourse in the preceding chapter but another dimension thereof can be discerned in this context by reference to the experience of Professor Arthur Schlesinger, Jr., when he found himself playing a dual role as a leading historian as well as an important consultant to the late President Kennedy. It is this dual responsibility which Schlesinger sought to rationalize and reconcile in his *Foreign Affairs*[19] article, to which we direct our attentions briefly.

Regarding the Dual Involvement of the Historian

Professor Schlesinger introduces his rationalization and reconciliation by commenting on the ambiguity of the term "history" and "historian" which he explains can relate to the actual experience and to the subsequent record thereof. The problem to which he addresses himself in his article is "the interaction between history, in both senses, and the historian." In introducing the arguments in opposition to any one person undertaking a responsibility in both senses Professor Schlesinger cites Walter Lippmann's views looking to the historian with the "disinterested mind," whose commitment is to history-as-record, not to history-as-experience, to its writing rather than making. The Lippmann creed, as quoted by Schlesinger, is put forward as follows:

> The world will go on somehow, and more crises will follow. It will go on best, however, if among us there are men who have stood apart, who refused to be anxious or too much concerned, who were cool and inquiring and had their eyes on a longer past and a longer future. By their example they can remind us that the passing moment is only a moment; by their loyalty they will have cherished those things which only the disinterested mind can use.[20]

Professor Schlesinger then proceeds to the justification of his own dual commitment; at various points his justification can be seen to parallel that of the proponents of our further involvement in management services. True, he says, "involvement has its hazards" but "it also offers its compensations"; if in no other way such a duality demonstrates to the historian the "precariousness of his calling" and thereby gives him a "proper humility." Further, the "disinterested mind, in any case, is an ideal, not an actuality," and "it may be more a consequence of temperament than of a preference for the ivory tower over the barricades."[21]

What lessons did Schlesinger learn from his very delicate burdens of leading such a "double life"? He concludes his paper:

> The conclusion is twofold. If exposure to history-as-experience may lead the historian to doubt a little the precision of history-as-record, it also persuades him that history-as-record forms a basic part of the intellectual climate which shapes the actual unfolding of history in the future—that a sense of history is the indispensable underpinning of statesmanship.
>
> It further persuades this historian that monistic and deterministic visions of history are, except in some broad and trivial sense, wrong—that the sense of history possessed by the great American leadership of our century, based on the belief in the reality of choice and the plurality of existence, is much more in the grain of the turning world.[22]

Undoubtedly there are those who will remain unconvinced by Professor Schlesinger's rationalization, just as there are those who have serious misgivings as to whether the attesting accountant can effectively fulfill this vital function when he involves himself in the management services which were considered in the preceding chapter. It may very well be (as Schlesinger asserts) that the two functions have a reciprocity or compatibility with each other; that someone who is well versed in the one dimension can thereby perform more effectively in the other. This is accepted; the gnawing question still remains: Can the same person be presumed to look back on his own involvement with the same "fair bias" with which he views the involvements of others? And even if he could so look back, should his audience, generally the public which has been denied a corresponding access to the facts of the particular history (i.e., the society, in the macrocosm), be constrained to presume such a consistent "fair bias," or a consistent standard of "objectivity"? Put otherwise, should not the readers of history (or the users of the financial statements) be permitted to judge for themselves the reliability of the facts, interpretation, and explanations promulgated by the historian (or the accountant) who has determined to undertake such a dual responsibility? In either case, where the professional historian or accountant pursues a dual responsibility he undoubtedly owes it to his audience to make them aware of his combined undertaking. This audience would thereby be able to determine for themselves whether the duality generates conflicting forces which might impinge on the historian or accountant so as to effect a result considered by the audience to be inimical to the professional's pursuit.

In brief and as a bare minimum: *Let the People Know!*

This is the way in which our discussion of the Schlesinger double involvement ended in the dissertation on which this work is principally based. And as was necessary in the case of Sorensen's commentary on the late President Kennedy as an autonomous decision maker, facts exposed after the assassination (and after our original writing) make it necessary to append a tragic and ironic postscript to our Schlesinger commentary. Thus, *The New York Times* on Thanksgiving Day, 1965, carried the following Washington news item under the caption "Schlesinger Says He Lied to Times":

> Arthur M. Schlesinger, Jr. said today he had lied to *The New York Times* in April, 1961, about the nature and size of the Cuban refugee landing in the Bay of Pigs.
>
> In his newly published book, "A Thousand Days," Mr. Schlesinger says that the Central Intelligence Agency, as early as December, 1960, abandoned its original plans for a guerrilla operation against Premier Fidel Castro in favor of "an amphibious invasion." The invasion force, he states, finally numbered 1,400 men.

> In a telephone interview today, Mr. Schlesinger was reminded that on April 17, the day of the landings, he had told *The Times's* Washington Bureau, for publication on a background basis, that the landing force numbered no more than 200 to 300 men. He said then that the operation was not an "invasion" . . .
>
> "Did I say that?" Mr. Schlesinger asked today. "Well, I was lying. This was the cover story. I apologize for having been involved in passing along the cover story."[23]

This ironic and tragic postscript merely fortifies our opposition to any corresponding duality of function, whether by the historian or our colleagues in the accounting profession.

Conclusion

This chapter was a recognized digression from the mainstream of accounting theorizing and did not especially speak to the problems of the accountant, nor of the body of knowledge he professes. And yet this chapter did speak directly to the reliability of communication, including communication in accountancy, hence the effectiveness of such communication. The principal purpose served by this digression was to move the discussion to a more general, a more pervasive, a higher, and more transcendent plane. This was done consistent with the view that the dilemmas of accountancy cannot be resolved by any study or studies concentrating on a particular problem, or even on all of the problems as problems. Instead, we believe that the long road to professional fulfillment must begin with the accountant first determining for himself just what should be the objectives of any profession in our society and then, specifically, of his chosen profession within our economic society. To the extent that he thereby determines that his professional commitment demands a dedication (corresponding to that of the historian, say) to discern truth and to communicate truth, he should then be commanded to acquire those capacities and capabilities, the habits of conscience and mind, as would permit him best to fulfill these commitments.

The foregoing discussions can be shown to be consistent with, and directly related to, the preceding discussions relating to the problems of research in accountancy, the communications process generally and, specifically, the performance of management services. All have pointed up the interdisciplinary implications of any pursuit entitled to the encomium of a "profession," permitting the professional to enjoy the perquisites and the prerogatives which stem from such status.

While it is the subject of the philosophy of history which has been shown to be especially helpful in the shaping of a corresponding philosophy for accountants this subject is but one important aspect of the *Weltanschauung* presumed to be indispensable for any accountant who professes to be a professional. As was suggested at the threshold to this chapter, these dilemmas regarding one's professional identity and meaning are pervasive in all such higher pursuits; however, it is accountancy to which the philosophy of history was shown to have a special message in the context of this work.

The common theme for the historian and the accountant, the scientist and the artist, the theologian and the educator, the judge and the philosopher, which was sought to be conveyed by this historical digression was most effectively expressed by A. Whitney Griswold when he concluded his essay on "Society's Need for Man," thus:

> The moral, then, is plain. To do good we must first know good; to serve beauty we must first know beauty; to speak the truth we must first know the truth. We must know these things ourselves, be able to recognize them by ourselves, . . . and wish to do so, when no one else is present to prompt us or bargain with us. We must hold true to that purpose. No price, no mess of pottage, can equal its value to our country and ourselves, its citizens.[24]

In the discussion which preceded, reference was made to the undoubted impact which such a higher commitment, the quest for a positive philosophy, could have on the education of aspirants for the profession. Consistent with this endeavor to expand, extend, and deepen these newly won insights, to help to emphasize this need to search for identity and purpose, and to point up these relationships for those practitioners who are now generally beyond the reach of formal education, it is here recommended that the American Institute of CPAs, or the Accounting Principles Commission as proposed in Chapter 3, or a university with the support of a foundation, consider the convening of an Accounting "Pugwash Conference," a Secular Ecumenical Council, or an accounting "teach-in." Such a conference, council, or teach-in would bring together representatives from the disciplines of law, economics, the natural, behavioral and social sciences, from history, philosophy, government, linguistics, as well as from the realms of banking, labor and finance, to comprise a "surmising forum" (to use the phrase of Bertrand de Jouvenal).[25] What would be the function of such an interdisciplinary forum? Briefly, it would serve the cross-pollinating function to which reference was made in several contexts; to make known to the accounting profession the patterns of thinking and discovery of these other branches of study which could, on reflection, be seen to have a most vital bearing on the resolution of the dilemmas of our chosen profession.

The idea of a "surmising forum" referred to above was advanced by de Jouvenal (in a context entirely unrelated to accountancy) in order to help "dispel the paradoxical feeling of impotence which in an age of rapidly increasing possibilities seems to afflict so many good minds."[26] In brief, such a forum would give greater meaning to the idea of self-determination for mankind generally—there is a corresponding need in accounting.

And finally, such an accounting "Pugwash Conference," could also be shown to be implementing the counsel offered by Père Teilhard, referred to in the Introduction to this work. We there referred to his view that mankind's evolution can only be fulfilled through a "convergent integration," through the *"enroulement organique sur soi-même"*; or, in Huxley's terms, by achieving the "more complex, and more integrated mental activity, which can guide the human species up the path of progress to higher levels of hominisation."[27]

8

All this will not be finished in the first 100 days. Nor will it be finished in the first 1,000 days, . . . nor even perhaps in our lifetime on this planet. But let us begin.
President Kennedy's Inaugural Address [1]

Conclusion

This brings us to the summing up, to the bringing together of the principal themes and streams developed by our study and analysis. This work has dealt with the single, unitary subject of the effectiveness of communication in accounting. In the development of the subject we have demonstrated that the communciations gap confronting the accounting profession is indeed a serious one. This follows from the fact that a central objective of the accounting process has been, traditionally, the ascertaining of the economic truths of the entity which is the subject of the accountant's study and then the transmission of the results to the various groups in our society who are entitled to know them. That the need for such effective communication has intensified with time is apparent from the fact of the expansion in the size and role of the corporations comprising our economic society and the concurrent increase in the parties who are presumed to have an interest in such corporations; these parties are the participants in the dispersed ownership thereof or are otherwise touched by the far-flung activities of the corporations. Further, the separation of the corporate ownership from the control of the corporation's properties has intensified the need for bridging the communications gap; instead the gap can be seen to be widening into a chasm producing a confidence and credibility gap.

The development and consideration of the communications

problem was uniformly related to our research. This research was of two kinds: The primary study involved the development of a questionnaire appropriate for this study and the analysis of the data derived therefrom; the secondary study called for the review of the literature of accountancy, as well as in other fields which were seen to be related thereto. Both studies were undertaken for the dual purpose of determining the nature and extent of the communications problem, and making our recommendations for its mitigation.

As has been made clear throughout the preceding text, both the primary and the secondary studies furnished substantial and significant evidence to prove the existence of major dilemmas in each of the aspects of the accounting function reviewed by us; these major dilemmas have been described by some writers as having assumed a crisis, or "showdown," proportion. The communications gap was seen to prevail in all of the areas investigated; i.e., there is a lack of understanding by the financial community of the independent reporting function of the accounting profession, of the circumstances or environment in which the profession pursues this function, and of the structure and mode of development of the underlying body of accounting theory (its generally accepted accounting principles).

Further, and equally significant in this connection, is the additional fact developed by this study, namely, that this confounding of tongues is also indigenous to the accounting profession itself in that there are serious divergencies among the several major groups comprising the profession; so it is that we saw disparities in the views of the practitioners and academicians who were the subject of this inquiry, and in some cases the views of the practitioners with the major accounting firms were shown to contrast sharply with those of practitioners with the other firms.

The Major Areas of Communications Breakdown

Our primary study demonstrated this failure in accounting communications in the following significant areas:

There was shown to be an inability to develop a consensus regarding the meaning of the "opinion clause" of the auditor's certificate. This demonstrates a lack of comprehension regarding the very "hallmark" of the attest function.

There is an absence of anything approaching a consensus with respect to the terms assumed to be at the very foundations of our present-day accounting theory and practice; thus, there is no consensus regarding terms like "objectivity," "consistency," and "conservatism" in accountancy. Such a failure in reaching a common understanding, at these fundamental levels, could make mere shibboleths of these basic terms and permit their interpretation along a broad spectrum.

Similarly, major divergencies were discerned regarding the comprehension of the special idiom in accountancy both as to the accounting principles which now prevail as well those which should prevail. Among the areas where such major divergencies were discerned are: the reporting of extraordinary gains or losses, long-term leases, inventories determined on a LIFO basis, business combinations and consolidations, and the accounting for pension costs and research and development costs. Again, these gaps in comprehension were shown to exist not only between the financial community and the accounting profession, but also between component groups within the profession itself.

That the gap is recognized, even if not accepted, may be evidenced by the responses to several of the questions which reflected a dismal view regarding the presumed understanding of the aforementioned special idiom by such segments of our economic society as investment advisers, economists, and government personnel—groups who must use accounting statements as an important aspect of their decision making. (Especially presumed to be ignorant of our principles of accounting are the individual investors, and their putative advisers, the customers' men with brokerage firms.)

This serious communications gap is further evidenced by the prevalence of the view that the financial statements are inadequately responsive to the needs of such important users as financial analysts and substantial investors.

While there is a general understanding that the management of the corporation has the primary role and responsibility in the formulation of its financial statements, we have, nevertheless, shown that there is confusion as to whether it is this management or the independent auditor who would determine the applicable principles in any particular situation. There is even greater uncertainty regarding the manner in which a dispute involving such alternative principles would be resolved.

Consistent with the foregoing, the data obtained from the financial community indicate an almost unanimous belief that where the auditor believes some other alternative principle preferable to the one adopted by management, he would at least describe this other alternative (in fact, almost 70 per cent of the community expected him to do more, i.e., take an exception, qualify, or interpose his own determination). All this was shown to have been presumed by the statement users months before the Council of the American Institute of CPAs addressed itself to this condition, and then responded in only an attenuated and compromised form. And even then there were those who voted for this resolution in the hope that before its actual implementation (generally not until 1967) the Council would "see the light" and reverse its position.

Regarding the nature and scope of the attesting

auditor's practice, it has been shown that while the AICPA is proselytizing in favor of the profession's further involvement in management services, concurrent with its performance of the attest function, the preponderant view from the financial community is diametrically opposed thereto. While the Institute asserts that it is thereby voicing the views of the profession (and it points to various spokesmen within the profession to justify its position) the responses from the financial community indicate an abysmal ignorance regarding the nature of the services comprising the management services nexus; and, even more significantly, they have asserted a consensual view that if they comprehended the kinds of services intended to be swept into the compound of management services they would be opposed to their performance by the attesting firm. Possibly of equal, if not greater, significance is the marked difference of opinion among the several segments of the accounting profession as to whether these services should be thus expanded and extended. In fact only a single group—respondents from the major, the "Big-Eight," firms—was shown by the study to be aligned with the established position of the Institute.

The Institute's Research Division is now seen to be structured in a manner which we believe to be inimical to the advances of the kind of research urgently required for the mitigation of the dilemmas here exposed and considered. That this present structuring and organization are inconsistent with the vision of those who initially proposed the establishment of such a division has been demonstrated.

The foregoing conclusions, among others, buttressed by the supporting evidence obtained from the collateral studies of the literature, all served to point up the magnitude and complexity of the communications dilemma.

Our Principal Recommendations

Based on the foregoing analysis and evaluation we recommend the following:

> There is an urgent need to bridge the so-called "gap in GAAP," to narrow the areas of difference and divergence in the alternative accounting principles which might be deemed to be generally acceptable for a particular circumstance or event. To this end, we propose the establishment of a commission, comprised of representatives from within and without the profession, and charged with the responsibility for determining and promulgating the body of principles presumed to be generally accepted. The reasons for believing that such a pluralistically constituted commission would be more effective than the Accounting Principles Board were described in the text.
>
> Proceeding from the foregoing, we urge that the irreducible gap in the applicable principles should be bridged by greater disclosure and the better education of the user groups. Through such disclosure and education, they would become better informed and the "myth of certitude" exorcised.
>
> Again, as part of the foregoing pattern of recommendations: Since determinations are ultimately required to be made regarding the economic truths of the particular corporation, we propose that it be the auditor (rather than the management) who should be explicitly charged with the burden of choosing from among the available alternatives. The auditor's assumption of the role of surrogate is justified because he is best suited by temperament, training, and tradition to fulfill this role. If he should refuse it, or fail in his endeavors, some other profession or agency will have to emerge and undertake this vital responsibility to the detriment of the professional status of accounting.

Such an absolute assumption of responsibility by the auditor is essential because the mere disclosure of alternatives or divergencies in footnotes, or otherwise, merely shifts the burden to the user groups; to groups which lack the sophistication, competence and access to the facts which the auditor possesses.

The analysis of the problems of research in accountancy demonstrated that the present concentration thereof in the American Institute of CPAs is inimical to the objectives of such research; so undertaken, we believe that this research endeavor is destined to fail in its mission. We therefore urge that such research be centered in the universities; only there, in our opinion, is there the environment which is felicitous to the pursuit of "truths," an environment relatively unfettered by the vested interests of the professional establishment. Only within the universities do the conditions conducive to the process of continuity exist; this is a process which is essential to the continuing evolution of a body of knowledge. Only in the universities can there be the essential interdisciplinary cross-pollination so essential to moving the body of knowledge to the levels required by our professional commitment.

To advance the foregoing research endeavor we recommend the creation of a foundation for accounting research supported by funds received from both within and without the profession, which would stipulate the broad areas in which this research should be undertaken and supported.

As the corollary to the third recommendation we recommend that the profession determine first for itself, and then make generally known, whether it envisages the objects of its communication to be the public at large or some special segment thereof. Is it for the vulgar mass, or is it for some hierarchy? Until the profession makes this clear, for itself and our society generally, it will seek to please all the people all the time, and thereby be destined to please none. Unless this dispersal and confusion of objectives is cleared up our communications must lose clarity and focus, and the profession will fail to fulfill its attest function.

Because of the lack of awareness by the financial community and by many within the accounting profession regarding the types of ancillary services which might be appropriately performed by public accounting firms, we recommend that the American Institute of CPAs and the Securities and Exchange Commission ascertain the kinds of services presently being performed by CPA firms and the circumstances under which they are being performed. The Institute and the SEC should then define those services which are deemed to be out-of-bounds for the firm performing the attest function where such services are deemed to be inimical to the audit firm's independence, in appearance if not in fact.

Of transcendent significance, accountancy and accountants should be committed to the development of a philosophy going far beyond the "pragmatic," which is now conceived by us to be synonomous with the expeditious, or at least the practical.

The foregoing would necessitate a major reappraisal of the education for those aspiring for admission to the accounting profession. Further, it would demand a major thrust into continuing education for the practitioner in areas which at first blush might be deemed to be outside the frame of professional knowledge and responsibility. To emphasize the importance of the interdisciplinary aspects, the recommendation was made that the American Institute of CPAs, the American Accounting Association, foundations, universities—collectively if possible, alone if need be—convene an accounting "Pugwash Conference."

The Vital Impact of Our Proposals

We concede that these recommendations would effect precipitous changes in the organization and functioning of the accounting profession; these major shifts would include:

The principal orientation in accountancy would be shifted from the presumed "objective" or "scientific" to the recognized "subjective" or "interpretative," thereby making both the function and the man that much more vital and significant.

Our recommendations would change the nature of the accountant's services, of his education, and the pattern of his relationships with the corporation's management. This shift would stem from the overt recognition of the accountant's unavoidable involvement in the subject matter, and the entity to which he is rendering his professional services. This reciprocity between recognition of involvement and changes in function should give rise to a "new type of objectivity . . . attainable not through the exclusion of evaluations but through the critical awareness and control of them."[2]

These recommendations, if implemented, would direct a reappraisal of what is an important assumption (if not actually a postulate) of present-day accountancy, namely, that the corporate entity as now conceived will and should enjoy perpetual existence. Such a shift might give rise to alternatives to the corporate enterprise, or at least suggest alternative values and objectives for the corporate society. In turn, such a shift of presumption should cause the auditor to recognize the need for some fulcrum standing in the balance between, or among, the countervailing forces which are recognized in our economic society. He should recognize that his training, temperament, and traditions should permit him to fulfill this "fulcrum function" most effectively; this would be so only if he concurrently recognizes the significance and implications of the power-property dichotomy in our publicly held enterprises; and provided further that upon such recognition he dedicates himself to the avoidance of entangling alliances with any of these vectors in the calculus.

And we would shift the center of interest of the accountant's study from the techniques and the practices of *accountancy* to the study of the *accountant;* this is the very shift anticipated by the prediction made when concluding the introductory chapter to this work. There, the saga of Siddhartha was retold: He (like we) set out on a long quest in search of the "ultimate meaning," the answer to the enigma of Man's role on earth. After a tortuous road he (like we) discovered that the answer was always within the Self, and it is there that we are constrained to search for it.

So Let Us Begin!

We know now that the program outlined by the late President Kennedy in his Inaugural Address was not fulfilled in his first 1,000 days as President. Nor will the program and the shifts outlined above be finished in 1,000 days "nor even perhaps in our lifetime on this planet." While we can accept a spirit of deliberate speed we nevertheless believe that the profession should move forthwith to implement two of the recommendations made above which, it can be shown, look only to the communication of that which the statement preparer presently presumes (but which we know is not being effectively communicated to him), thus:

The profession knows that "the accounts of a company are primarily the responsibility of manage-

> ment," but the statement user is not thus knowledgeable. Therefore let us change the wording of the final clause of the opinion paragraph of the auditor's certificate so as to read that the statements were prepared: "in conformity with the generally accepted accounting principles adopted by the corporation's management, which principles were applied on a basis consistent with that of the preceding year."
>
> The profession knows that "management service activities are a proper function of CPAs," but the statement user is not correspondingly sophisticated. Therefore, let us move to make known to the user that which we know so well. This, it is believed, can be done most expeditiously through the disclosure of the nonaudit or peripheral services (and the compensation derived therefrom) as a part of the proxy material distributed as incident to the obtaining of the shareholders' consent to the designation of the company's auditors.

Again, neither of these procedures recommended for immediate implementation would, in and of itself, change the status quo. Instead, each of them seeks to make certain that the inferences drawn from the financial statements are consistent with the implications intended with respect thereto by their preparers. This would appear to be a most important and logical first step in the bridging of the communications gap.

And yet these mere procedural changes could have a profound effect on the evolution of accountancy and the practice thereof. It may be anticipated that through the reactions to these explicit disclosures the profession would be better able to determine whether that which they presume to meet with the approbation of the statement users does, in fact, attract such a response. It might well be that the shock of recognition of what are presumed to be old "realities" may reveal the existence of some old "myths." This very process of inviting a dialogue around that which the profession presumes to be commonly known and accepted could, through the dialectic process, generate change, if change is shown to be needed.

Clearly we have directed some serious criticism against our chosen profession—for its failure to fulfill what we believe to be its responsibility in assuring fair corporate reporting and accountability. This criticism, not without its polemical aspects, is motivated by a love of the profession of accountancy, a profession which is capable of rewarding us so generously and in so many ways. This jeremiad flows from a deeply held sense that we are pursuing a collision course destined to make this felicitous profession most seriously vulnerable—a position in which the reaction from the financial community (and society generally) will cause the pendulum to swing much further than is really warranted.

Appendix

As I look to the future I am . . . troubled by two misgivings: that there will be less and less place for the small experimenter, and that the time of all of us will be increasingly commandeered by administrative mechanical details. In view of these misgivings I cannot help wondering as I look back on the past whether, if I were to start over again now, I could or would be able to do again what I have done.

Bridgman, *Reflections of a Physicist*[1]

The Methodology of the Research

Frequent reference was made throughout the study to the primary research which was undertaken in connection with this work. To facilitate the task of those within the profession or the universities who may determine to use this study as a point of departure, this appendix describes in some detail the nature of this research, the manner in which it was pursued, and those who were the subjects for our questionnaire.

The Summary Data Obtained from Our Primary Study

The results obtained from this study are presented in summary form as Appendix C, which sets forth the percentage distribution derived from the responses from the seventy-two respondents comprising the "Financial Community Category" (as described heretofore), and the sixty-four respondents constituting the "Accounting Profession Category."

The Form and Content of the Questionnaire

The questionnaire, as submitted to the respondents, is found in Appendix B.

The questions sought to determine the consensus of the financial community regarding its understanding of the audit function and the circumstances of its fulfillment, and its understanding of the body of knowledge which is the special responsibility of the accounting profession, i.e., its generally accepted accounting principles. The questions were promulgated along the following lines:

Series A Questions:

A-1 and 2 —requested information regarding the respondents—their function in the financial community and any formal accounting training which they may have had.

A-3 and 4 —sought to determine the respondents' views as to the nature of the economic environment in which the audit function is being performed.

A-5 —was an extension of the preceding questions and sought to ascertain the respondents' understanding of the central responsibility for the financial statements.

A-6 —was designed to elicit the respondents' understanding of the so-called opinion clause in the auditor's certificate.

A-7, 8, and 9 —were general in nature and sought to determine the extent of the respondents' satisfaction with the published statements taken as a whole.

A-10 —was an extension of the three preceding questions and sought the respondents' evaluation of the degree of responsiveness of published financial statements to each of eight important groups of "users" of financial statements. (The user-groups enumerated in this question were determined from our readings to comprise the groups in our economic society who require information regarding corporate entities. With the exception of "customer's men," each of the groups described in the Arthur Andersen *Postulate*[2] was included in the question. In addition, the "financial analysts" and "anyone who is willing and competent to read the statements . . ." groups were indicated by the readings as being properly includable.)

A-11, 12, 13, and 14 —related to the respondents' understanding of the "economic environment in which the auditor fulfills [his audit] function" and even more explicitly, the respondents' understanding of, and judgment regarding, "the nature and extent of the auditor's involvement in modern corporate society." Accordingly, these questions related to the appropriateness of the auditors' involvements in management services, extensive tax consultative services, and the combination thereof. (The specific thrust of the questions, i.e., the compatibility of these services with the traditions and independence of the auditing profession, was determined by the readings to be areas of important controversy.)

A-15 —proceeded from the foregoing general questions; there were listed twelve areas of service offered by the Peat, Marwick, Mitchell & Co., Management Controls Department, as set forth in their mimeographed bulletin entitled "Services to Management." Categories of services (a) through (f) as included in the questionnaire were set forth in the Peat, Marwick bulletin as follows:

GENERAL MANAGEMENT

General Surveys
Review all phases of a business in connection with plan to expand profits, liquidate a loan, undertake new financing, buy the business, or reorganize the company; long-range planning.

Organization
Appraisal of organization structure; preparation of organization manual defining responsibilities and authorities; executive development programs.

Executive Compensation
Basic compensation; executive incentive plans; fringe benefits.

The next four categories of services, enumerated in the questionnaire as (g) through (j), were set forth in the Peat, Marwick mimeograph as follows:

MARKETING

Sales Control
Sales forecasting and budgeting; determining market potentials; planning profitable sales territories; establishing sales quotas; recommending proper sales reports; control of selling costs; developing salesmen's incentives.

Products and Pricing
Determining profitability of product groups and items; increasing volume and profits through improved pricing methods.

The last two such categories, (k) and (l) of Question A-15, were derived from the mimeographed bulletin, wherein they appeared in the following context:

PERSONNEL

Job Evaluation
Analysis of job functions, responsibilities, and authorities; classification and rating of positions; determining relative contribution of positions.

Series B Questions:

B-1 —sought to determine the respondents' views and judgments regarding the persons in our economic society who are presumed to be knowledgeable regarding the body of generally accepted accounting principles. The groups who were thus enumerated were intended to include all persons believed to have an important responsibility with respect to accounting data, either as the "producers" thereof or as "users."

B-2 —sought a general consensus regarding the existence of a body of principles, and the respondents' judgments as to the way in which it should be determined.

B-3 and 4 —as was the case with Question A-5, these questions sought to elicit the respondents' understanding regarding the economic environment in which the auditor fulfills his function, except that these "B" questions probed specifically for the central responsibility for the selection and application of accounting principles in a particular situation.

B-5(a) and (b)	—also related to the environment in which the audit function is fulfilled and to the auditor's relationship with management.
B-5(c) through (f)	—sought to arrive at a consensus regarding the meaning and acceptability of such concepts as "consistency" and "comparability."
B-6	—like B-2, was a general question and sought to ascertain whether the respondents believed a body of principles of accounting to exist.
B-7	—sought the respondents' views on the question revealed by the literature to be crucial, i.e., whether a uniform body of principles is to be preferred to a nexus of alternatives. The specific question herein was suggested by assertions by Savoie in his *Harvard Business Review* article.[3]

Series C Questions:

These questions were predicated on what we believed to be the significant areas of accounting and reporting which were revealed by the secondary study to be unresolved and with respect to which major controversy prevails. To confirm our selection of the subjects to be probed in this series of questions, reference was made to Arthur Andersen's *Accounting and Reporting Problems of the Accounting Profession—1962;*[4] this monograph set forth twenty-five of what were considered to be the more important accounting and reporting problems facing the profession. These problems, and where appropriate the question wherein the particular problem was submitted to the respondents herein, were as follows:

	Arthur Andersen Problems[5]	*Series C Questions*
1.	Price-level accounting	C-14
2.	Pension plans	C-13
3.	Leases	C-5
4.	Significance of net income	C-1
5.	Income-tax allocation	Not considered
6.	Income-tax benefits from operating loss carry-forward credits	C-2, 3
7.	Deferred income taxes . . . for public utility rate-making . . .	Not considered
8.	Deferred income taxes on installment sales	Not considered
9.	Pooling of interests	C-9, 11
10.	Stock options	C-4
11.	LIFO versus FIFO	C-6, 7
12.	Research and development costs	C-15
13.	Gross sales	Not considered
14.	Intangible development costs applicable to productive oil and gas properties	C-8
15.	Oil and gas exploration costs	Not considered
16.	Producing oil and gas working interests	Not considered
17.	Auditors' opinions on regulated companies	Not considered
18.	Accounting by railroads	Not considered
19.	Accounting by insurance companies	Not considered
20.	Bank holding companies	Not considered
21.	Goodwill	C-11
22.	Working capital	Not considered
23.	Savings and loan associations	Not considered
24.	Long-term construction contracts	Not considered
25.	Intercorporate investments	C-10, 12

The Results from the Research Cross-Referenced to the Text

Our commentaries on the results obtained from the research are included in the text as follows:

Questions	*Considered in Detail in Chapter(s)*
A-1, 2	Not considered especially
A-3	5
A-4	5
A-5	5

A-6	1
A-7, 8, and 9	Not considered especially
A-10	5
A-11 through 15	6
B-1	2 and 4
B-2	Not considered especially
B-3, 4	4
B-5	1 and 3
B-6	Not considered especially
B-7	2
C-1 through 15	2

The Population Which Was the Subject of this Research

There were, in all, 138 respondents to our questionnaire; while the responses of two such respondents were received too late for inclusion in the tabulations they were, nevertheless, considered by us in our evaluation. Of these respondents 123 consented to their being identified in an alphabetical roster included herein as Appendix D.

The respondents whose views were included in the data recapitulated in this work were categorized by us as follows:

The Financial Community Groups:		
Investment Analysts with Advisory Services, and Financial Writers		15
Investment Analysts with Brokerage Firms		11
Investment Analysts with Banks		13
Investment Analysts with Mutual Funds, Insurance Companies, and Associations		18
Others, including: Officials with Governmental Agencies, Lawyers extensively engaged in securities underwriting		15
Total Financial Community		72
The Accounting Profession Groups:		
Practitioners of Accountancy		
With the major firms (the so-called "Big-Eight")	17	
With other firms	14	31
Professors of Accountancy		21
Others, including Financial Executives of publicly owned corporations, Execu-		

tive Personnel with the American Institute of CPAs	12
Total Accounting Profession	64
Total All Respondents	136

The Procedures for Selecting the Population

It should be evident from the foregoing categories of respondents (as well as from Appendix D) that a very deliberate attempt was made to obtain a representative population or "universe." The subjects were not selected randomly, but instead were solicited with a view toward obtaining a representative sampling from various segments of the financial community, as well as from the several sectors of the accounting profession. Further, as will be pointed out below, the selection also involved geographical considerations.

This selection was achieved through three separate procedures, as follows:

1. The initial selection was made on the basis of our direct, close knowledge of persons within the financial community and the profession who were believed to possess sufficient direct knowledge of the problems here being probed, enabling them to provide significant responses. This group numbers approximately thirty-five, or about 25 per cent of the entire population.

2. A further selection was made on the basis of what might be referred to as "once removed." Thus, to obtain the responses from a group of chartered financial analysts the cooperation of Professor C. Stewart Sheppard was invited; to obtain the responses from persons within the insurance field, Charles H. Pritchard, who is actively identified as a reinsurance intermediary, was asked to select and to solicit ten persons engaged in the analysis of financial statements as an incident to their guiding the investment decisions of insurance companies. Similarly, Louis Stone (of Hayden Stone & Co.) and A. W. Zelomek helped solicit the cooperation of financial writers for both the general press and specialized financial publications. From these "once removed" solicitations a group of about twenty-five respondents (approximating 20 per cent of the entire population) was obtained.

3. The remainder, constituting the majority of the subjects, was obtained by the use of four different (but essentially consistent) form letters, as follows:

a) A form letter was directed to a group of analysts selected from the *1963 Membership Directory (15th Edition) of The Financial Analysts Federation.*[6] The *Directory* subdivided the membership into the twenty-nine member organizations comprising the Federation. By reference to this geographical division, and the institutional identification of the members, the solicitation sought to obtain both geographical and institutional diversification.
b) A group of practitioners was obtained by writing to colleagues on the American Institute of CPAs Federal Tax Committee. This solicitation was deemed necessary in order to obtain responses from practitioners, especially outside the New York metropolitan area.
c) In order to bring together a group of professors of accountancy in universities in various parts of the country, a form letter was sent to authors of articles appearing in *The Accounting Review* where the writings demonstrated that the writer was concerned with the problems of accounting theory, or financial reporting generally.
d) Another form letter was sent to the chief financial officers of a group of publicly owned corporations; these were selected at random.

Each of the aforementioned letters was consistent insofar as substance was concerned; each letter described the circumstances under which the research was to be undertaken and the nature of the study. Illustrative of this description are the following paragraphs taken from the form letter soliciting the cooperation of the principal financial executives:

My study was undertaken to determine whether the

financial community understands the audit function; the nature of our economic environment in which the auditor fulfills this function; the structure of our present-day accounting theory (and the way in which this theory is determined). Further, the study would seek to determine whether this financial community accepts and is satisfied with the way in which the accounting profession is now structured and functions. (By "financial community" I mean all those responsible for the making or guiding of major investment decisions, and thereby capable of affecting significantly the allocation of economic resources of our society).

The questionnaire which is the medium for my research is being sent to a relatively small select group (100-200) of leaders in this community (including practitioners and professors in the accounting discipline to see whether their understanding is consistent with that of the financial community). I very much believe that the study can make a most vital contribution to the future development of the profession and of our standards of reporting.

The Forwarding of the Questionnaire

Beginning in May, 1964, the questionnaires were forwarded to the 177 subjects who had previously indicated that they would be willing to complete them. Completed questionnaires were received (all by mid-July, 1964) from 138 of these subjects.

The Tabulation of the Data

As the questionnaires were received, the identification stubs included at the end of the questionnaire were detached, and the responses coded, tabulated, and summarized. These summaries were then verified; the especially critical data were the subject of further review and verification.

Appendix B

The questionnaire, in the form submitted to the prospective respondents, is reproduced herein as Appendix B. (The original dimensions of the questionnaire were 8½ x 11.)

QUESTIONNAIRE

to determine

THE EFFECTIVENESS OF ACCOUNTING COMMUNICATION TO VARIOUS GROUPS IN THE FINANCIAL COMMUNITY

With Particular Reference to

The Fairness of the Financial Statements Which Have Been the Subject of Review by the Independent Auditors

Prepared by:
ABRAHAM J. BRILOFF, C.P.A.
30 Broad Street, New York 4, N. Y.
(In connection with an independent research project undertaken by him)

DESCRIPTION OF THE OBJECTIVES AND NATURE OF THIS QUESTIONNAIRE

This questionnaire is the principal research medium developed in connection with the research recently undertaken by me for a study entitled "The Effectiveness of Accounting Communication to Various Segments of the Financial Community." This study is being undertaken privately, without foundation or organization sponsorship. It is to be the basis for a doctoral dissertation to be submitted by me to the Graduate School of Business Administration of the New York University.

As used in this study the term "financial community" is intended to include all those persons who are responsible for making or guiding major investment decisions, and who are thereby capable of affecting significantly the allocation of the economic resources of our society.

This questionnaire is intended to determine the understanding by the financial community of the auditor's independent reporting function; of the nature of our economic environment in which the auditor fulfills this function; and of the structure of the accounting theory which underlies financial recording and reporting, as well as the way in which this accounting theory evolves. In addition, the questionnaire is intended to help ascertain the extent to which the financial community accepts and is satisfied with the way in which the accounting profession now performs its independent audit function. This phase of the questionnaire also calls for you to indicate your value judgments regarding the nature and extent of the auditor's involvement in modern corporate society, as well as your judgments relating to the theoretical, structural basis of our profession, usually described as our "generally accepted accounting principles."

In addition to being submitted to leading representatives of the financial community, this questionnaire will also be submitted to active practitioners in the profession of Accountancy as well as to academicians in this discipline. The results to be obtained from this phase of the research should demonstrate whether the understanding by these practitioners and teachers of the problems here being considered is consistent with that of the members of the financial community responding thereto.

The questions are grouped in three categories, as follows:

(1) The "A" series of questions is general in nature, and is intended to determine your particular involvement in the financial community and your views regarding the present-day economic environment. Also included in this section are questions intended to determine your understanding of, and degree of satisfaction with, the services rendered by accounting firms for the corporate entities whose statements are then the subject of independent audit by such firms.

(2) The "B" series of questions is intended to determine your degree of satisfaction with the way in which the accounting theory which underlies financial recording and reporting evolves. In addition, questions in this section are intended to determine your views on the extent to which this body of theory is both understood and accepted.

(3) The "C" series of questions sets forth various accounting transactions and business events in areas which are now considered to be the subject of significant study by the accounting profession. While the questions in this section are, of necessity, technical in nature, they are not designed to test your technical background in accountancy. Instead, they are intended to help ascertain whether the financial community shares the concern of the accounting profession regarding these areas; further, these questions should help to determine whether the profession has effectively communicated the financial and accounting implications of these transactions and events to this community.

Your responses will be kept in complete confidence. They will not be set forth in any form or context that would permit identification of any particular respondent, of his firm, or his institutional association. A summary of the data obtained by this questionnaire will be forwarded to you as soon as it becomes available.

Your cooperation in this research project is earnestly solicited and will be greatly appreciated.

ABRAHAM J. BRILOFF, C.P.A.

The questions in this section are general in nature. They are intended to determine your particular involvement in the financial community and your views regarding the shareholders' relationship to the modern corporate society. Also included in this section are questions intended to determine your satisfaction with the nature and extent of the services which might be rendered by accounting firms to the corporate entities for which they also render the independent audit function.

A-1 (a) You would best describe your position and role in the financial community as:

....

....

(b) Are you a Certified Public Accountant? Yes ☐ (In what State ....) No ☐

(c) Are you a Chartered Financial Analyst? Yes ☐ No ☐

(d) Are you a member of any Financial Analysts Organization? Yes ☐ No ☐

If so, which organization(s)?

....

....

A-2 If you pursued formal courses in Accountancy in a college or university indicate the areas of such courses.

Fundamentals of Accounting..............................	☐	Auditing	☐
Intermediate Accounting	☐	Contemporary Accounting Theory.....................	☐
Advanced Accounting	☐	Managerial Accounting	☐
Financial Statement Analysis.............................	☐	Taxation	☐
Cost Accounting	☐	Other (Describe)	☐

....

....

A-3 (a) Your view of the present-day corporate society, and particularly the relative roles of the publicly owned corporations and their shareholders, can best be described as:

(Check One)

One wherein the shareholders are directly concerned in the operations of the entity and seek knowledge with respect thereto for their guidance and action.. ☐

One wherein the shareholders have delegated all essential responsibility to the corporate management and where the shareholders then look to it for results.. ☐

Neither of the foregoing (in which case would you describe our present-day economic society as you envisage it?).. ☐

....

....

(b) Based on your view of the corporate society, is the shareholder getting the information essential for his effective performance in such society? Yes ☐ No ☐ No Definite View ☐

(c) Is the shareholder generally capable of comprehending and utilizing the information which he is getting for investment decision-making? Yes ☐ No ☐ No Definite View ☐

A-4 In your opinion which of the following relationships best describes that which prevails between the management and the shareholders of a major American publicly owned corporation:

(Check One)

- Employee *vis à vis* Employer ☐
- Agent *vis à vis* Principal ☐
- Borrower of Property *vis à vis* Lender of Property ☐
- Independent Manager of property *vis à vis* Persons entitled to the fruits of their investments in the property ☐
- None of the foregoing (In which case would you describe the relationship as you see it?) ☐

....

....

A-5 In your evaluation of published financial statements do you assume that they have been:

(Check One)

- Prepared by Management of the corporation and then examined by the Independent Auditor? ☐
- Prepared by the Independent Auditor? ☐
- Prepared jointly by the Management of the corporation and the Independent Auditor? ☐

If the third alternative was indicated, assuming disagreement between the Auditor and Management which of the two would make the ultimate decision?

As Prevails Presently: ....

As Should Prevail: ....

A-6 As you know the opinion paragraph of the Auditors' Certificate reads as follows: "In our opinion, the accompanying consolidated balance sheet and consolidated statements of income and surplus present fairly the financial position of The X Company as of December 31, 1963, and the results of its operations for the year then ended, in conformity with generally accepted accounting principles applied on a basis consistent with that of the preceding year."

The clause "present fairly . . . in conformity with generally accepted accounting principles" means that:

(Check One)

- In the Auditor's opinion the statements are both fair and in accordance with generally accepted accounting principles ☐
- In the Auditor's opinion the statements are fair because they are in accordance with generally accepted accounting principles ☐
- In the Auditor's opinion the statements are fair only to the extent that generally accepted accounting principles are fair ☐
- None of the foregoing (In which case would you describe the meaning of the clause as you see it?) ☐

....

....

A-7 In your evaluation of the published financial statements received and reviewed by you, you find that:

(Check One)

- They are generally adequate, and consistent with your expectations ☐
- Useful principally as a point of departure for your independent analysis ☐
- They are unsatisfactory except as one of the sources of data ☐

A-8 In your evaluation of the published financial statements, you cannot reach any judgments unless and until you have:

	(Check as many as you consider appropriate)
Made certain arbitrary assumptions concerning the entity's accounting procedures and policies	☐
Read the entire text of the report (including the President's commentary)	☐
Read all of the footnotes and other explanatory material	☐
Reviewed the S.E.C. Form 10K and other explanatory material	☐
Compared the statements with listing applications filed with the Stock Exchange	☐
Reviewed speeches by Management at annual meetings and otherwise	☐
None of the foregoing (because you are able to make your determinations from the statements themselves)	☐

A-9 In your view should it have been necessary for you to proceed along the foregoing (A-8) lines?

Yes ☐ No ☐

If "No"—Do you have any alternative procedures which would permit you to proceed more expeditously?

....

....

A-10 In your opinion to what extent are published financial statements responsive to the needs and requirements of each of the groups noted below:

	Fully	Substantially	Adequately	Inadequately
	(CHECK ONE ON EACH LEVEL)			
a) Management	☐	☐	☐	☐
b) Shareholders owning a substantial interest	☐	☐	☐	☐
c) Shareholders owning a minor interest	☐	☐	☐	☐
d) Financial Analysts	☐	☐	☐	☐
e) Creditors	☐	☐	☐	☐
f) Labor	☐	☐	☐	☐
g) Government	☐	☐	☐	☐
h) Anyone who is willing and competent to read the statements carefully and with discrimination	☐	☐	☐	☐

A-11 In your opinion the rendering of management services by CPAs in situations where they will also be fulfilling the independent audit function will:

	(Check One)
Enhance the significance of the auditor's opinion	☐
Detract from the significance of this opinion	☐
Have no important effect on the significance of this opinion	☐
No definite views thereon	☐

A-12 In your opinion the rendering of *management services* by CPAs in situations where they will also be fulfilling the independent audit function is:

(Check one in each group)

a) Compatible with the traditions of the Auditor.......... ☐
Incompatible with these traditions.......... ☐
No definite views thereon.......... ☐

b) Compatible with the independence of the Auditor.......... ☐
Incompatible with such independence.......... ☐
No definite views thereon.......... ☐

c) An involvement which should be encouraged and extended.......... ☐
An involvement which should be discouraged and restricted.......... ☐
No definite views thereon.......... ☐

A-13 In your view the rendering of *extensive tax consultative services* by CPAs in situations where they will also be fulfilling the independent audit function is:

(Check one in each group)

a) Compatible with the traditions of the Auditor.......... ☐
Incompatible with these traditions.......... ☐
No definite views thereon.......... ☐

b) Compatible with the independence of the Auditor.......... ☐
Incompatible with such independence.......... ☐
No definite views thereon.......... ☐

c) An involvement which should be encouraged and extended.......... ☐
An involvement which should be discouraged and restricted.......... ☐
No definite views thereon.......... ☐

A-14 In your view, the rendering of *both* management services and tax consultative services by CPAs in circumstances where they are also performing the audit function is:

(Check one in each group)

a) Compatible with the traditions of the Auditor.......... ☐
Incompatible with these traditions.......... ☐
No definite views thereon.......... ☐

b) Compatible with the independence of the Auditor.......... ☐
Incompatible with such independence.......... ☐
No definite views thereon.......... ☐

c) An involvement which should be encouraged and extended.......... ☐
An involvement which should be discouraged and restricted.......... ☐
No definite views thereon.......... ☐

-15 Listed below are a number of categories of management services which might be required by corporations. For each category indicate:

(A) Whether you believe such services *are now* being offered by public accounting firms to corporations for whom they are already performing the independent audit function.

(B) Whether in your opinion they *should be* so offered.

	(A) DO YOU BELIEVE THAT THEY ARE BEING OFFERED?			(B) DO YOU BELIEVE THAT THEY SHOULD BE OFFERED?		
	Yes	No	Do Not Know	Yes	No	No Opinion
	(CHECK ONE ON EACH LEVEL)			(CHECK ONE ON EACH LEVEL)		
a) Review all phases of a business in connection with a plan to expand profits	☐	☐	☐	☐	☐	☐
b) Review all phases of a business in connection with a plan of the accounting firm's client to buy the business	☐	☐	☐	☐	☐	☐
c) Review all phases of a business in connection with a plan to reorganize the company	☐	☐	☐	☐	☐	☐
d) Appraise the organizational structure of the entity and the preparation of a manual defining responsibilities and lines of authority	☐	☐	☐	☐	☐	☐
e) Prepare an executive development program	☐	☐	☐	☐	☐	☐
f) Develop a plan of Executive Compensation (including "fringe benefits")	☐	☐	☐	☐	☐	☐
g) Develop sales forecasts and budgeting in connection with sales controls	☐	☐	☐	☐	☐	☐
h) Determine market potentials and plan profitable sales territories	☐	☐	☐	☐	☐	☐
i) Determine sales quotas and salesmen's incentives	☐	☐	☐	☐	☐	☐
j) Determine programs for increasing volume and profits through improved pricing methods	☐	☐	☐	☐	☐	☐
k) Analyze job functions and responsibilities of the entity's personnel	☐	☐	☐	☐	☐	☐
l) Determine the relative contributions of the entity's personnel	☐	☐	☐	☐	☐	☐

The questions that follow are intended to determine your satisfaction, generally, with the way in which the underlying theory of accountancy (i.e., the body of generally accepted accounting principles) is determined, with the extent to which such body of principles is generally known and accepted, and with the manner in which it is applied in practice.

B-1 For the purposes of this question assume that such a body of generally accepted accounting principles does exist. In your opinion:

(A) To which of the several groups described below are these principles reasonably well known?

(B) To which of these groups should they be thus known?

	(A) THEY ARE REASONABLY WELL KNOWN			(B) THEY SHOULD BE REASONABLY WELL KNOWN		
	Probably Yes	Probably No	No Definite Opinion	Probably Yes	Probably No	No Definite Opinion
	(CHECK ONE ON EACH LEVEL)			(CHECK ONE ON EACH LEVEL)		
a) Members of the accounting professions extensively engaged in the audit function	☐	☐	☐	☐	☐	☐
b) Members of the profession principally engaged in management or "Internal Accounting"	☐	☐	☐	☐	☐	☐
c) Professors of Accountancy	☐	☐	☐	☐	☐	☐
d) Management of major corporations	☐	☐	☐	☐	☐	☐
e) Chief financial officers of major corporations	☐	☐	☐	☐	☐	☐
f) Certified Financial Analysts	☐	☐	☐	☐	☐	☐
g) Investment advisers generally	☐	☐	☐	☐	☐	☐
h) Individual investors generally	☐	☐	☐	☐	☐	☐
i) Accountants with the S.E.C.	☐	☐	☐	☐	☐	☐
j) Economists generally	☐	☐	☐	☐	☐	☐
k) Governmental personnel responsible for the determination of fiscal policy	☐	☐	☐	☐	☐	☐
l) Governmental personnel with regulatory agencies	☐	☐	☐	☐	☐	☐
m) "Customers' men" with stock brokerage firms	☐	☐	☐	☐	☐	☐

B-2 It has been urged that a body of clearly and readily identified accounting principles which would have universal applicability should be developed.

Do you agree that such a body of principles with universal applicability should be developed?

Yes ☐ No ☐ No definite opinion ☐

In the development of such a body of principles the responsibility should be with:

(Indicate by number the *order of preference,* with "1" being most preferred.)

The practitioners in the profession of public accountancy ☐

Corporate management charged with financial statement matters ☐

Professors of accountancy ☐

Bankers and the financial community generally ☐

Governmental agencies ☐

Other (Please indicate who should be thus responsible) ☐

....

No definite opinion ☐

B-3 The particular principle or principles which may be selected in a particular situation, to apply to a particular transaction, will be determined primarily by:

(Check One)

- The corporation's management ☐
- The independent public accountant ☐
- Other (Please indicate who should make the determination) ☐

  ....

- No definite opinion ☐

In your opinion this selection should be determined primarily by:

(Check One)

- The corporation's management ☐
- The independent public accountant ☐
- Other (Please indicate who should be thus responsible) ☐

  ....

- No definite opinion ☐

B-4 Assume that management has selected a particular principle to apply, but the independent auditor considers another such principle to be preferable. Assuming the matter to be significant and material, the auditor will presumably:

(Check One)

- Take an exception to the selection made by management ☐
- Describe the alternative principles but otherwise permit management's selection to prevail ☐
- Qualify his opinion ☐
- Prepare the statement on the basis of his own selection ☐
- None of the foregoing ☐
- No definite opinion ☐

In your opinion, what action should the auditor take in the foregoing circumstance?

(Check One)

- Take an exception to the selection made by management ☐
- Describe the alternative principles but otherwise permit management's selection to prevail ☐
- Qualify his opinion ☐
- Prepare the statement on the basis of his own selection ☐
- None of the foregoing (In which case would you describe your preferred alternative?) ☐

  ....

- No definite opinion ☐

B-5 Each of the statements below sets forth a view regarding accounting theory in general, or some aspect thereof. In each case you are asked to indicate:

(A) Whether the view expressed is currently consistent with "generally accepted accounting principles" (GAAP)

and

(B) Whether such view would result in a fairer presentation of corporate financial statements (and accordingly should be deemed to be consistent with such principles).

	(A) IS IT IN ACCORD WITH GAAP?			(B) SHOULD IT BE IN ACCORD WITH GAAP?		
	Yes	No	No Definite Knowledge	Yes	No	No Definite Opinion
	(CHECK ONE ON EACH LEVEL)			(CHECK ONE ON EACH LEVEL)		
a) Since management knows of the various alternative principles in advance of entering into a transaction, it can so structure the transaction that it will correspond to that principle which it believes will be most desirable for its purposes...........	☐	☐	☐	☐	☐	☐
b) The Independent Auditor (who will ultimately be the one to perform the audit function) may describe in advance the several alternative principles which can be made to apply to a particular kind of transaction and emphasize for management the particular principle which will apply, dependent on the form of the transaction.....................	☐	☐	☐	☐	☐	☐
c) In the event that there is a doubt as to the particular principle which should be applied in a particular situation, the one that will show lesser earnings is to be selected...............................	☐	☐	☐	☐	☐	☐
d) More important than the particular principle selected in a particular entity situation is that the same principle be made applicable to all entities in the same or similar industry...........	☐	☐	☐	☐	☐	☐
e) More important than the particular principle selected in a particular situation is that the same principle be selected for that situation year-in and year-out..	☐	☐	☐	☐	☐	☐
f) The consistency rule assumes that even though different companies may use divergent principles for the same transaction, the incomes of the several companies are usually quite comparable because the turnover of items being accounted for tends to cancel out differences in method.......................................	☐	☐	☐	☐	☐	☐

B-6 The preceding questions have generally been predicated on the assumption that there is such a body of accounting principles which has met with general acceptance.

In your opinion is there such a body of principles? Yes ☐ No ☐ No definite opinion ☐

B-7 It has been suggested that the welfare of the various groups comprising our economic society is best served by having a multiplicity of alternative principles permitting a diversity of individual judgment rather than through having centralized decisions arrived at by the few.

Do you agree with this statement? Yes ☐ No ☐ No definite opinion ☐

If you have responded "Yes" to the preceding question, do you believe that the "individual judgment" is being well exercised at present? Yes ☐ No ☐ No definite opinion ☐

In this section various accounting transactions and business events will be set forth. In each case various alternatives for financial statement presentation are indicated. You are then asked with respect to each such alternative:

(A) Whether you believe the alternative indicated is in accordance with "generally accepted accounting principles" (GAAP), and

(B) Whether you believe the alternative indicated should be in accordance with such principles.

	(A) IS IT IN ACCORD WITH GAAP?			(B) SHOULD IT BE IN ACCORD WITH GAAP?		
	Yes	No	No Definite Knowledge	Yes	No	No Definite Opinion
	(CHECK ONE ON EACH LEVEL)			(CHECK ONE ON EACH LEVEL)		
C-1 The corporation has realized a very substantial and extraordinary gain from the liquidation of an investment. This gain is shown:						
a) On the income statement as a part of the corporation's income for the year	☐	☐	☐	☐	☐	☐
b) On the income statement, but only after the income for the year is determined	☐	☐	☐	☐	☐	☐
c) Not shown on the income statement at all	☐	☐	☐	☐	☐	☐
C-2 The corporation has a substantial loss for the year:						
a) This loss is reduced by any tax refund to which it is entitled by reason of the carry-back of such loss	☐	☐	☐	☐	☐	☐
b) A carry-back is not available; however, the reported loss is reduced by reason of the fact that the corporation expects to have taxable income in the future (to which the loss could be carried forward)	☐	☐	☐	☐	☐	☐
C-3 The corporation has very substantial earnings during the current year. However, no income taxes are required to be paid this year because of a substantial loss carry-forward.						
a) The current year's income is stated without any provision for income tax	☐	☐	☐	☐	☐	☐
b) The current year's income is reduced by the amount of tax which would otherwise have been payable (and the tax being saved is credited to earned surplus)	☐	☐	☐	☐	☐	☐
C-4 Stock options have been granted to an executive entitling him to purchase shares at 100 (when they are worth 100) exercisable at any time within five years. The option is exercised when the shares are selling for $140.						
a) The $40 differential is additional compensation and is deducted as a cost on the income statement for the year when the option is exercised	☐	☐	☐	☐	☐	☐
b) The option is valued by a "Put and Call" option dealer and is deducted as a cost of the year when the option is granted	☐	☐	☐	☐	☐	☐
c) While the option is deemed to be a method of compensating the executive, it is nevertheless properly ignored in the determination of income	☐	☐	☐	☐	☐	☐
d) In order to prevent dilution of the corporation's stock the corporation goes into the market place and buys its shares at 140 (which it then resells to the executive at 100). The $40 differential is then shown as a cost for the year (thereby reducing its income)	☐	☐	☐	☐	☐	☐

	(A) IS IT IN ACCORD WITH GAAP?			(B) SHOULD IT BE IN ACCORD WITH GAAP?		
	Yes	No	No Definite Knowledge	Yes	No	No Definite Opinion
	(CHECK ONE ON EACH LEVEL)			(CHECK ONE ON EACH LEVEL)		
C-5 This question relates to the problem of accounting for long-term leases.						
a) Whenever the circumstances indicate that a long-term lease is (by its nature or terms) essentially equivalent to a purchase of the property, the transaction is required to be shown as such a purchase (with the related liability disclosed)........................	☐	☐	☐	☐	☐	☐
b) Such an accounting treatment (i.e., as though it were a purchase) is especially prevalent where it is apparent that the leasing (rather than actual purchase) was determined upon in order to avoid showing a debt in the balance sheet......................	☐	☐	☐	☐	☐	☐
c) This treatment (i.e., as though it were a purchase) is particularly urgent where various debt restriction covenants are contained in bond indentures (and where the "purchase" might indicate a breach of these covenants)..	☐	☐	☐	☐	☐	☐
d) This treatment (i.e., as though it were a purchase) is particularly urgent where it is apparent to the auditor that the rentals in the early years are especially reduced in order to permit greater income to be shown in these early years...............	☐	☐	☐	☐	☐	☐
e) This treatment (i.e., as though it were a purchase) is particularly urgent where it is apparent to the auditor that the rentals in the early years are especially high in order to permit a reduction in income in these earlier years (and correspondingly greater amounts in the later years)...	☐	☐	☐	☐	☐	☐
f) Regardless of the manner of accounting treatment, the rental for the ensuing year is required to be shown as a current liability (just as the ensuing year's debt amortization would be thus shown)	☐	☐	☐	☐	☐	☐
g) This reflection of the current liability is especially urgent where the auditor sees that the working capital ratios would be vitally affected by such an inclusion of additional current debt	☐	☐	☐	☐	☐	☐
C-6 An important silver producer carries its inventories of metals on the Last-in, First-out (LIFO) basis. These inventories aggregate $120 million as of the close of 1963.						
a) Inasmuch as there had been a very precipitous rise in silver prices during the year 1963, the market values of the inventories at the beginning and end of the year are required to be shown	☐	☐	☐	☐	☐	☐
b) Assuming that the silver is really worth $250 million the management can, in its sole discretion, realize income of $130 million (or any portion thereof), subject, of course, to the applicable income taxes. The income so realized would be included in the annual income statement.......................................	☐	☐	☐	☐	☐	☐
c) If management determined that it desired earnings of $4.50 per share but saw the corporation realizing only $4.00 from operations otherwise, it could dispose of enough of its silver inventories so as to produce the additional 50¢ per share. The income for the year would then be stated at $4.50 per share....	☐	☐	☐	☐	☐	☐

	(A) IS IT IN ACCORD WITH GAAP?			(B) SHOULD IT BE IN ACCORD WITH GAAP?		
	Yes	No	No Definite Knowledge	Yes	No	No Definite Opinion
	(CHECK ONE ON EACH LEVEL)			(CHECK ONE ON EACH LEVEL)		
C-7 This question also relates to the Last-in, First-out (LIFO) method of inventory valuation and assumes that price levels are increasing.						
a) The balance sheet of a company which carries its inventories on the LIFO basis is more conservatively stated than its competitors' which use the First-in, First-out (FIFO) basis..........	☐	☐	☐	☐	☐	☐
b) The annual income statement of a company which carries its inventories on a LIFO basis is more conservatively stated than its competitors' which use the FIFO basis....................................	☐	☐	☐	☐	☐	☐
C-8 This question relates to the accounting problems of the oil and gas industry.						
a) Where the corporation incurs costs for Intangible Drilling Costs of productive oil and gas properties these costs are charged to expense in the year when incurred..	☐	☐	☐	☐	☐	☐
b) These costs are entirely capitalized and then amortized over the expected productivity resulting from these costs..................	☐	☐	☐	☐	☐	☐
c) These costs are first to be reduced by any immediate tax saving resulting from the cost, the excess is then amortized over the expected productive life of the facility...	☐	☐	☐	☐	☐	☐
C-9 In order to acquire the entire capital stock of the S corporation which owns a very valuable patent (carried on the S books at $10,000) and nothing else, the P corporation issues 1,000 shares of its $1 par value stock which then has a market price of $40 a share (hence an aggregate value of $40,000):						
a) In accounting for the transaction on the consolidated balance sheet of P, the patents thus acquired will be carried at $10,000 (i.e., their book value on the S books).............................	☐	☐	☐	☐	☐	☐
b) In accounting for the transaction as above, future operations will be charged with amortization of patent cost of $10,000........	☐	☐	☐	☐	☐	☐
c) This accounting for $10,000 would be possible for P even though, in order to avoid any dilution of its shares, P went out into the open market and bought in 1,000 shares at $40 (hence for $40,000)	☐	☐	☐	☐	☐	☐
d) In all future comparative financial statements, the previous year's operations will be restated so as to reflect the combined operations of both P and S during these previous years................	☐	☐	☐	☐	☐	☐
C-10 This question relates to problems of consolidated financial statements.						
a) The C company is a major producer of silver, copper and other metals. It owns a "more than 50%" interest in the Z corporation which owns major mines in Australia. The financial statements of C and Z are undoubtedly to be presented on a consolidated basis	☐	☐	☐	☐	☐	☐
b) The D corporation, engaged in food retailing, owns 100% of the outstanding shares of T (a trading stamp company). The operations of D and T are undoubtedly to be presented on a consolidated basis	☐	☐	☐	☐	☐	☐

	(A) IS IT IN ACCORD WITH GAAP?			(B) SHOULD IT BE IN ACCORD WITH GAAP?		
	Yes	No	No Definite Knowledge	Yes	No	No Definite Opinion
	(CHECK ONE ON EACH LEVEL)			(CHECK ONE ON EACH LEVEL)		

C-11 The A corporation desires to obtain for itself competent management now with the X corporation. To accomplish this result A exchanges 100,000 of its shares (representing a 25% interest in itself) for all of the X corporation shares and thereupon obtains this management together with inventory worth $100,000 (but with a book value on the books of X of $15,000). At the time of the exchange the shares of A are quoted on a stock exchange at 7 (hence $700,000 in the aggregate for the 100,000 shares).

a) This transaction will be reflected on a consolidated statement of A so as to show:

Inventories	$100,000
Goodwill (the amount presumed to represent the value of the management taken over)	600,000
Total (the amount equal to the value of the shares given up by A)	700,000

☐ ☐ ☐ ☐ ☐ ☐

b) The Goodwill shown above will undoubtedly be written off over the years when the newly acquired management will be making its contribution to the consolidated income ☐ ☐ ☐ ☐ ☐ ☐

c) In all future comparative financial statements, the previous years' operations will be restated so as to reflect the combined operations of A and X ☐ ☐ ☐ ☐ ☐ ☐

C-12 Oil company B has a 50% interest in petrochemical company Y which uses B's product for the manufacture of various consumer and industrial commodities.

a) 50% of profits earned by Y will be reflected year-by-year in the B financial statements ☐ ☐ ☐ ☐ ☐ ☐

b) It may be that B management will determine that it will pick up its share of the profits only when it receives a dividend from Y ☐ ☐ ☐ ☐ ☐ ☐

c) It may be (assuming that there are no significant dividends paid over the years) that the B management might determine to reflect the bulk of its share of Y income in a particular year through a disposition of its interest in Y ☐ ☐ ☐ ☐ ☐ ☐

d) A very substantial gain on the disposition or liquidation by B of its investment in Y would be credited directly to B's earned surplus (and not to the year's income) ☐ ☐ ☐ ☐ ☐ ☐

	(A) IS IT IN ACCORD WITH GAAP?			(B) SHOULD IT BE IN ACCORD WITH GAAP?		
	Yes	No	No Definite Knowledge	Yes	No	No Definite Opinion
	(CHECK ONE ON EACH LEVEL)			(CHECK ONE ON EACH LEVEL)		
C-13 This question relates to the problems of accounting for pension cost.						
a) Corporation E has an established pension plan entitling its employees to a stipulated pension on attaining retirement age. Assuming that E does not have a prefunded pension plan, no charge need be made to annual operations until it is called upon to make payments to retired employees	☐	☐	☐	☐	☐	☐
b) Assuming that F does have a prefunded pension plan with some discretion allowed to the corporation in making contributions under the plan. The amount charged to annual operations will be equal to the amount which management determined to fund that year	☐	☐	☐	☐	☐	☐
c) Because the pension fund referred to in (b) above will have earnings and capital appreciation, the annual charge to operations for F's pension cost will be affected by such earnings, etc., of the fund	☐	☐	☐	☐	☐	☐
d) Company G has no pension plan but is in an industry where most other major firms do have such a plan. Company G's operations will be charged with an amount equal to what the pension cost would be if the company had a plan consistent with that common in the industry	☐	☐	☐	☐	☐	☐
C-14 During 1958 company H acquired an extensive new plant at a cost of $100,000 which had an estimated life of ten years. The replacement value of this plant is now considered to be $200,000 (new). Price levels have increased by 50% between 1958 and the present. The company uses the declining-balance method of depreciation for income tax purposes. The depreciation charged on the 1963 financial statements will be:						
a) $10,000 (one-tenth of the cost)	☐	☐	☐	☐	☐	☐
b) $6,600 (the amount deductible in 1963 for tax purposes)	☐	☐	☐	☐	☐	☐
c) $20,000 (one-tenth of the $200,000 replacement value)	☐	☐	☐	☐	☐	☐
d) $15,000 ($10,000 multiplied by 150%—the current price index in relation to 1958)	☐	☐	☐	☐	☐	☐
C-15 Company J is engaged in aircraft manufacture. It expended $500,000 in costs for Research and Development in the development of a prototype of a new supersonic aircraft. Company J will:						
a) Charge this $500,000 against the current year's operations	☐	☐	☐	☐	☐	☐
b) Capitalize this $500,000 and amortize it over a period of years	☐	☐	☐	☐	☐	☐
c) Capitalize this $500,000 and write it off when the aircraft design produces revenue	☐	☐	☐	☐	☐	☐

NOTES and COMMENTS

Please turn to inside back cover.

NOTE: THE SEGMENT BELOW WILL BE DETACHED BY ME IMMEDIATELY UPON RECEIPT. THEREAFTER, THIS QUESTIONNAIRE WILL BE IDENTIFIED SOLELY BY THE NUMBER ASSIGNED THERETO.

Number__________

Number__________

Please furnish the following information:

Name__________

Firm or Institutional Association__________

Business Address__________

Phone__________ May I 'phone you in the event that some clarification becomes necessary? ....Yes______ No______

Appendix

C

The results obtained from this study are presented in summary form in the following Table 12. This table sets forth the percentage distribution derived from the responses from the seventy-two respondents comprising the "Financial Community Category" and the sixty-four respondents constituting the "Accounting Profession Category."

TABLE 12

The Percentage Distribution of Responses
Obtained from the Questionnaire to Determine
The Effectiveness of Accounting Communication

Financial Community Category (C) — Frequency 72
Accounting Profession Category (P) — Frequency 64
Combined Frequency — 136

The questions in this section are general in nature. They are intended to determine your particular involvement in the financial community and your views regarding the shareholders' relationship to the modern corporate society. Also included in this section are questions intended to determine your satisfaction with the nature and extent of the services which might be rendered by accounting firms to the corporate entities for which they also render the independent audit function.

A-1 (a) You would best describe your position and role in the financial community as:

....

....

(b) Are you a Certified Public Accountant? Yes ☐ (In what State .... Yes: C* 4.2 P* 75.0

(c) Are you a Chartered Financial Analyst? Yes: C 13.9 P 0

(d) Are you a member of any Financial Analysts Organization? Yes: C 68.1 P 7.8

If so, which organization(s)?

....

....

A-2 If you pursued formal courses in Accountancy in a college or university indicate the areas of such courses.

Fundamentals of Accounting	☐	Auditing	☐
Intermediate Accounting	☐	Contemporary Accounting Theory	☐
Advanced Accounting	☐	Managerial Accounting	☐
Financial Statement Analysis	☐	Taxation	☐
Cost Accounting	☐	Other (Describe)	☐

NOT TABULATE[D] HEREIN

....

....

A-3 (a) Your view of the present-day corporate society, and particularly the relative roles of the publicly owned corporations and their shareholders, can best be described as:

	C	P
One wherein the shareholders are directly concerned in the operations of the entity and seek knowledge with respect thereto for their guidance and action	6.9	0
One wherein the shareholders have delegated all essential responsibility to the corporate management and where the shareholders then look to it for results	88.9	96.9
Neither of the foregoing (in which case would you describe our present-day economic society as you envisage it?)	4.2	1.6

....

....

* "C" indicates responses from The Financial Community Category
"P" indicates responses from The Accounting Profession Category

(b) Based on your view of the corporate society, is the shareholder getting the information essential for his effective performance in such society?

Yes: C 59.7 P 45.6 No: C 20.8 P 46.9

(c) Is the shareholder generally capable of comprehending and utilizing the information which he is getting for investment decision-making?

Yes: C 20.8 P 21.9 No: C 61.1 P 65.6

A-4 In your opinion which of the following relationships best describes that which prevails between the management and the shareholders of a major American publicly owned corporation:

	C	P
Employee *vis à vis* Employer	4.2	1.6
Agent *vis à vis* Principal	9.7	6.3
Borrower of Property *vis à vis* Lender of Property	0	0
Independent Manager of property *vis à vis* Persons entitled to the fruits of their investments in the property	76.4	85.9
None of the foregoing (In which case would you describe the relationship as you see it?)	8.3	4.7

....

....

A-5 In your evaluation of published financial statements do you assume that they have been:

	C	P
Prepared by Management of the corporation and then examined by the Independent Auditor?	43.6	65.6
Prepared by the Independent Auditor?	4.2	1.6
Prepared jointly by the Management of the corporation and the Independent Auditor?	43.1	32.3

If the third alternative was indicated, assuming disagreement between the Auditor and Management which of the two would make the ultimate decision?

As Prevails Presently: ....

As Should Prevail: ....

A-6 As you know the opinion paragraph of the Auditors' Certificate reads as follows: "In our opinion, the accompanying consolidated balance sheet and consolidated statements of income and surplus present fairly the financial position of The X Company as of December 31, 1963, and the results of its operations for the year then ended, in conformity with generally accepted accounting principles applied on a basis consistent with that of the preceding year."

The clause "present fairly . . . in conformity with generally accepted accounting principles" means that:

	C	P
In the Auditor's opinion the statements are both fair and in accordance with generally accepted accounting principles	44.4	34.4
In the Auditor's opinion the statements are fair because they are in accordance with generally accepted accounting principles	22.2	29.7
In the Auditor's opinion the statements are fair only to the extent that generally accepted accounting principles are fair	27.8	20.3
None of the foregoing (In which case would you describe the meaning of the clause as you see it?)	5.6	15.6

....

....

A-7 In your evaluation of the published financial statements received and reviewed by you, you find that:

	C	P
They are generally adequate, and consistent with your expectations	25.0	32.8
Useful principally as a point of departure for your independent analysis	61.1	46.9
They are unsatisfactory except as one of the sources of data	9.7	18.8

A-8 In your evaluation of the published financial statements, you cannot reach any judgments unless and until you have:

(Check as many as you consider appropriate)

Made certain arbitrary assumptions concerning the entity's accounting procedures and policies........ ☐

Read the entire text of the report (including the President's commentary)........ ☐

Read all of the footnotes and other explanatory material........ ☐ NOT TABULATED HEREIN

Reviewed the S.E.C. Form 10K and other explanatory material........ ☐

Compared the statements with listing applications filed with the Stock Exchange........ ☐

Reviewed speeches by Management at annual meetings and otherwise........ ☐

None of the foregoing (because you are able to make your determinations from the statements themselves)........ ☐

A-9 In your view should it have been necessary for you to proceed along the foregoing (A-8) lines?

Yes ☐ No ☐

If "No"—Do you have any alternative procedures which would permit you to proceed more expeditously?

.... NOT TABULATED

.... HEREIN

A-10 In your opinion to what extent are published financial statements responsive to the needs and requirements of each of the groups noted below:

		Fully	Substantially	Adequately	Inadequately
a) Management	C	12.5	18.1	15.3	48.6
	P	14.1	14.1	10.9	57.8
b) Shareholders owning a substantial interest	C	5.6	22.2	22.2	45.8
	P	1.6	18.8	32.8	46.9
c) Shareholders owning a minor interest	C	16.7	30.6	34.7	16.7
	P	10.9	31.3	34.4	23.4
d) Financial Analysts	C	0	12.5	30.6	52.8
	P	0	10.9	26.6	62.5
e) Creditors	C	2.8	19.4	29.2	43.1
	P	1.6	32.8	42.2	23.4
f) Labor	C	22.2	16.7	29.2	25.0
	P	10.9	17.2	29.7	42.2
g) Government	C	16.7	15.3	26.4	30.6
	P	10.9	18.8	34.4	31.3
h) Anyone who is willing and competent to read the statements carefully and with discrimination	C	8.3	23.6	36.1	20.8
	P	6.3	18.8	34.4	31.3

A-11 In your opinion the rendering of management services by CPAs in situations where they will also be fulfilling the independent audit function will:

	C	P
Enhance the significance of the auditor's opinion	16.7	7.8
Detract from the significance of this opinion	52.8	21.9
Have no important effect on the significance of this opinion	18.1	68.8
No definite views thereon	11.1	1.6

A-12 In your opinion the rendering of *management services* by CPAs in situations where they will also be fulfilling the independent audit function is:

	C	P
a) Compatible with the traditions of the Auditor	22.2	65.6
Incompatible with these traditions	48.6	21.9
No definite views thereon	25.0	12.5
b) Compatible with the independence of the Auditor	22.2	71.9
Incompatible with such independence	58.3	21.9
No definite views thereon	16.7	4.7
c) An involvement which should be encouraged and extended	18.1	59.4
An involvement which should be discouraged and restricted	54.2	21.9
No definite views thereon	26.4	15.6

A-13 In your view the rendering of *extensive tax consultative services* by CPAs in situations where they will also be fulfilling the independent audit function is:

	C	P
a) Compatible with the traditions of the Auditor	66.7	87.5
Incompatible with these traditions	20.8	9.4
No definite views thereon	8.3	3.1
b) Compatible with the independence of the Auditor	69.4	34.4
Incompatible with such independence	25.0	14.1
No definite views thereon	4.2	0
c) An involvement which should be encouraged and extended	48.6	76.6
An involvement which should be discouraged and restricted	27.8	10.9
No definite views thereon	23.6	9.4

A-14 In your view, the rendering of *both* management services and tax consultative services by CPAs in circumstances where they are also performing the audit function is:

	C	P
a) Compatible with the traditions of the Auditor	26.4	75.0
Incompatible with these traditions	45.8	17.2
No definite views thereon	20.8	6.3
b) Compatible with the independence of the Auditor	26.4	75.0
Incompatible with such independence	56.9	18.8
No definite views thereon	11.1	3.1
c) An involvement which should be encouraged and extended	23.6	62.5
An involvement which should be discouraged and restricted	52.8	18.8
No definite views thereon	18.1	15.6

A-15 Listed below are a number of categories of management services which might be required by corporations. For each category indicate:

(A) Whether you believe such services *are now* being offered by public accounting firms to corporations for whom they are already performing the independent audit function.

(B) Whether in your opinion they *should be* so offered.

		(A) DO YOU BELIEVE THAT THEY ARE BEING OFFERED?		(B) DO YOU BELIEVE THAT THEY SHOULD BE OFFERED?	
		Yes	No	Yes	No
a) Review all phases of a business in connection with a plan to expand profits	C	36.2	26.4	27.8	59.7
	P	71.9	17.2	64.1	28.1
b) Review all phases of a business in connection with a plan of the accounting firm's client to buy the business	C	62.5	13.9	59.7	31.9
	P	84.4	7.8	75.0	20.3
c) Review all phases of a business in connection with a plan to reorganize the company	C	58.3	15.3	52.8	36.1
	P	82.9	10.9	71.9	25.0
d) Appraise the organizational structure of the entity and the preparation of a manual defining responsibilities and lines of authority	C	19.4	26.4	8.3	68.0
	P	76.6	7.8	60.9	31.2
e) Prepare an executive development program	C	8.4	34.7	2.8	82.0
	P	37.6	28.1	31.3	56.2
f) Develop a plan of Executive Compensation (including "fringe benefits")	C	33.4	11.1	29.2	55.5
	P	76.6	6.3	68.7	21.9
g) Develop sales forecasts and budgeting in connection with sales controls	C	29.2	27.8	19.5	69.5
	P	63.1	11.0	49.1	32.8
h) Determine market potentials and plan profitable sales territories	C	8.4	40.3	2.8	86.2
	P	51.6	25.0	31.2	50.0
i) Determine sales quotas and salesmen's incentives	C	7.0	38.9	5.6	84.8
	P	48.5	2.5	29.7	30.6
j) Determine programs for increasing volume and profits through improved pricing methods	C	30.6	20.9	30.6	57.0
	P	74.9	9.4	67.1	25.0
k) Analyze job functions and responsibilities of the entity's personnel	C	22.3	29.2	5.6	80.6
	P	71.9	10.9	53.1	35.9
l) Determine the relative contributions of the entity's personnel	C	18.0	29.2	8.3	79.2
	P	54.7	18.8	45.4	43.8

The questions that follow are intended to determine your satisfaction, generally, with the way in which the underlying theory of accountancy (i.e., the body of generally accepted accounting principles) is determined, with the extent to which such body of principles is generally known and accepted, and with the manner in which it is applied in practice.

B-1 For the purposes of this question assume that such a body of generally accepted accounting principles does exist. In your opinion:

(A) To which of the several groups described below are these principles reasonably well known?

(B) To which of these groups should they be thus known?

		(A) THEY ARE REASONABLY WELL KNOWN		(B) THEY SHOULD BE REASONABLY WELL KNOWN	
		Yes	No	Yes	No
a) Members of the accounting professions extensively engaged in the audit function	C	98.6	1.4	97.2	1.4
	P	98.5	1.5	93.8	3.2
b) Members of the profession principally engaged in management or "Internal Accounting"	C	88.9	5.6	93.1	2.8
	P	84.4	12.5	95.3	3.1
c) Professors of Accountancy	C	97.2	0	97.2	0
	P	98.5	1.6	98.5	0
d) Management of major corporations	C	44.5	37.5	79.2	12.5
	P	28.2	59.3	70.3	21.9
e) Chief financial officers of major corporations	C	91.7	4.2	97.3	1.4
	P	84.4	9.4	97.0	0
f) Certified Financial Analysts	C	70.8	19.5	95.8	0
	P	54.7	28.2	95.4	1.6
g) Investment advisers generally	C	40.3	41.7	79.2	11.1
	P	17.2	67.2	89.1	7.8
h) Individual investors generally	C	4.2	88.8	26.4	61.1
	P	3.1	95.3	34.4	48.4
i) Accountants with the S.E.C.	C	93.1	2.8	96.8	1.4
	P	93.8	6.2	96.9	0
j) Economists generally	C	23.6	49.9	56.9	27.8
	P	4.7	82.8	76.6	12.5
k) Governmental personnel responsible for the determination of fiscal policy	C	40.3	41.7	66.6	22.3
	P	15.6	70.3	71.9	14.1
l) Governmental personnel with regulatory agencies	C	40.3	37.5	79.2	13.9
	P	28.0	59.4	76.6	12.5
m) "Customers' men" with stock brokerage firms	C	2.8	83.3	48.6	38.9
	P	1.6	89.0	45.4	35.9

B-2 It has been urged that a body of clearly and readily identified accounting principles which would have universal applicability should be developed.

Do you agree that such a body of principles with universal applicability should be developed?

Yes: C 70.8 P 81.3 No: C 8.3 P 14.1

In the development of such a body of principles the responsibility should be with:

(Indicate by number the *order of preference,* with "1" being most preferred.)

The practitioners in the profession of public accountancy ☐

Corporate management charged with financial statement matters ☐

Professors of accountancy ☐

Bankers and the financial community generally ☐

Governmental agencies ☐

Other (Please indicate who should be thus responsible) ☐

....

No definite opinion ☐

NOT TABULATED HEREIN

B-3 The particular principle or principles which may be selected in a particular situation, to apply to a particular transaction, will be determined primarily by:

	C	P
The corporation's management	50.0	82.8
The independent public accountant	34.7	10.9
Other (Please indicate who should make the determination)	4.2	3.1
....		
No definite opinion		

In your opinion this selection should be determined primarily by:

	C	P
The corporation's management	36.1	57.8
The independent public accountant	55.6	25.0
Other (Please indicate who should be thus responsible)	1.4	10.9
....		
No definite opinion		

B-4 Assume that management has selected a particular principle to apply, but the independent auditor considers another such principle to be preferable. Assuming the matter to be significant and material, the auditor will presumably:

	C	P
Take an exception to the selection made by management	22.2	17.2
Describe the alternative principles but otherwise permit management's selection to prevail	25.0	21.9
Qualify his opinion	45.8	23.4
Prepare the statement on the basis of his own selection	1.4	0
None of the foregoing	2.8	28.1
No definite opinion		

In your opinion, what action should the auditor take in the foregoing circumstance?

	C	P
Take an exception to the selection made by management	34.9	21.9
Describe the alternative principles but otherwise permit management's selection to prevail	12.5	18.8
Qualify his opinion	37.5	28.1
Prepare the statement on the basis of his own selection	11.1	4.7
None of the foregoing (In which case would you describe your preferred alternative?)	2.8	18.1
....		
No definite opinion		

B-5 Each of the statements below sets forth a view regarding accounting theory in general, or some aspect thereof. In each case you are asked to indicate:

(A) Whether the view expressed is currently consistent with "generally accepted accounting principles" (GAAP)

and

(B) Whether such view would result in a fairer presentation of corporate financial statements (and accordingly should be deemed to be consistent with such principles).

		(A) IS IT IN ACCORD WITH GAAP?		(B) SHOULD IT BE IN ACCORD WITH GAAP?	
		Yes	No	Yes	No
a) Since management knows of the various alternative principles in advance of entering into a transaction, it can so structure the transaction that it will correspond to that principle which it believes will be most desirable for its purposes...........	C	50.0	12.5	52.8	18.0
	P	84.4	6.3	61.0	34.4
b) The Independent Auditor (who will ultimately be the one to perform the audit function) may describe in advance the several alternative principles which can be made to apply to a particular kind of transaction and emphasize for management the particular principle which will apply, dependent on the form of the transaction........	C	75.0	0	81.9	2.8
	P	89.1	3.1	76.6	15.6
c) In the event that there is a doubt as to the particular principle which should be applied in a particular situation, the one that will show lesser earnings is to be selected........	C	18.1	37.6	26.4	39.0
	P	32.8	51.6	12.5	76.6
d) More important than the particular principle selected in a particular entity situation is that the same principle be made applicable to all entities in the same or similar industry...........	C	34.7	30.6	62.5	12.5
	P	14.1	75.1	51.6	40.7
e) More important than the particular principle selected in a particular situation is that the same principle be selected for that situation year-in and year-out........	C	58.4	15.3	68.1	16.7
	P	60.9	34.4	71.9	25.0
f) The consistency rule assumes that even though different companies may use divergent principles for the same transaction, the incomes of the several companies are usually quite comparable because the turnover of items being accounted for tends to cancel out differences in method........	C	8.4	37.5	26.5	40.3
	P	40.6	45.3	26.5	59.4

B-6 The preceding questions have generally been predicated on the assumption that there is such a body of accounting principles which has met with general acceptance.

In your opinion is there such a body of principles? Yes: C 65.3 P 60.9 No: C 20.8 P 34.4

B-7 It has been suggested that the welfare of the various groups comprising our economic society is best served by having a multiplicity of alternative principles permitting a diversity of individual judgment rather than through having centralized decisions arrived at by the few.

Do you agree with this statement? Yes: C 43.1 P 43.8 No: C 40.3 P 45.3

If you have responded "Yes" to the preceding question, do you believe that the "individual judgment" is being well exercised at present?

In this section various accounting transactions and business events will be set forth. In each case various alternatives for financial statement presentation are indicated. You are then asked with respect to each such alternative:

(A) Whether you believe the alternative indicated is in accordance with "generally accepted accounting principles" (GAAP), and

(B) Whether you believe the alternative indicated should be in accordance with such principles.

		(A) IS IT IN ACCORD WITH GAAP?		(B) SHOULD IT BE IN ACCORD WITH GAAP?	
		Yes	No	Yes	No
C-1 The corporation has realized a very substantial and extraordinary gain from the liquidation of an investment. This gain is shown:					
a) On the income statement as a part of the corporation's income for the year	C	23.7	51.4	9.8	69.4
	P	25.0	65.7	23.5	70.3
b) On the income statement, but only after the income for the year is determined	C	72.3	2.8	77.8	9.8
	P	89.1	7.8	78.1	17.2
c) Not shown on the income statement at all	C	20.9	38.9	26.5	44.5
	P	57.8	31.3	25.0	61.0
C-2 The corporation has a substantial loss for the year:					
a) This loss is reduced by any tax refund to which it is entitled by reason of the carry-back of such loss	C	73.6	11.2	69.4	16.7
	P	82.8	7.8	75.0	17.2
b) A carry-back is not available; however, the reported loss is reduced by reason of the fact that the corporation expects to have taxable income in the future (to which the loss could be carried forward)	C	5.6	70.8	7.0	80.5
	P	7.8	87.5	25.0	68.7
C-3 The corporation has very substantial earnings during the current year. However, no income taxes are required to be paid this year because of a substantial loss carry-forward.					
a) The current year's income is stated without any provision for income tax	C	69.4	12.5	54.1	33.3
	P	87.6	9.4	61.0	32.8
b) The current year's income is reduced by the amount of tax which would otherwise have been payable (and the tax being saved is credited to earned surplus)	C	19.5	47.3	39.0	34.8
	P	29.8	68.8	36.0	57.9
C-4 Stock options have been granted to an executive entitling him to purchase shares at 100 (when they are worth 100) exercisable at any time within five years. The option is exercised when the shares are selling for $140.					
a) The $40 differential is additional compensation and is deducted as a cost on the income statement for the year when the option is exercised	C	4.2	57.0	16.7	56.9
	P	12.6	76.6	29.7	57.9
b) The option is valued by a "Put and Call" option dealer and is deducted as a cost of the year when the option is granted	C	0	57.0	4.2	50.0
	P	15.7	62.6	26.6	53.2
c) While the option is deemed to be a method of compensating the executive, it is nevertheless properly ignored in the determination of income	C	57.0	8.3	55.5	16.7
	P	76.6	14.1	34.4	54.7
d) In order to prevent dilution of the corporation's stock the corporation goes into the market place and buys its shares at 140 (which it then resells to the executive at 100). The $40 differential is then shown as a cost for the year (thereby reducing its income)	C	20.9	32.0	29.3	34.7
	P	28.2	57.9	46.6	42.3

		(A) IS IT IN ACCORD WITH GAAP?		(B) SHOULD IT BE IN ACCORD WITH GAAP?	
		Yes	No	Yes	No
C-5 This question relates to the problem of accounting for long-term leases.					
a) Whenever the circumstances indicate that a long-term lease is (by its nature or terms) essentially equivalent to a purchase of the property, the transaction is required to be shown as such a purchase (with the related liability disclosed)	C	19.4	37.6	55.6	19.5
	P	71.9	18.8	89.1	3.2
b) Such an accounting treatment (i.e., as though it were a purchase) is especially prevalent where it is apparent that the leasing (rather than actual purchase) was determined upon in order to avoid showing a debt in the balance sheet	C	15.3	44.4	44.4	26.4
	P	34.5	40.7	59.4	17.2
c) This treatment (i.e., as though it were a purchase) is particularly urgent where various debt restriction covenants are contained in bond indentures (and where the "purchase" might indicate a breach of these covenants)	C	16.7	38.8	52.8	22.2
	P	39.1	40.7	56.3	21.9
d) This treatment (i.e., as though it were a purchase) is particularly urgent where it is apparent to the auditor that the rentals in the early years are especially reduced in order to permit greater income to be shown in these early years	C	11.1	40.3	50.0	27.8
	P	32.3	48.4	55.7	23.5
e) This treatment (i.e., as though it were a purchase) is particularly urgent where it is apparent to the auditor that the rentals in the early years are especially high in order to permit a reduction in income in these earlier years (and correspondingly greater amounts in the later years)	C	9.7	41.7	52.2	27.8
	P	34.4	26.0	35.4	21.9
f) Regardless of the manner of accounting treatment, the rental for the ensuing year is required to be shown as a current liability (just as the ensuing year's debt amortization would be thus shown)	C	25.0	34.8	57.0	19.5
	P	25.0	65.6	57.8	35.9
g) This reflection of the current liability is especially urgent where the auditor sees that the working capital ratios would be vitally affected by such an inclusion of additional current debt	C	19.4	32.0	52.7	19.5
	P	18.8	62.6	45.4	39.1
C-6 An important silver producer carries its inventories of metals on the Last-in, First-out (LIFO) basis. These inventories aggregate $120 million as of the close of 1963.					
a) Inasmuch as there had been a very precipitous rise in silver prices during the year 1963, the market values of the inventories at the beginning and end of the year are required to be shown	C	19.4	43.1	59.7	16.7
	P	6.3	81.3	62.6	26.5
b) Assuming that the silver is really worth $250 million the management can, in its sole discretion, realize income of $130 million (or any portion thereof), subject, of course, to the applicable income taxes. The income so realized would be included in the annual income statement	C	30.5	41.7	23.6	59.7
	P	65.6	31.3	45.3	53.1
c) If management determined that it desired earnings of $4.50 per share but saw the corporation realizing only $4.00 from operations otherwise, it could dispose of enough of its silver inventories so as to produce the additional 50¢ per share. The income for the year would then be stated at $4.50 per share	C	45.9	19.4	40.3	43.0
	P	85.1	1.6	51.6	34.5

		(A) IS IT IN ACCORD WITH GAAP?		(B) SHOULD IT BE IN ACCORD WITH GAAP?	
		Yes	No	Yes	No
C-7 This question also relates to the Last-in, First-out (LIFO) method of inventory valuation and assumes that price levels are increasing.					
a) The balance sheet of a company which carries its inventories on the LIFO basis is more conservatively stated than its competitors' which use the First-in, First-out (FIFO) basis	C	68.1	8.4	64.9	4.2
	P	85.9	3.2	46.9	37.5
b) The annual income statement of a company which carries its inventories on a LIFO basis is more conservatively stated than its competitors' which use the FIFO basis	C	66.7	8.4	62.5	4.2
	P	84.5	4.7	50.0	34.4
C-8 This question relates to the accounting problems of the oil and gas industry.					
a) Where the corporation incurs costs for Intangible Drilling Costs of productive oil and gas properties these costs are charged to expense in the year when incurred	C	44.4	19.5	44.5	25.0
	P	84.3	3.1	23.4	51.5
b) These costs are entirely capitalized and then amortized over the expected productivity resulting from these costs	C	45.8	12.5	44.4	24.6
	P	59.5	10.9	43.8	17.2
c) These costs are first to be reduced by any immediate tax saving resulting from the cost, the excess is then amortized over the expected productive life of the facility	C	16.7	26.4	25.0	29.2
	P	51.6	21.9	39.2	37.5
C-9 In order to acquire the entire capital stock of the S corporation which owns a very valuable patent (carried on the S books at $10,000) and nothing else, the P corporation issues 1,000 shares of its $1 par value stock which then has a market price of $40 a share (hence an aggregate value of $40,000):					
a) In accounting for the transaction on the consolidated balance sheet of P, the patents thus acquired will be carried at $10,000 (i.e., their book value on the S books)	C	36.2	27.8	34.8	38.9
	P	56.3	34.4	23.5	64.1
b) In accounting for the transaction as above, future operations will be charged with amortization of patent cost of $10,000	C	34.8	23.6	37.5	32.0
	P	61.0	32.8	26.5	62.5
c) This accounting for $10,000 would be possible for P even though, in order to avoid any dilution of its shares, P went out into the open market and bought in 1,000 shares at $40 (hence for $40,000)	C	19.5	36.1	18.1	44.4
	P	48.9	37.5	15.6	67.7
d) In all future comparative financial statements, the previous year's operations will be restated so as to reflect the combined operations of both P and S during these previous years	C	38.9	29.2	47.1	25.1
	P	48.4	36.0	42.2	37.5
C-10 This question relates to problems of consolidated financial statements.					
a) The C company is a major producer of silver, copper and other metals. It owns a "more than 50%" interest in the Z corporation which owns major mines in Australia. The financial statements of C and Z are undoubtedly to be presented on a consolidated basis	C	22.2	47.2	41.6	38.9
	P	40.6	48.5	65.6	18.8
b) The D corporation, engaged in food retailing, owns 100% of the outstanding shares of T (a trading stamp company). The operations of D and T are undoubtedly to be presented on a consolidated basis	C	47.2	26.4	68.0	18.1
	P	51.6	42.2	75.0	14.1

		(A) IS IT IN ACCORD WITH GAAP?		(B) SHOULD IT BE IN ACCORD WITH GAAP?	
		Yes	No	Yes	No
C-11 The A corporation desires to obtain for itself competent management now with the X corporation. To accomplish this result A exchanges 100,000 of its shares (representing a 25% interest in itself) for all of the X corporation shares and thereupon obtains this management together with inventory worth $100,000 (but with a book value on the books of X of $15,000). At the time of the exchange the shares of A are quoted on a stock exchange at 7 (hence $700,000 in the aggregate for the 100,000 shares).					
a) This transaction will be reflected on a consolidated statement of A so as to show: Inventories $100,000; Goodwill (the amount presumed to represent the value of the management taken over) 600,000; Total (the amount equal to the value of the shares given up by A) 700,000	C	37.6	20.9	44.5	20.9
	P	65.6	23.5	61.0	26.6
b) The Goodwill shown above will undoubtedly be written off over the years when the newly acquired management will be making its contribution to the consolidated income	C	40.3	20.8	59.7	16.7
	P	32.9	53.1	48.5	34.4
c) In all future comparative financial statements, the previous years' operations will be restated so as to reflect the combined operations of A and X	C	38.9	22.3	50.0	20.9
	P	37.5	45.4	48.5	35.9
C-12 Oil company B has a 50% interest in petrochemical company Y which uses B's product for the manufacture of various consumer and industrial commodities.					
a) 50% of profits earned by Y will be reflected year-by-year in the B financial statements	C	26.4	40.3	40.2	36.2
	P	56.3	37.5	71.8	21.9
b) It may be that B management will determine that it will pick up its share of the profits only when it receives a dividend from Y	C	65.3	5.6	56.9	20.9
	P	92.3	1.6	34.4	53.2
c) It may be (assuming that there are no significant dividends paid over the years) that the B management might determine to reflect the bulk of its share of Y income in a particular year through a disposition of its interest in Y	C	50.1	13.9	37.6	32.0
	P	78.1	17.2	36.0	59.4
d) A very substantial gain on the disposition or liquidation by B of its investment in Y would be credited directly to B's earned surplus (and not to the year's income)	C	55.5	15.3	54.2	20.8
	P	78.1	15.6	42.2	45.3

		(A) IS IT IN ACCORD WITH GAAP?		(B) SHOULD IT BE IN ACCORD WITH GAAP?	
		Yes	No	Yes	No
C-13 This question relates to the problems of accounting for pension cost.					
a) Corporation E has an established pension plan entitling its employees to a stipulated pension on attaining retirement age. Assuming that E does not have a prefunded pension plan, no charge need be made to annual operations until it is called upon to make payments to retired employees	C	27.7	31.9	19.4	55.5
	P	51.6	40.7	11.0	82.8
b) Assuming that F does have a prefunded pension plan with some discretion allowed to the corporation in making contributions under the plan. The amount charged to annual operations will be equal to the amount which management determined to fund that year	C	59.7	9.7	38.9	37.3
	P	64.1	28.1	20.3	75.0
c) Because the pension fund referred to in (b) above will have earnings and capital appreciation, the annual charge to operations for F's pension cost will be affected by such earnings, etc., of the fund	C	47.2	16.7	50.0	25.0
	P	78.2	12.5	71.9	21.9
d) Company G has no pension plan but is in an industry where most other major firms do have such a plan. Company G's operations will be charged with an amount equal to what the pension cost would be if the company had a plan consistent with that common in the industry	C	0	66.7	13.9	62.5
	P	3.2	90.7	9.5	84.5
C-14 During 1958 company H acquired an extensive new plant at a cost of $100,000 which had an estimated life of ten years. The replacement value of this plant is now considered to be $200,000 (new). Price levels have increased by 50% between 1958 and the present. The company uses the declining-balance method of depreciation for income tax purposes. The depreciation charged on the 1963 financial statements will be:					
a) $10,000 (one-tenth of the cost)	C	40.3	25.0	36.2	29.1
	P	89.0	4.7	64.1	25.0
b) $6,600 (the amount deductible in 1963 for tax purposes)	C	55.6	11.1	48.6	15.3
	P	79.6	14.0	51.5	34.3
c) $20,000 (one-tenth of the $200,000 replacement value)	C	2.8	56.9	8.3	52.7
	P	3.2	89.1	12.5	68.8
d) $15,000 ($10,000 multiplied by 150%—the current price index in relation to 1958)	C	2.8	58.3	12.5	50.0
	P	3.2	90.7	28.2	56.3
C-15 Company J is engaged in aircraft manufacture. It expended $500,000 in costs for Research and Development in the development of a prototype of a new supersonic aircraft. Company J will:					
a) Charge this $500,000 against the current year's operations	C	48.7	16.7	50.1	26.4
	P	79.7	9.4	40.7	46.9
b) Capitalize this $500,000 and amortize it over a period of years	C	50.0	13.9	43.0	33.3
	P	78.2	14.0	54.7	32.8
c) Capitalize this $500,000 and write it off when the aircraft design produces revenue	C	36.1	30.5	30.5	46.8
	P	79.7	12.5	73.5	18.8

Appendix

D

Roster of Respondents to the Questionnaire

Names of the 123 respondents who gave their consent are listed here; institution or firm affiliations are indicated for identification only.

The consent given by the persons identified below does not necessarily imply that they concur in the conclusions or recommendations drawn by us from our research.

Name of Respondent	Firm or Institution	City
Albrecht, Philip E.	Merrill, Lynch, Pierce, Fenner & Smith	New York, N. Y.
Alkire, Durwood L.	Touche Ross, Bailey & Smart	Seattle, Wash.
Anderson, Corliss D.	Northwestern University	Evanston, Ill.
Anderson, Harry G., Jr.	Hale & Dorr	Boston, Mass.
Anreder, Steven S.	Barron's Weekly	New York, N. Y.
Anthony, Robert N.	Harvard University, School of Business	Boston, Mass.
Barnett, Bernard	Apfel & Englander	New York, N. Y.
Baum, Dwight C.	Eastman Dillon, Union Securities & Co.	Los Angeles, Calif.
Becker, Stephen W.	Lionel D. Edie & Co.	New York, N. Y.
Bekaert, Charles J.	Cherry, Bekaert & Holland	Wilmington, N. C.
Bell, W. Edward	Crocker-Citizens National Bank	San Francisco, Calif.
Bergeron, Virgil O.	Brockway, Bergeron. Booth & Co.	Minneapolis, Minn.
Bernstein, Leopold A.	The City College of New York, Baruch School	New York, N. Y.
Birmingham, John M., Jr.	Wellington Management Co.	Philadelphia, Pa.
Blanchard, C. Ford	Public Utility Specialist	Washington, D. C.
Block, Frank E.	Citizens & Southern National Bank	Atlanta, Ga.
Block, Max	Anchin, Block & Anchin	New York, N. Y.
Bohrer, Seymour M.	Peat, Marwick, Mitchell & Co.	New York, N. Y.
Borini, Mario P.	Hurdman and Cranstoun	New York, N. Y.
Broderick, Kirby L.	Chase Manhattan Bank	New York, N. Y.
Cahn, Bernard D.	Attorney	New York, N. Y.
Carter, Leonard H.	Blumberg, Block & Carter	New York, N. Y.
Chamberlin, Lawrence N.	Chamberlin and Company	Pittsburgh, Pa.
Chambers, R. J.	University of Sydney	Sydney, Australia
Clark, William J.	Kansas State University	Manhattan, Kansas
Colen, Louis M.	Consolidated Cigar Corporation	New York, N. Y.
Collins, Charles J.	Investment Counsellor	Grosse Point, Mich.
Comrie, Allan	Great American Insurance Company	New York, N. Y.
Davidson, Sidney	University of Chicago Graduate School of Business	Chicago, Ill.
Dennis, Gerald S.	The Shelby Mutual Insurance Co.	Shelby, Ohio
Dreiman, Jack J.	Main, Lafrentz & Company	Oakland, Calif.
Ende, Joseph	United Artists Corporation	New York, N. Y.
Engel, W. Keith	Touche, Ross, Bailey & Smart	Washington, D. C.
Falck, Edward	Public Utility Consultant	Washington, D. C.
Ferretti, Andrew P.	Keystone Custodian Funds, Inc.	Boston, Mass.
Fitzgerald, Richard D.	Price Waterhouse & Co.	New York, N. Y.
Friedman, Hortense	University of Chicago	Chicago, Ill.
Fuld, James J.	Proskauer Rose Goetz & Mendelsohn	New York, N. Y.
Goldberg, Louis	University of Melbourne	Victoria, Australia
Goodwin, W. C.	St. Paul Fire & Marine Insurance Co.	St. Paul, Minn.
Gray, William S.	Harris Trust and Savings Bank	Chicago, Ill.
Grimstad, Clayton R.	Ohio State University	Columbus, Ohio
Groh, Reinhold	Groh, Gough & Company	Chicago, Ill.
Grossman, Harry I.	Altschuler, Melvoin & Glasser	Chicago, Ill.
Gumperz, Julian	Basic Economic Appraisals, Inc.	New York, N. Y.
Harwood, Dale S., Jr.	University of Oregon School of Business Administration	Eugene, Oregon
Henning, Fred M.	Main, Lafrentz & Company	Los Angeles, Calif.
Higgins, Thomas G.	Arthur Young & Co.	New York, N. Y.
Ho, Herbert	Standard & Poor's Corp.	New York, N. Y.
Hoffman, L. R.	Ohio Farmers Insurance Group	LeRoy, Ohio
Hollander, T. Edward	The City College of New York, Baruch School	New York, N. Y.
Isensee, C. T.	Ernst & Ernst	Houston, Texas
Jacobs, William K., Jr.	Abacus Fund, Inc.	New York, N. Y.
Jiler, Harry	Commodity Research Bureau, Inc.	New York, N. Y.
Johnston, Lee R.	University of Virginia Graduate Business School	Charlottesville, Va.
Kappelman, Allan E.	Sage, Rutty & Company	Rochester, N. Y.
Kelly, Lester J.	General Motors Overseas Operations	New York, N. Y.
Kelly, Robert E., Jr.	Foreign Credit Insurance Assn.	New York, N. Y.
Koehner, Frederick E.	Cinerama, Inc.	New York, N. Y.
Ladd, Dwight R.	University of New Hampshire Whittemore School of Business & Economics	Durham, N. H.
Lambourne, Richard W.	Insurance Securities Incorporated	San Francisco, Calif.
Lane, Joseph E., Jr.	University of Alabama	University, Alabama
Leslie, Donald S., Jr.	Hammermill Paper Company	Erie, Pa.

MacNeill, James H.	Fordham University, School of Business	Bronx, N. Y.
Marcum, Joseph L.	Ohio Casualty Insurance Company	Hamilton, Ohio
Massengale, John E.	Paul, Weiss, Rifkind, Wharton & Garrison	New York, N. Y.
Mattay, Arnold K.	First National Bank in Dallas	Dallas, Texas
Matusiak, Louis W.	Alexander Grant & Company	Chicago, Ill.
Mautz, Robert K.	University of Illinois	Urbana, Ill.
Mellman, Martin	The City College of New York, Baruch School	New York, N. Y.
Miles, Francis I.	Arthur Andersen & Company	New Orleans, La.
Moonitz, Maurice	University of California	Berkeley, Calif.
Morehouse, M. Dutton	Brown Brothers, Harriman & Company	Chicago, Ill.
Morrissey, Leonard E., Jr.	Dartmouth College, Amos Tuck School of Business Administration	Hanover, N. H.
Naess, Ragnar D.	Naess & Thomas	New York, N. Y.
Nelson, Carl L.	Columbia University	New York, N. Y.
Newman, Benjamin	New York University, School of Commerce	New York, N. Y.
O'Connor, Lawrence J., Jr.	Federal Power Commission	Washington, D. C.
Olson, Norman O.	Arthur Andersen & Co.	Chicago, Ill.
Parker, C. Reed	Duff, Anderson & Clark	Chicago, Ill.
Paul, Richard H.	Paul, Weiss, Rifkind, Wharton & Garrison	New York, N. Y.
Phelps, Thomas W.	Scudder, Stevens & Clark	New York, N. Y.
Phoenix, J. W., Jr.	Haskins & Sells	New York, N. Y.
Platt, Lawrence T.	Dick & Merle-Smith	New York, N. Y.
Plumb, Charles	State Teachers Retirement System	Columbus, Ohio
Plum, Robert J., Jr.	American Smelting & Refining Co.	New York, N. Y.
Powell, William J.	Federal Power Commission	Washington, D. C.
Pryor, Thomas C.	White Weld & Co.	New York, N. Y.
Purdy, Thurlow	Lehman Brothers	New York, N. Y.
Rapoport, Leonard A.	Calmenson Abramson & Co.	St. Paul, Minn.
Rappaport, L. H.	Lybrand, Ross Bros. & Montgomery	New York, N. Y.
Robinson, William J.	Insurance Co. of North America	Philadelphia, Pa.
Russ, Alexander	Henry Brout & Co.	New York, N. Y.
Savage, E. Linwood	New England Merchants National Bank	Boston, Mass.
Savoie, Leonard M.	Price Waterhouse & Co.	New York, N. Y.
Schwarz, R. H.	Kaiser Aluminum & Chemical Corporation	Oakland, Calif.
Seidman, J. S.	Seidman & Seidman	New York, N. Y.
Sellin, Henry	New York University	New York, N. Y.
Shea, George E., Jr.	The Wall Street Journal	New York, N. Y.
Singer, Frank A.	University of Massachusetts	Amherst, Mass.
Skelton, Aubrey D.	Irving Trust Company	New York, N. Y.
Smith, Frank P.	Lybrand, Ross Bros. & Montgomery	New York, N. Y.
Smith, Harold C.	YMCA Retirement Fund	New York, N. Y.
Smith, Raymond D., Jr.	Bankers Trust Corp.	New York, N. Y.
Smith, Willis A.	Main, Lafrentz & Company	New York, N. Y.
Stanley, Curtis Holt	Yale University	New Haven, Conn.
Stone, Louis	Hayden Stone, Inc.	New York, N. Y.
Storey, Reed K.	American Institute of Certified Public Accountants	New York, N. Y.
Tailer, T. Suffern	Private Investor	New York, N. Y.
Tappan, John R.	American Re-Insurance Co.	New York, N. Y.
Tharsing, Howard C.	Dean Witter & Co.	San Francisco, Calif.
Upton, William W. B.	Philadelphia National Bank	Philadelphia, Pa.
Werntz, William W.	Touche, Ross, Bailey & Smart	New York, N. Y.
Willie, Howard E.	Piedmont Advisory Corporation	New York, N. Y.
Williams, David D.	National Bank of Detroit	Detroit, Mich.
Wilson, Douglas B.	Bankers Trust Co.	New York, N. Y.
Windal, Floyd W.	Michigan State University	East Lansing, Mich.
Wintermute, Mary C.	Standard & Poor's Corp.	New York, N. Y.
Wolf, Mildred B.	Standard & Poor's Corp.	New York, N. Y.
Wolk, Elliot K.	Salomon Brothers & Hutzler	New York, N. Y.
Wray, Robert T.	Sentry Insurance Company	Stevens Point, Wis.
Zeff, Stephen A.	Tulane University	New Orleans, La.
Zelomek, A. W.	International Statistical Bureau, Inc.	New York, N. Y.

Appendix E

Table 3 (at pages 38-44) sets forth the percentage of responses to the Series C questions of the questionnaire which solicited the respondents' views regarding the accounting alternatives for selected business transactions. The graphs which follow are designed to demonstrate the degree of relationships of the responses received to these Series C questions, as summarized in Table 3.

Figures 1, 5, and 9 each charted the relationships between the responses from two populations to the first probe of these questions, i.e., whether they believed the alternative *to be* in accord with generally accepted accounting principles. Figures 2, 6, and 10 each charted the relationships between two populations of respondents for their answers to the second probe of these questions, i.e., whether they believed the alternatives suggested *should be* in accord with such principles.

The remaining figures numbered 3, 4, 7, and 8 are each for a single population and show the shifts or divergence between that population's responses to the "it is" and "should be" probes.

Specifically, and in greater detail, the relationships shown by these ten graphs are the following:

Figure 1, reflects the relationships between the affirmative responses received from the financial community and accounting profession categories to the first probe of the Series "C" questions to wit: "Whether you believe the alternative indicated is in accordance with generally accepted accounting principles."

Figure 2, reflects the relationships between the same categories with respect to the second probe of the Series "C" questions, to wit: "Whether you believe the alternative indicated should be in accordance with such principles."

Figure 3, shows the relationships between affirmative responses received from the financial community category to the first probe of the Series "C" questions (whether the alternative is in accordance with GAAP), with responses received from the same category to the second probe thereof (whether the alternative should be in accordance with GAAP).

Figure 4, reflects the same relationships as figure 3, except that they are here shown for the accounting profession category.

Figure 5, shows the same set of relationships reflected by figure 1 (i.e., the "is it" probe), except that the populations here being compared are the accounting practitioner and accounting professor groups (both of which are included in the accounting profession category).

Figure 6, shows the same relationships reflected by figure 2 (i.e., the "should it be?" probe) except that here again the populations being compared are the practitioner and professor of accounting groups.

Figure 7, this graph is consistent with figures 3 and 4,

excepting that the relationships between the "is it?" and "should it be?" responses are here being shown for the accounting practitioner group.

Figure 8, correspondingly, this graph shows the "is" and "should be" affirmative responses for the professor of accounting groups.

Figure 9, reflects the relationships between the affirmative responses received from prartitioners with the national ("Big-Eight") firms and such responses received from other practitioners with reference to the first probe (i.e., "is it in accord with GAAP?"). This graph is consistent with Figures 1 and 5.

Figure 10, reflects the relationship between the affirmative responses received from the practitioners with such "Big-Eight" firms and from other practitioners, with reference to the second ("should it be?") probe. This graph is, accordingly, consistent with Figures 2 and 6.

A 45° curve (solid line) has been superimposed on each graph; any point along this curve would reflect agreement in the affirmative responses received with respect to the particular question from the two populations being measured (or for the two probes from the same population as the case may be). The extent of departure from this 45° curve would measure the degree of divergence of one population from another (or where appropriate measure the divergence between the "It Is" and "It Should Be" responses from a single population).

In addition broken lines paralleling this 45 degree curve have been drawn to measure "20 percentage point" deviations from the aforementioned "identity of agreement" curve. For purposes of the analysis of the graphs and the underlying data any deviation or divergence in excess of such "20 percentage points" (and therefore causing the relationship to fall outside these "broken lines") was presumed to be a "major divergence." A description of the major divergencies disclosed by each graph is included at the bottom thereof.

FIGURE 1

Relationships Between Affirmative Responses from Financial Community and Accounting Profession Re Question C Queries: "IS It in Accord with Generally Accepted Accounting Principles?"

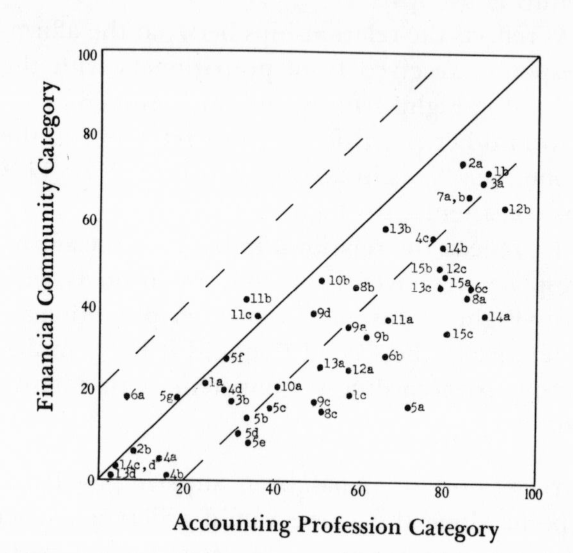

Divergencies in Excess of "20 percentage points" Evidenced by Figure 1

For twenty-four of the responses (out of fifty) the Accounting Profession's affirmative assertion of its awareness exceeded by more than the "20 percentage point" standard used herein the corresponding expression of awareness by the Financial Community that the suggested accounting treatment was "in accordance with generally accepted accounting principles." These areas of what might be described as those revealing major divergency are:

Question	*Subject*
C-1 (c)	extraordinary income
C-5 (a) (c) (d) (e)	long-term leases
C-6 (b) (c)	LIFO inventories
C-8 (a) (c)	accounting for oil and gas
C-9 (a) (b) (c)	a "pooling of interest" situation
C-11 (a)	another "pooling of interest" situation
C-12 (a) (b) (c) (d)	a jointly held (associated entity) situation
C-13 (a) (c)	accounting for pension cost
C-14 (a) (b)	depreciation accounting
C-15 (a) (b) (c)	research and development cost

FIGURE 2

Relationships Between Affirmative Responses from
Financial Community and Accounting Profession Re Question C Queries:
"SHOULD It Be in Accord with Generally Accepted
Accounting Principles?"

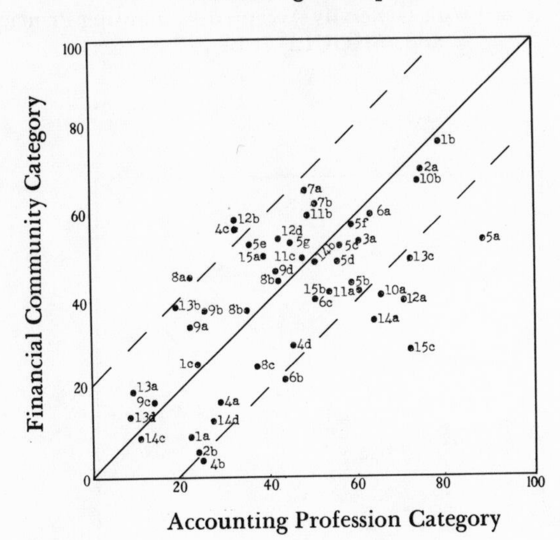

Divergencies in Excess of "20 percentage points" Evidenced by Figure 2

In eleven situations (out of fifty) there were divergencies which exceeded "20 percentage points" between the affirmative responses for what the Financial Community thought "should be" in accord with generally accepted accounting principles as contrasted with the corresponding views from the Accounting Profession.

Instances in which the affirmative responses from the Profession exceeded those from the Community were:

Question	*Subject*
C-4 (b)	stock options
C-5 (a)	long-term leases
C-6 (b)	LIFO inventories
C-10 (a)	an affiliated entity situation
C-12 (a)	a jointly held (associated entity) situation
C-13 (c)	accounting for pension cost
C-14 (a)	depreciation accounting
C-15 (c)	research and development cost

Instances in which affirmative responses from the Community exceeded those from the Profession:

C-4 (c)	stock options
C-8 (a)	oil and gas industry
C-12 (b)	a jointly held entity situation

FIGURE 3

Relationships Between Affirmative Responses from the
Financial Community Re Question C Queries:
"IS It in Accord with Generally Accepted Accounting Principles"
and "SHOULD It Be . . ."

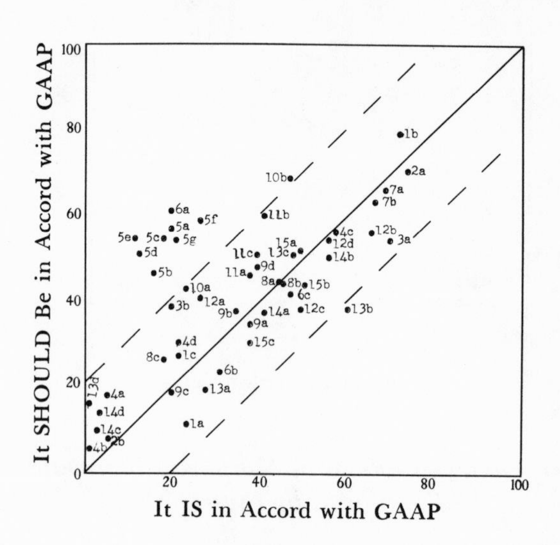

Divergencies in Excess of "20 percentage points" Evidenced by Figure 3

In ten instances (out of fifty) the Financial Community evidenced a shift of more than "20 percentage points" in their affirmative responses for the "is in accord" to the "should be in accord" aspects of the Series C questions. In all but one of the instances the Community manifested a greater desire to see certain precepts become accepted than their corresponding state of awareness of present practice, thus:

Question	*Subject*
C-5 (a) (b) (c) (d) (e) (f) (g)	long-term leases
C-6 (a)	LIFO inventories
C-10 (b)	an affiliated entity situation

The situation in which the Community's affirmative responses as to what "should be" showed an only slightly more than "20 percentage point" retrogression from "what is," was C-13 (b) relating to the accounting for pension cost.

FIGURE 4

Relationships Between Affirmative Responses from
Accounting Profession Re Question C Queries:
"IS It in Accord with Generally Accepted Accounting Principles"
and "SHOULD It Be . . ."

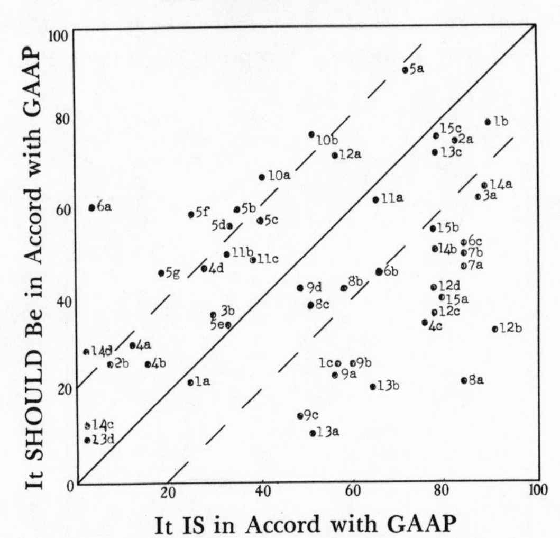

Divergencies in Excess of "20 percentage points" Evidenced by Figure 4

In twenty-seven instances (out of fifty) the Accounting Profession's affirmative responses to the "what is" diverged from the "should be" aspects of the Series C questions by more than the "20 percentage point" margin.

The more than "20 percentage point" shifts from the "is" to "should be" occurred in the following eight cases:

Question	*Subject*
C-5 (b) (d) (f) (g)	long-term leases
C-6 (a)	LIFO inventories
C-10 (a) (b)	an affiliated entity situation
C-14 (d)	depreciation accounting

Correspondingly, the nineteen situations in which there was a greater than "20 percentage point" *regression* from the "is" to "should be," were as follows:

C-1 (c)	extraordinary income
C-3 (a)	accounting for income taxes
C-4 (c)	stock options
C-6 (c)	LIFO inventories
C-7 (a) (b)	LIFO inventories
C-8 (a)	accounting for oil and gas
C-9 (a) (b) (c)	a "pooling of interest" situation
C-12 (b) (c) (d)	a jointly held entity situation
C-13 (a) (b)	accounting for pension cost
C-14 (a) (b)	depreciation accounting
C-15 (a) (b)	research and development costs

FIGURE 5

Relationships Between Affirmative Responses from Practitioners and Professors of Accountancy Re Question C Queries: "IS It in Accord with Generally Accepted Accounting Principles?"

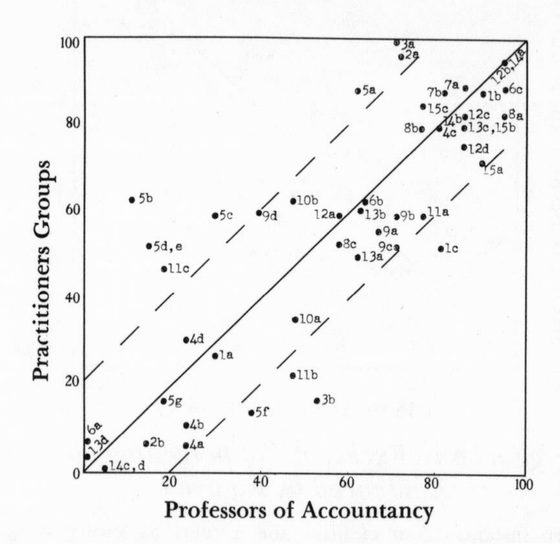

Divergencies in Excess of "20 percentage points" Evidenced by Figure 5

In twelve cases (out of fifty) the assertion of awareness by the Professors as to what "is" diverged from the corresponding awareness on the part of the Practitioners by more than "20 percentage points."

Those situations in which the Practitioners' affirmative responses exceeded those of the Professors by more than the aforementioned margin were:

Question	*Subject*
C-2 (a)	accounting for income taxes
C-3 (a)	accounting for income taxes
C-5 (a) (b) (c) (d) (e)	long-term leases
C-11 (c)	a "pooling of interest" situation

Correspondingly, the four situations in which the Professors asserted an awareness which was greater by more than "20 percentage points" than the awareness of the Practitioners, were with respect to:

C-1 (c)	extraordinary income
C-3 (b)	accounting for income taxes
C-5 (f)	long-term leases
C-11 (b)	a "pooling of interest" situation

FIGURE 6

Relationships Between Affirmative Responses from Practitioners and Professors of Accountancy Re Question C Queries: "SHOULD It Be in Accord with Generally Accepted Accounting Principles?"

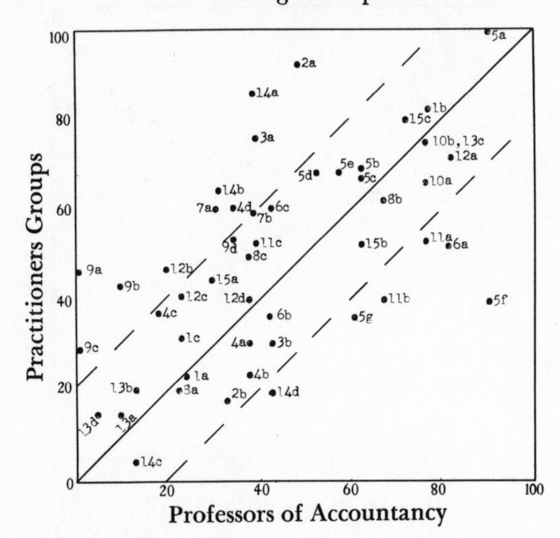

Divergencies in Excess of "20 percentage points" Evidenced by Figure 6

In sixteen cases (out of fifty) there were divergencies which exceeded "20 percentage points" between the affirmative responses for what the Professors thought "should be" in accord with GAAP, as contrasted with the corresponding views from the Practitioners.

The ten instances in which the "should be" responses from the Practitioners exceeded those of the Professors by more than this "20 percentage point" margin were:

C-2 (a)	accounting for income taxes
C-3 (a)	accounting for income taxes
C-4 (d)	stock options
C-7 (a)	LIFO inventories
C-9 (a) (b) (c)	a "pooling of interest" situation
C-12 (b)	a jointly held entity situation
C-14 (a) (b)	depreciation accounting

The six instances in which the Professors' responses as to what "should be" exceeded those from the Practitioners by more than the aforementioned margin were:

Question	*Subject*
C-5 (f) (g)	long-term leases
C-6 (a)	LIFO inventories
C-11 (a) (b)	a "pooling of interest" situation
C-14 (d)	depreciation accounting

FIGURE 7

Relationships Between Affirmative Responses from the Practitioners Group Re Question C Queries: "IS It in Accord with Generally Accepted Accounting Principles" and "SHOULD It Be . . ."

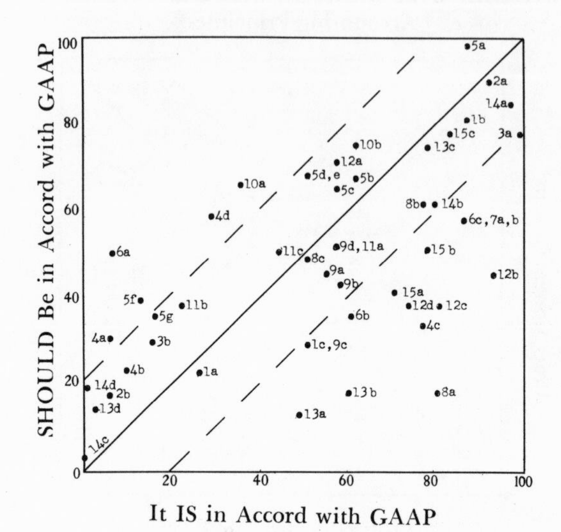

Divergencies in Excess of "20 percentage points" Evidenced by Figure 7

In twenty-one cases (out of fifty) the Practitioners' affirmative responses to the "what is" diverged from the "should be" aspects of the Series C questions by more than the "20 percentage point" margin.

Such more than standard shifts from the "is" to the "should be" occurred in the following five instances:

Question	*Subject*
C-4 (a) (d)	stock options
C-5 (f)	long-term leases
C-6 (a)	LIFO inventories
C-10 (a)	an affiliated entity situation

Correspondingly, the sixteen situations in which there was more than a "20 percentage point" *regression* from the "is" to "should be" were the following:

C-1 (c)	extraordinary income
C-3 (a)	accounting for income taxes
C-4 (c)	stock options
C-6 (b) (c)	LIFO inventories
C-7 (a) (b)	LIFO inventories
C-8 (a)	accounting for oil and gas
C-9 (c)	a "pooling of interest" situation
C-12 (b) (c) (d)	a jointly held entity situation
C-13 (a) (b)	accounting for pension cost
C-15 (a) (b)	research and development cost

FIGURE 8

Relationships Between Affirmative Responses from the Professors of Accountancy Group Re Question C Queries: "IS It in Accord with Generally Accepted Accounting Principles" and "SHOULD It Be . . ."

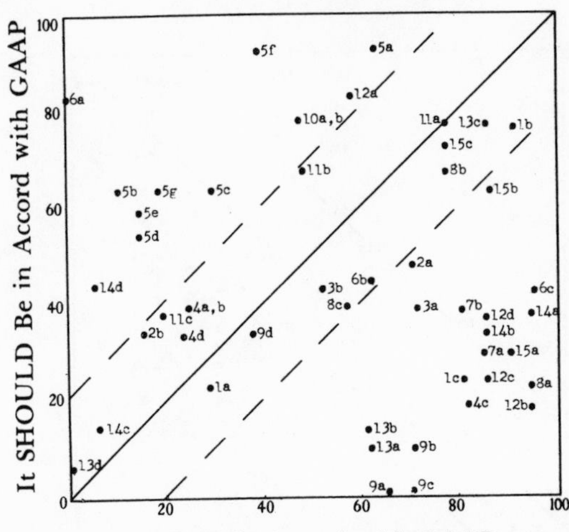

It IS in Accord with GAAP

Divergencies in Excess of "20 percentage points" Evidenced by Figure 8

In thirty-two cases (out of fifty) the Professors' affirmative responses to the "what is" diverged from the "should be" aspects of the Series C questions by more than the "20 percentage point" margin.

These more than standard shifts from the "is" to the "should be" occurred in the following twelve instances:

Question	*Subject*
C-5 (a) (b) (c) (d) (e) (f) (g)	long-term leases
C-6 (a)	LIFO inventories
C-10 (a) (b)	an affiliated entity situation
C-12 (a)	a jointly held entity situation
C-14 (d)	depreciation accounting

Correspondingly, the twenty situations in which there was more than a "20 percentage point" *regression* from the "is" to "should be" were the following:

C-1 (c)	extraordinary income
C-2 (a)	accounting for income taxes
C-3 (a)	accounting for income taxes
C-4 (c)	stock options
C-6 (c)	LIFO inventories
C-7 (a) (b)	LIFO inventories
C-8 (a)	accounting for oil and gas
C-9 (a) (b) (c)	a "pooling of interest" situation
C-12 (b) (c) (d)	a jointly held entity situation
C-13 (a) (b)	accounting for pension cost
C-14 (a) (b)	depreciation accounting
C-15 (a) (b)	research and development cost

FIGURE 9

Relationships Between Affirmative Responses from Practitioners with "Big-Eight" Firms and Other Practitioners Re Question C Queries: "IS It in Accord with Generally Accepted Accounting Principles?"

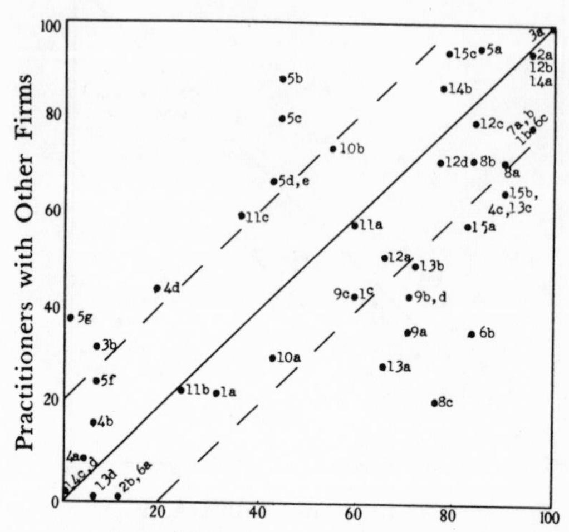

Divergencies in Excess of "20 percentage points" Evidenced by Figure 9

In nineteen cases (out of fifty) the assertions of awareness by the Practitioners with the so-called "Big-Eight" firms as to what "is" diverged from the corresponding awareness on the part of Other Practitioners by more than "20 percentage points."

Those eleven situations in which the "Big-Eight" affirmative responses exceeded those of the Other Practitioners by more than the aforementioned margin were:

Question	*Subject*
C-4 (c)	stock options
C-6 (b)	LIFO inventories
C-8 (c)	accounting for oil and gas
C-9 (a) (b) (d)	a "pooling of interest" situation
C-13 (a) (b) (c)	accounting for pension cost
C-15 (a) (b)	research and development cost

Correspondingly, the eight situations in which the Other Practitioners asserted an awareness which was greater by more than "20 percentage points" than the awareness of the respondents from the "Big-Eight" firms were:

C-3 (b)	accounting for income taxes
C-4 (d)	stock options
C-5 (b) (c) (d) (e) (g)	long-term leases
C-11 (c)	a "pooling of interest" situation

FIGURE 10

Relationships Between Affirmative Responses from Practitioners With "Big-Eight" Firms and Other Practitioners Re Question C Queries: "SHOULD It Be in Accord with Generally Accepted Accounting Principles?"

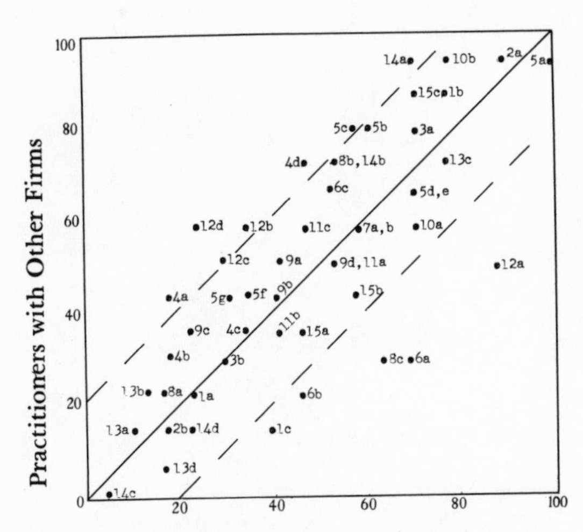

Practitioners with "Big-Eight" Firms

Divergencies in Excess of "20 percentage points" Evidenced by Figure 10

In twelve cases (out of fifty) there were divergencies which exceeded the "20 percentage points" between the affirmative responses for what Practitioners with the so-called "Big-Eight" firms thought "should be" in accord with GAAP, as contrasted with the corresponding views from the Other Practitioners.

The five instances in which the "Big-Eight" affirmative responses exceeded those of the Other Practitioners by more than the aforementioned margin were:

Question	*Subject*
C-1 (c)	extraordinary income
C-6 (a) (b)	LIFO inventories
C-8 (c)	accounting for oil and gas
C-12 (a)	a jointly held entity situation

The seven instances in which the "should be" responses from the Other Practitioners exceeded those of the "Big-Eight" respondents by more than this "20 percentage point" margin were:

C-4 (a) (d)	stock options
C-5 (c)	long-term leases
C-12 (b) (c) (d)	a jointly held entity situation
C-14 (a)	depreciation accounting

Appendix F

Table 11 (at page 161) summarized the respondents' views regarding specific kinds of management services by CPAs who were concurrently rendering the independent audit function. The graphs which follow are designed to demonstrate the degree of relationships of the responses received to the queries in Question A-15 of the questionnaire.

Figures 11 and 15 each charted the relationship between the responses from two different populations to the first probe of these questions, i.e., whether they believed the particular category of management service was now being offered by the attesting firm. Figures 12 and 16 each charted the relationships between two different populations for their answers to the second probe of these questions, i.e., whether they believed the particular kind of service should be offered by the auditing firm.

Figures numbered 13, 14, 17, 18, and 19 are each for a single population and show the shifts or spreads between that population's responses to the "are now" and "should be" probes.

Figure 20 is a collage, bringing together Figures 13 and 19.

Specifically, and in greater detail, the relationships shown by these ten graphs are the following:

Figure 11: Relationships between affirmative responses received from the financial community and the accounting profession categories to the first probe of the Question A-15 queries: "(A) Whether you believe such [management] services are now being offered by public accounting firms to corporations for whom they are already performing the independent audit function."

Figure 12: Reflects the relationships between the same population categories with respect to the second probe of the Question A-15 queries: "(B) Whether in your opinion they should be so offered."

Figure 13: Relationships between affirmative responses received from the financial community category to the first probe of the Question A-15 queries (whether the services are now being thus offered), with responses received from the same category to the second probe thereof (whether they should be so offered).

Figure 14: Reflects the same relationships as Figure 13, except that they are here shown for the accounting profession category.

Figure 15: Shows the same set of relationships reflected by Figure 11 (i.e., the "are they now being offered" probe) except that the populations here being compared are the accounting practitioner and accounting professor groups (both of which are included in the accounting profession category).

Figure 16: Shows the same relationships reflected by Figure 12 (i.e., the "should they be offered" probe) except that here again (as in Figure 15) the populations being compared are the practitioners and professors of accounting groups.

Figure 17: This graph is consistent with Figures 13 and 14, except that here the relationships between the "are now" and "should be" responses are being shown for the accounting practitioners group.

Figure 18: Correspondingly, this graph reflects the relationships between the "are now" and "should be" affirmative responses from the professors of accounting group.

Figure 19: This figure is consistent with Figure 17, excepting that the relationships between the "are now" and "should be" affirmative responses are here being shown for the practitioners with the national ("Big-Eight") firms. (These respondents are included in the practitioners groups and accordingly their responses are also reflected in Figure 17 above.)

Figure 20: This graph is a collage of Figures 13 and 19 and therefore reflects the relationships between the "are now" and "should be" responses received from the financial community category, as well as the same relationships of responses from the practitioners with the "Big-Eight" firms.

A 45° curve (solid line) has been superimposed on each graph. Any point along this curve would reflect agreement in the affirmative responses received with respect to the particular question from the two populations being measured (or for the two probes from the same population, as the case may be). The extent of departure from this 45° curve would measure the degree of divergence of one population from another (or measure the divergence between the "are now" and "should be" responses from a single population).

In addition, broken lines paralleling this 45° curve have been drawn to measure "20 percentage point" deviations from the aforementioned "identity of agreement" curve. For purposes of this commentary any deviation or divergence in excess of such "20 percentage points" (and therefore causing the relationship to fall outside these "broken lines") was presumed to be a major divergence. A description of the major divergencies disclosed by each graph is included at the bottom thereof.

FIGURE 11

Relationships Between Affirmative Responses from Financial Community and Accounting Profession Re Question A-15 Queries: "Do You Believe the Category of Management Service IS Being Offered?"

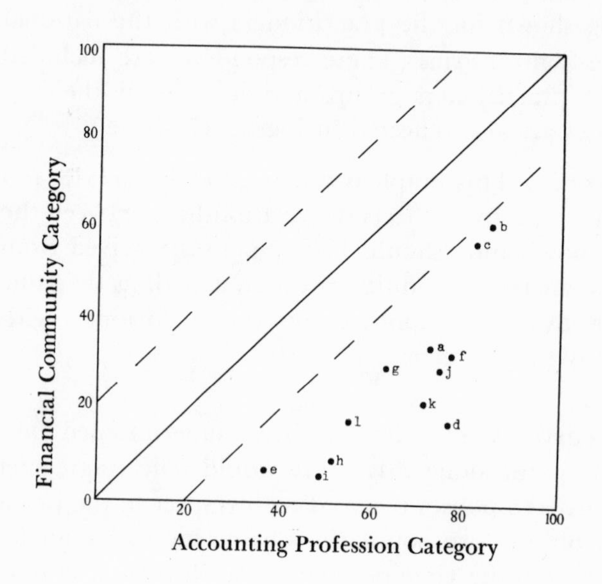

Divergencies in Excess of "20 percentage points" Evidenced by the Above

Such a divergency occurred for each of the twelve categories of services described in the Question A-15. In each instance the Accounting Profession furnished affirmative responses which were greater by this "20 percentage point" margin than the corresponding responses from the Financial Community. These divergencies evidence a greater recognition by the Accounting Profession that the services set forth in the question are being offered under the circumstances described by the question.

FIGURE 12

Relationships Between Affirmative Responses from Financial Community and Accounting Profession Re Question A-15 Queries: "Do You Believe the Category of Management Service SHOULD Be Offered?"

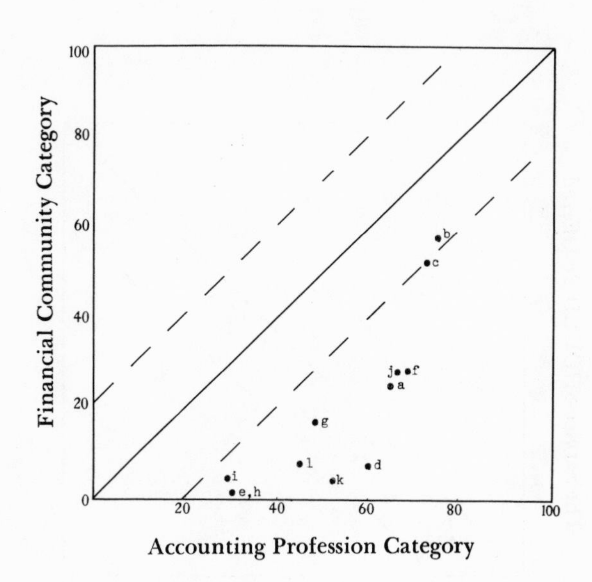

Divergencies in Excess of "20 percentage points" Evidenced by the Above

Excepting for services (b) and (c) (relating to a review of a business in connection with a plan to buy or reorganize the business, respectively), the Accounting Profession's view that the services "should be" rendered exceeded the corresponding view from the Financial Community category by more than the "20 percentage point" margin here used as the standard.

FIGURE 13

Relationships Between Affirmative Responses from the Financial Community Re Question A-15 Queries: "IS the Category . . . Being Offered?" and "SHOULD It Be Offered?"

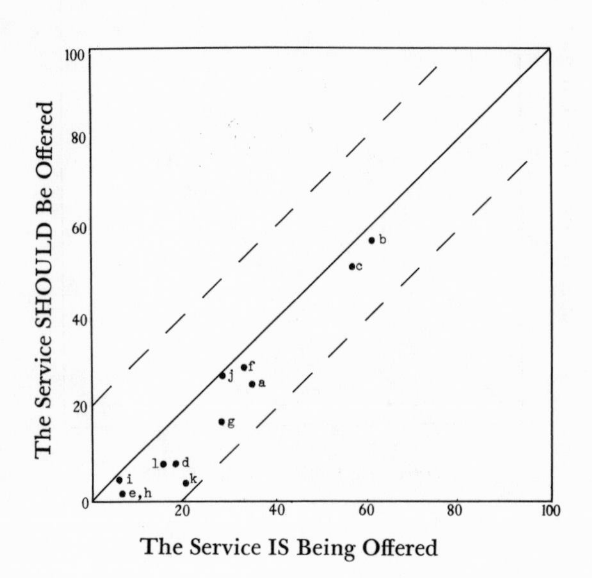

Divergencies in Excess of "20 percentage points" Evidenced by Above

There were no such divergencies. With the exception of service categories (b) and (c) relating to a review of the business in connection with a plan to buy or reorganize it, respectively, the responses from the Financial Community category were concentrated at the lower end of the scale both with respect to what prevails presently as well as to what should prevail.

FIGURE 14

Relationships Between Affirmative Responses from the Accounting Profession Re Question A-15 Queries: "IS the Category . . . Being Offered?" and "SHOULD It Be Offered?"

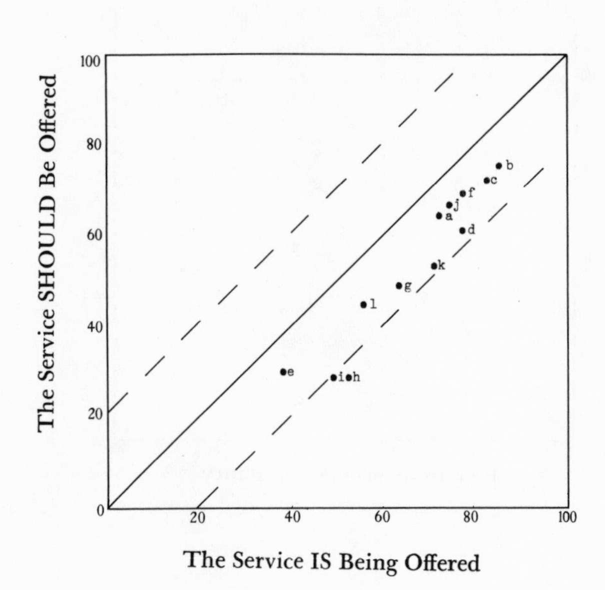

Divergencies in Excess of "20 percentage points" Evidenced by Above

Excepting for a minimal excess for service category (h) (relating to the determination of market potentials and profit planning), the Accounting Profession's views as to what should prevail did not diverge by more than the "20 percentage point" margin from its views as to what now prevails.

FIGURE 15

Relationships Between Affirmative Responses from Practitioner and Professor of Accountancy Groups Re Question A-15 Queries: "Do You Believe the Category of Management Service IS Being Offered?"

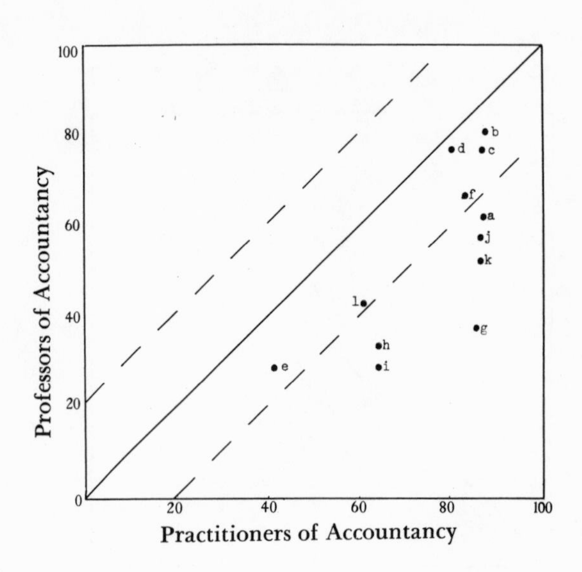

Divergencies in Excess of "20 percentage points" Evidenced by Above

For six categories of services, out of twelve, the Practitioners of Accountancy indicated an awareness that the services are now being offered which exceeded the corresponding awareness by the Professors of Accountancy by a margin in excess of the standard herein used, i.e., "20 percentage points." These six categories of major divergence are:

a) review business to expand profits
g) develop sales forecasts and sales controls
h) determine market potentials and profit planning
i) determine sales quotas and incentives
j) determine volume, profit, pricing programs
k) analyze job functions and responsibilities

FIGURE 16

Relationships Between Affirmative Responses from Practitioner and Professor of Accountancy Groups Re Question A-15 Queries: "Do You Believe the Category of Management Service SHOULD Be Offered?"

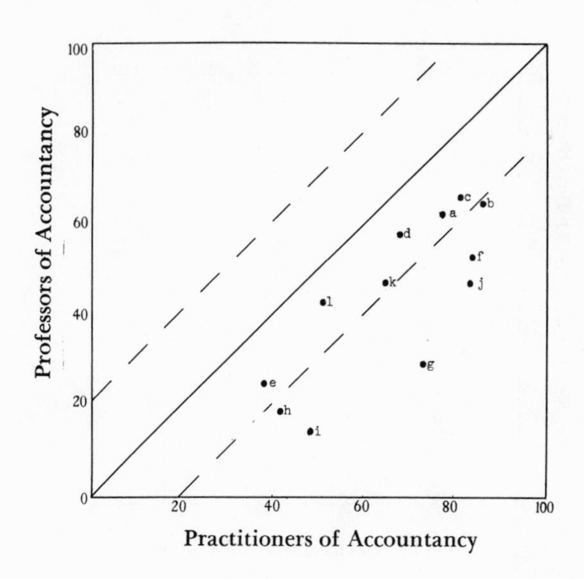

Divergencies in Excess of "20 percentage points" Evidenced by Above

For six categories of services, out of twelve, the Practitioners of Accountancy manifested an affirmative belief that the services should be rendered, which exceeded the corresponding views of the Professors of Accountancy by a margin in excess of the "20 percentage point" standard. These major divergencies related to:

b) review of the business with a view toward its purchase
f) development of a plan of executive compensation
g) develop sales forecasts and sales controls
h) determine market potentials and profit planning
i) determine sales quotas and incentives
j) determine volume, profit, pricing programs

FIGURE 17

Relationships Between Affirmative Responses from Practioners of Accountancy Group Re Question A-15 Queries: "IS the Category of Service Being Offered?" and "SHOULD It Be Offered?"

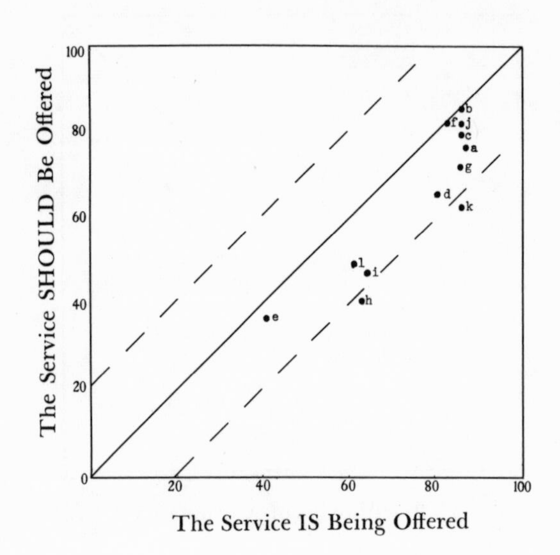

Divergencies in Excess of "20 percentage points" Evidenced by Above

Only with respect to service categories (h), the determination of market potentials and profit planning, and (k), the analysis of job functions and responsibilities, were there such divergencies beyond the margin here assumed. And for each of these divergencies, the excess over the standard was minor. The meaning of this graph is that the belief of the Practitioners of Accountancy regarding the services which should be rendered were essentially consistent with their indicated state of awareness that they are being thus rendered.

FIGURE 18

Relationships Between Affirmative Responses from Professors of Accountancy Group Re Question A-15 Queries: "IS the Category of Service Being Offered?" and "SHOULD It Be Offered?"

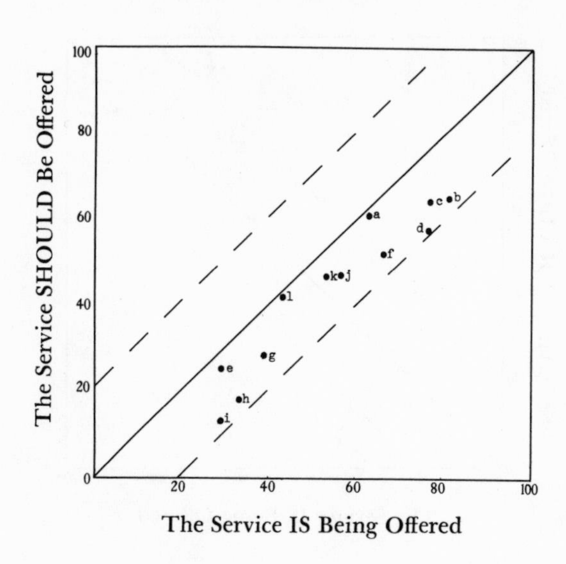

Divergencies in Excess of "20 percentage points" Evidenced by Above

For all categories of service suggested by Question A-15 the Professors' views as to which services should be rendered under the circumstances did not deviate by more than the "20 percentage point" margin from their views as to what services are now being rendered.

FIGURE 19

Relationships Between Affirmative Responses from
Practitioners with "Big-Eight" Firms Re Question A-15 Queries:
"IS the Category of Service Being Offered?"
and "SHOULD It Be Offered?"

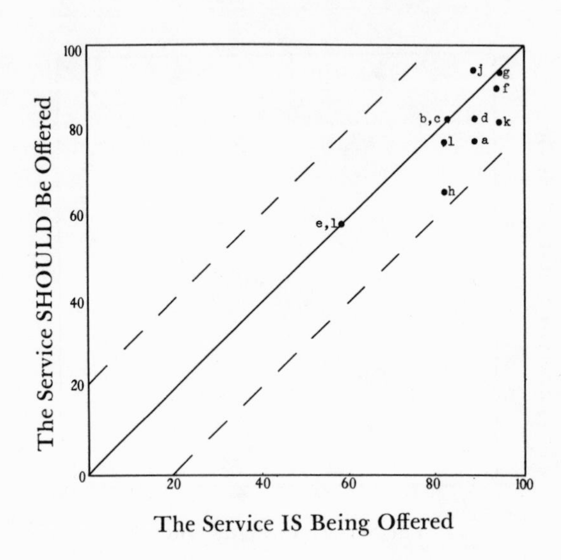

Divergencies in Excess of "20 percentage points" Evidenced by Above

For all categories of service suggested by Question A-15, the Practitioners with the national ("Big-Eight") firms' views as to which services should be rendered under the circumstances did not deviate by more than the "20 percentage point" margin from their views as to what services are now being rendered.

FIGURE 20

Relationships Between Affirmative Responses from the
Financial Community Category Re Question A-15 Queries:
"IS the Category of Service Being Offered?"
and "SHOULD It Be Offered?"
and the Same Relationships for the Practitioners with the
"Big-Eight" Firms

Key
a . . . l Relationships of Responses from "Big-Eight" Firms
A . . . L Relationships of Responses from Financial Community

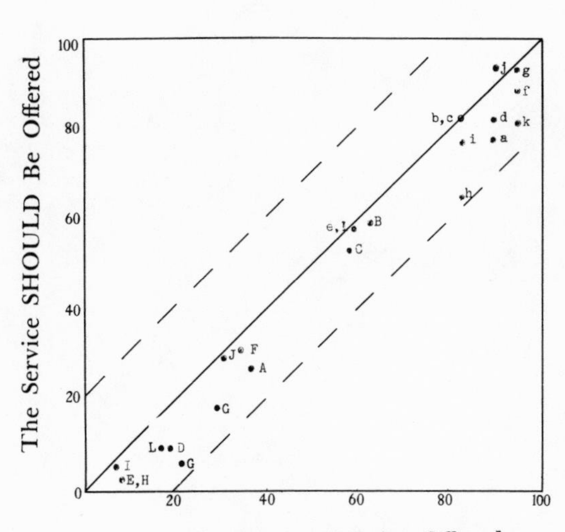

The Service IS Being Offered

The Inferences to Be Drawn from this Collage

The graph above combines Figure 13 (which reflects the responses from the Financial Community category) with the preceding Figure 19 (which reflects such responses from Practitioners with the "Big-Eight" firms). The obvious polarization of the respective responses is the subject of extended discussion in the text.

Notes

Preface

1. "Unaccountable CPAs," *Forbes* editorial, October 15, 1966, p. 15.
2. "CPAs Under Fire—Auditors' Critics Seek Wider, Faster Action in Reform of Practices," *The Wall Street Journal,* November 15, 1966, p. 1.
3. *Ibid.*
4. "Accounting Profession, Vexed by Lawsuits, Weighs Responsibility to Shareholders," *The New York Times,* November 20, 1966, sec. 3, p. 1.

Chapter 1

1. American Accounting Association, *A Statement of Basic Accounting Theory* (Evanston, Ill.: American Accounting Association, 1966), p. 20.
2. *Accounting Research and Terminology Bulletins* (final ed.; "Accounting Terminology Bulletins"; New York: American Institute of Certified Public Accountants, 1961), pp. 18-19.
3. John L. Carey (ed.), *The Accounting Profession—Where Is It Headed?* (New York: American Institute of Certified Public Accountants, 1962), p. 47.
4. Charles Frankel, *The Democratic Prospect* (New York: Harper & Row, 1962), pp. 158-59.
5. Everett C. Hughes, "Professions," *Daedalus* (Fall, 1963), pp. 655-56, *passim.*
6. A. C. Littleton and V. K. Zimmerman, *Accounting Theory: Continuity and Change* (Englewood Cliffs, N. J.: Prentice-Hall, Inc., 1962), p. 46.
7. John L. Carey (ed.), *The CPA Plans for the Future* (New York: American Institute of Certified Public Accountants, 1965), p. 117.

8. Francis W. Pixley, *Auditors: Their Duties and Responsibilities* (8th ed.; London: Henry Good & Son, 1901), pp. 2-3.
9. U.S., Securities and Exchange Commission, *Special Study of Securities Markets,* House Document No. 95, Pt. 3, 88th Cong., 1st Sess., 1963, p. 1.
10. Carey, *The Accounting Profession, op. cit.,* p. 53.
11. *A Statement of Basic Accounting Theory, op. cit.,* p. 13.
12. *Ibid.,* p. 64.
13. Leonard M. Savoie, "Accounting Improvement: How Fast, How Far?," *Harvard Business Review* (July/August, 1963), p. 153.
14. Weldon Powell, "The Development of Accounting Principles," *The Journal of Accountancy* (September, 1964), p. 43.
15. Paul Grady, *Inventory of Generally Accepted Accounting Principles for Business Enterprises* ("Accounting Research Study," No. 7; New York: American Institute of Certified Public Accountants, 1965), p. 381.
16. *The Wall Street Journal,* January 21, 1964, p. 1.
17. U.S., Congress, House, Subcommittee on Commerce and Finance of the Committee on Interstate and Foreign Commerce, Hearings on H.R. 6789, H.R. 6793, S. 1642, 88th Cong., 1st and 2nd Sess., p. 1298.
18. J. Howard Laeri, "The Audit Gap," Address before the American Bankers Association Credit Policy Committee, New York, February 1, 1966.
19. Jack M. Whitney II, Address before the Washington, D. C., Society of Investment Analysts, February 5, 1963, quoted in *The Journal of Accountancy* (March, 1963), p. 9.
20. Dwight R. Ladd, *Contemporary Corporate Accounting and the Public* (Homewood, Ill.: Richard D. Irwin, Inc., 1963), pp. 7-8.
21. David F. Hawkins, "The Development of Modern Financial Reporting Practices Among American Manufacturing Corporations," *Business History Review,* XXXVII, 3 (Autumn, 1963), 165-66.

22. Howard C. Greer, "How To Succeed in Confusing People Without Even Trying," *The Journal of Accountancy* (March, 1963), p. 61.
23. Carey, *The CPA Plans for the Future, op. cit.*, p. 130.
24. Weldon Powell, "Putting Uniformity in Financial Accounting into Perspective," *Uniformity in Financial Accounting*, published as the Autumn, 1965, ed. of *Law and Contemporary Problems* (Durham, N. C.: Duke University School of Law, 1966), p. 689. [This work will henceforth be cited as *Uniformity in Financial Accounting*.]
25. Leonard Spacek, "Are Double Standards Good Enough for Investors But Unacceptable to the Securities Industry?," Address before The New York Society of Security Analysts, New York, September 30, 1964.
26. Carey, *The CPA Plans for the Future, op. cit.*, p. 149.
27. Thomas G. Higgins, "The Accounting Principles Board and Uniformity in Financial Accounting," *Twenty-fifth Annual Institute on Accounting Proceedings* (Columbus: Ohio State University, 1963), p. 71.
28. *Report of AICPA Special Committee on Opinions of the Accounting Principles Board* (New York: American Institute of Certified Public Accountants, 1965), p. 14.
29. *Supra*, pp. 7-8.
30. *Supra*, p. 7.
31. Introduction by Julian Huxley, Père Teilhard de Chardin, *The Phenomenon of Man* (New York: Harper & Row, 1959), p. 17.

Chapter 2

1. John L. Carey (ed.), *The Accounting Profession—Where Is It Headed?* (New York: American Institute of Certified Public Accountants, 1962), p. 54.
2. Everett C. Hughes, "Professions," *Daedalus* (Fall, 1963), p. 656.
3. Andrew Barr, "Financial Statements—How Reliable?," *NAA Bulletin* (September, 1963), p. 3.

4. Reed K. Storey, *The Search for Accounting Principles* (New York: American Institute of Certified Public Accountants, 1964), pp. 1-2.
5. Thomas Henry Sanders, Henry Rand Hatfield, and Underhill Moore, *A Statement of Accounting Principles* (New York: American Institute of Certified Public Accountants, 1938), p. xii.
6. Adolf A. Berle, Jr. and Gardiner C. Means, *The Modern Corporation and Private Property* (New York: Macmillan & Co., 1932), p. 202.
7. Arthur Andersen & Co., *The Postulate of Accounting—What It Is, How It Is Determined, How It Should Be Used* (Chicago, Ill.: Arthur Andersen & Co., 1960), p. 9.
8. Robert N. Anthony, "Showdown on Accounting Principles," *Harvard Business Review* (May/June, 1963), p. 99.
9. David F. Hawkins, "The Development of Modern Financial Reporting Practices Among American Manufacturing Corporations," *Business History Review,* XXXVII, 3 (Autumn, 1963), 168.
10. T. A. Wise and the eds. of *Fortune, The Insiders* (Garden City, N. Y.: Doubleday & Company, Inc., 1962), especially pp. 21-23.
11. *Report of AICPA Special Committee on Opinions of the Accounting Principles Board* (New York: American Institute of Certified Public Accountants, 1965), p. 15.
12. Paul Grady, *Inventory of Generally Accepted Accounting Principles for Business Enterprises* ("Accounting Research Study," No. 7; New York: American Institute of Certified Public Accountants, 1965), pp. 373-79.
13. *Ibid.,* p. 33.
14. Leonard M. Savoie, "Accounting Improvement: How Fast, How Far?," *Harvard Business Review* (July/August, 1963), pp. 149-50.
15. *Ibid.,* p. 144.
16. *Supra,* p. 7.
17. John L. Hennessy, "Unrealities in Accounting Reporting," *Proceedings of the Eighth Annual Institute on Accounting* (Boulder: University of Colorado, 1961), p. 23.

18. Allan R. Drebin, "Cash-Flowitis: Malady or Syndrome," *Journal of Accounting Research,* II, 1 (Spring, 1964), 26.
19. Robert M. Trueblood, "To Improve Financial Reporting," Remarks to Council of the AICPA, Boca Raton, Fla., May 2, 1966.
20. George C. Holdren, "Toward Greater Comparability of Financial Statements," *Financial Analysts Journal* (April, 1963), pp. 103-4.
21. *The Wall Street Journal,* January 21, 1964, p. 1.
22. U.S., Congress, House, Subcommittee on Commerce and Finance of the Committee on Interstate and Foreign Commerce, Hearings on H.R. 6789, H.R. 6793, S. 1642, 88th Cong., 1st and 2nd Sess., p. 1298.
23. William L. Cary, "The SEC and Accounting," *The Journal of Accountancy* (December, 1963), p. 50.
24. Manuel F. Cohen, as reported in *The Journal of Accountancy* (August, 1966), p. 59.
25. *Ibid.*
26. *Supra,* p. 27.
27. *Carey, op. cit.,* p. 58.
28. *Ibid.,* p. 55.
29. *Ibid.,* p. 58.
30. John L. Carey (ed.), *The CPA Plans For the Future* (New York: American Institute of Certified Public Accountants, 1965), pp. 147-48.

Chapter 3

1. Corliss D. Anderson (ed.), *Corporate Reporting for the Professional Investor* (Auburndale, Mass.: The Financial Analysts Federation, 1962).
2. Alan Robert Cerf, *Corporate Reporting and Investment Decisions* (Berkeley: University of California, 1961), p. 40.
3. *Supra,* p. 34.
4. Cerf, *op. cit.,* p. 70.
5. *Ibid.,* p. 120.
6. *Supra,* p. 27.
7. George Richmond Walker, "Art, Science and Reality," *Bulletin of the Atomic Scientists* (September, 1964), p. 12.

8. *Ibid.*
9. Weldon Powell, "The Development of Accounting Principles," *The Journal of Accountancy* (September, 1964), p. 43.
10. *Supra,* p. 32.
11. American Institute of Certified Public Accountants, *Transcript of Proceedings, Seminar on Long-Range Planning,* Rye, N. Y., May 21-22, 1965, p. 297.
12. Curtis Holt Stanley, "The Role of Objectivity in Accounting" (unpublished Ph.D. dissertation, Microfilm No. 63-5022; Ann Arbor, Mich.: University Microfilms, Inc., 1963).
13. *Ibid.,* conclusion to Chap. IV.
14. Sir James Jeans, *Physics and Philosophy* (Ann Arbor, Mich.: The University of Michigan Press, 1958, originally published 1942), p. 53.
15. Werner Heisenberg, *The Physicist's Conception of Nature* (New York: Harcourt, Brace & World, Inc., 1958), pp. 15-16.
16. Walker, *op. cit.,* p. 10.
17. Robert J. Oppenheimer, *The Flying Trapeze: Three Crises for Physicists* (London: Oxford University Press, 1964), pp. 52-53.
18. American Association for the Advancement of Science, Committee on Science in the Promotion of Human Welfare, *The Integrity of Science,* Report submitted December 31, 1964.
19. J. Bronowski, *Science and Human Values* (New York: Harper & Row, 1956), p. 61.
20. Edwin H. Caplan, "Behavioral Assumptions of Management Accounting," *The Accounting Review,* XLI, 3 (July, 1966), 498.
21. Oliver Wendell Holmes, "The Path of the Law," an address delivered at Boston University School of Law, January 8, 1897, reproduced in Julius J. Marke (ed.), *The Holmes Reader* (New York: Oceana Publications, 1955), p. 63.
22. Accounting Principles Board, AICPA, *Status of Accounting Research Bulletins* ("Opinion" No. 6; New York: American Institute of Certified Public Accountants, 1965).

23. Robert M. Trueblood, "To Improve Financial Reporting," Remarks to Council of the AICPA, Boca Raton, Fla., May 2, 1966.
24. *Ibid.*
25. Grant McConnell, *Private Power and American Democracy* (New York: Alfred A. Knopf, 1966), pp. 287-88.
26. Arthur Andersen & Co., *The Postulate of Accounting—What It Is, How It Is Determined, How It Should Be Used* (Chicago, Ill.: Arthur Andersen & Co., 1960), p. 31.
27. *Ibid.*, pp. 4-8, *passim.*
28. Arthur Andersen & Co., *Establishing Accounting Principles—A Crisis in Decision Making* (Chicago, Ill.: Arthur Andersen & Co., 1965), p. 9.
29. Morris R. Cohen, *The Faith of a Liberal* (New York: Henry Holt and Company, 1946), p. 138.
30. Jeans, *op. cit.*, p. 84.
31. Ludwig Von Mises, *Bureaucracy* (New Haven, Conn.: Yale University Press, 1944), pp. 32-33, *passim.*
32. Roscoe Pound, *An Introduction to the Philosophy of Law* (New Haven, Conn.: Yale University Press, 1922), pp. 58-59.
33. Jerome Frank, *Law and The Modern Mind* (Anchor Books ed; Garden City, N. Y.: Doubleday & Company, Inc.; 1963, originally published 1930), pp. 5-7.
34. *Ibid.*, pp. 20-21.
35. *Ibid.*, p. 203.
36. *Ibid.*, p. 271.
37. Benjamin N. Cardozo, *The Growth of the Law* (New Haven, Conn.: Yale University Press, 1924), pp. 64-67.
38. Powell, *op. cit.*, pp. 39-40.
39. Leonard M. Savoie, "Accounting Improvement: How Fast, How Far?," *Harvard Business Review* (July/August, 1963), p. 146.
40. Alvin R. Jennings, "The Accounting Profession's Responsibility in Determining Accounting Principles," Speech delivered at New York University Graduate School of Business Administration, New York, November 14, 1963.
41. Clark C. Havighurst (ed.), Foreword, in *Uniformity in Financial Accounting* (Durham, N. C.: Duke University

School of Law, 1966), p. 622.

42. *Supra,* p. 78.
43. Abraham J. Briloff, "Needed: A Revolution in the Determination and Application of Accounting Principles," *The Accounting Review,* XXXIX, 1 (January, 1964), 15.
44. Cardozo, *op. cit.,* pp. 7-9.
45. Benjamin N. Cardozo, *The Nature of the Judicial Process* (New Haven, Conn.: Yale University Press, 1921), p. 20.
46. *Ibid.,* p. 21.
47. *Ibid.,* p. 141.
48. Frank, *op. cit.,* p. 277 (in concluding his essay on Mr. Justice Oliver Wendell Holmes).

Chapter 4

1. Everett C. Hughes, "Professions," *Daedalus* (Fall, 1963), p. 656.
2. *Ibid.,* p. 657.
3. Alfred North Whitehead, *Adventures of Ideas* (New York: The New American Library, 1955, originally published 1933), p. 64.
4. *Ibid.,* pp. 64-65, *passim.*
5. Père Teilhard de Chardin, *The Phenomenon of Man* (New York: Harper & Row, 1961), pp. 278-79.
6. Simon Marcson, *The Scientist in American Industry* (New York: Harper & Row, for Princeton University, 1960), pp. 117-18.
7. G. Edward Philips, "Research In Major Public Accounting Firms," *The Journal of Accountancy* (June, 1964), pp. 37-38.
8. *Ibid.,* p. 40.
9. Reed K. Storey, *The Search for Accounting Principles* (New York: American Institute of Certified Public Accountants, 1964), pp. 6-7.
10. David F. Hawkins, "The Development of Modern Financial Reporting Practices Among American Manufacturing Corporations," *Business History Review,* XXXVII, 3 (Autumn, 1963), 166-67.
11. Alvin R. Jennings, "How Can CPAs Meet Present Day Challenges of Financial Reporting?," Address before

Seventieth Annual Meeting of the American Institute of CPAs, New Orleans, La., October 28, 1957.

12. *Ibid.*
13. Alving R. Jennings, "Accounting Research," *The Accounting Review,* XXXIII, 4 (October, 1958), 553.
14. Weldon Powell, "Report on the Accounting Research Activities of the American Institute of Certified Public Accountants," *The Accounting Review,* XXXVI, 1 (January, 1961), 29-30.
15. *Ibid.,* p. 31.
16. Storey, *op. cit.,* p. 58.
17. *Supra,* p. 90.
18. *Supra,* p. 92.
19. John William Ward, "The Intellectual in the University," *The American Scholar* (Winter, 1965-66), p. 113.
20. Leonard M. Savoie, "Accounting Principles: Where Do We Go From Here?," *The Price Waterhouse Review,* IX, 1 (Spring, 1964), 35.
21. J. W. Fulbright, *Old Myths and New Realities* (New York: Random House, 1964), p. 3.
22. John W. Gardner, *Self-Renewal: The Individual and The Innovative Society* (New York: Harper & Row, 1964), pp. 52-53.
23. Page Smith, *The Historian and History* (New York: Alfred A. Knopf, 1964), pp. 147-49.
24. Leonard Spacek, "The Treatment of Goodwill in the Corporate Balance Sheet," *The Journal of Accountancy* (February, 1964), p. 35.
25. As reported by the Editor, *The Journal of Accountancy* (July, 1964), p. 52.
26. Spacek, *op. cit.,* p. 40.
27. Leonard Spacek in "Letters," *The Journal of Accountancy* (July, 1964), p. 55.
28. R. K. Mautz, "Accounting As a Social Science," *The Accounting Review,* XXXVIII, 2 (April, 1963), 321.
29. Robert Aaron Gordon and James Edwin Howell, *Higher Education for Business* (New York: Columbia University Press, 1959), p. 377.
30. Frank C. Pierson, *et al., The Education of American*

Businessmen (New York: McGraw-Hill Book Company, 1959), pp. 310-11.

31. Committee for Economic Development, *Educating Tomorrow's Managers* (New York: Committee for Economic Development, 1964), p. 10.
32. *Ibid.,* p. 11.
33. Alfred North Whitehead, *The Aims of Education* (New York: Mentor Books, 1949, originally published 1929), p. 101.
34. *Ibid.,* p. 102.
35. *Ibid.*
36. John R. Platt, "Research and Development for Social Problems," *Bulletin of the Atomic Scientists* (June, 1964), pp. 27, 29.
37. Nathan M. Pusey, Address on Commencement Day, Harvard University, June 14, 1962.
38. James A. Perkins, *The University in Transition* (Princeton, N. J.: Princeton University Press, 1966).
39. Thomas S. Kuhn, *The Structure of Scientific Revolutions* (Chicago, Ill.: The University of Chicago Press, 1962), p. 10.
40. Gardner, *op. cit.,* pp. 37-38.
41. Report of The Commission on the Humanities (New York: The Commission, 1964), p. 8.
42. Letter to the author from R. K. Mautz dated March 1, 1963.
43. Clinton Rossiter and James Lare (eds.), *The Essential Lippmann* (New York: Random House, 1963), p. 29, quoting from *Drift and Mastery* (1914).
44. Gardner, *op. cit.,* pp. 14-15.
45. Leonard Spacek, "Are Double Standards Good Enough for Investors But Unacceptable to the Securities Industry?," Address before New York Society of Security Analysts, New York, September 30, 1964.

Chapter 5

1. Will Herberg, *The Writings of Martin Buber* (New York: Meridian Books, 1956), p. 14.
2. Leonard Spacek, "Are Double Standards Good Enough

for Investors But Unacceptable to the Securities Industry?," Address before New York Society of Security Analysts, New York, September 30, 1964.

3. *Ibid.*
4. C. P. Snow, *The Two Cultures and the Scientific Revolution* (Cambridge: Cambridge University Press, 1959), p. 17.
5. Max Lerner, *America As a Civilization* (New York: Simon and Schuster, Inc., 1957), p. 363.
6. John L. Carey (ed.), *The Accounting Profession—Where Is It Headed?* (New York: American Institute of Certified Public Accountants, 1962), p. 53.
7. Benjamin Graham, David L. Dodd, Sidney Cottle, *Security Analysis* (4th ed.; New York: McGraw-Hill Book Company, Inc., 1962), p. 674.
8. Paul Grady (ed.), *Memoirs and Accounting Thought of George O. May* (New York: The Ronald Press Co., 1962), pp. 295-96.
9. Edwin B. Cox, *Trends in the Distribution of Stock Ownership* (Philadelphia: University of Pennsylvania Press, 1963), p. 6.
10. A. C. Littleton, *Structure of Accounting Theory* (Urbana, Ill.: American Accounting Association, 1953), at p. 10, quoting a statement made (1937) by Colonel Robert H. Montgomery.
11. U.S., Congress, House, Subcommittee on Commerce and Finance of the Committee on Interstate and Foreign Commerce, Hearings on H.R. 6789, H.R. 6793, S. 1642, 88th Cong., 1st and 2nd Sess., p. 1304.
12. Paul O. Gaddis, *Corporate Accountability* (New York: Harper & Row, 1964), pp. 60-61.
13. Adolf A. Berle, Jr., *Power Without Property* (New York: Harcourt, Brace & World, Inc., 1959), p. 105.
14. *Ibid.*, pp. 108-9.
15. I. Joseph Brooks, "Stockholder Season," *The New Yorker* (October 8, 1966), p. 159.
16. R. K. Mautz and Hussein A. Sharaf, *The Philosophy of Auditing* (Madison, Wisc.: American Accounting Association, 1961), p. 196.
17. Berle, *op. cit.*, p. 105.

18. Corliss D. Anderson (ed.), *Corporate Reporting for the Professional Investor* (Auburndale, Mass.: The Financial Analysts Federation, 1962), Foreword.
19. *Supra,* p. 7.
20. James Allen (ed.), *William O. Douglas, Democracy and Finance* (New Haven, Conn.: Yale University Press, 1940), pp. 110-11.
21. American Accounting Association, *A Statement of Basic Accounting Theory* (Evanston, Ill.: American Accounting Association, 1966), p. 64.
22. *Accounting Research and Terminology Bulletins* (final ed.; "Accounting Terminology Bulletins"; New York: American Institute of Certified Public Accountants, 1961), pp. 18-19.
23. Andrew Barr, "Financial Statements—How Reliable," *NAA Bulletin* (September, 1963), pp. 4-5.
24. Louis H. Rappaport, *SEC Accounting Practice and Procedure* (2nd ed.; New York: The Ronald Press Co., 1963), paragraph 2.11.
25. Dwight R. Ladd, *Contemporary Corporate Accounting and the Public* (Homewood, Ill.: Richard D. Irwin, Inc., 1963), pp. 164-65.
26. John L. Hennessy, "Unrealities in Accounting Reporting," in *Proceedings of the Eighth Annual Institute on Accounting* (Boulder: University of Colorado, 1961), p. 12.
27. Patrick S. Kemp, "These Statements Present Fairly," *The New York Certified Public Accountant* (September, 1963) pp. 626-30.
28. Herbert E. Miller, "Audited Statements—Are They Really Management's," *The Journal of Accountancy* (October, 1964), p. 46.
29. *Ibid.*
30. Council of the AICPA, "Disclosure of Departures from Opinions of Accounting Principles Board" (New York: American Institute of Certified Public Accountants, 1964).
31. J. Howard Laeri, "The Audit Gap," Address before the American Bankers Association Credit Policy Committee, New York, February 1, 1966.
32. Clark C. Havighurst (ed.), Foreword, in *Uniformity in*

Financial Accounting (Durham, N.C.: Duke University School of Law, 1966), pp. 621-22.

33. Charles E. Johnson, "Management and Accounting Principles," in *Uniformity in Financial Accounting, op. cit.*, p. 705.
34. Douglas A. Hayes, "Accounting Principles and Investment Analysis," in *Uniformity in Financial Accounting, op. cit.*, p. 771.
35. Edwin J. Bradley, "Auditor's Liability and the Need for Increased Accounting Uniformity," in *Uniformity in Financial Accounting, op. cit.*, p. 921.
36. *Ultramares Corp. v. Touche,* 255 N.Y. 170, 174 N.E. 441 (1931).
37. T. A. Wise, "The Very Private World of Peat, Marwick, Mitchell," *Fortune* (July, 1966), pp. 89-90.
38. *Stephen Fischer, et al. v. Michael Kletz, et al.*, Proceedings in United States District Court, Southern District of New York, 65 Civ. 787, memorandum of the Securities and Exchange Commission, *amicus curiae,* in opposition to motion of Peat, Marwick, Mitchell & Co. to dismiss portions of the complaint, pp. 1-2.
39. *Ibid.*, pp. 2-3.
40. *Ibid.*, memorandum of Peat, Marwick, Mitchell & Co. in support of the motion, p. 4.
41. Abraham J. Briloff, "Old Myths and New Realities in Accountancy," *The Accounting Review,* XLI, 3 (July, 1966), 490.
42. Bradley, *op. cit.*, pp. 904-5, 909, 921.
43. Leonard M. Savoie, "Accounting Improvement: How Fast, How Far?," *Harvard Business Review* (July/August, 1963), p. 144.
44. Weldon Powell, "The Development of Accounting Principles," *The Journal of Accountancy* (September, 1964), p. 40.
45. *Supra,* pp. 116-17.
46. Encyclical *Pacem in Terris* of Pope John XXIII (from published text; New York: The America Press, 1964), p. 11.

Chapter 6

1. Resolution by Council of the AICPA (New York: American Institute of Certified Public Accountants, 1961).
2. Committee on Professional Ethics, AICPA, *Opinion re: "Independence"* (No. 12; New York: American Institute of Certified Public Accountants, 1963).
3. Committee on Professional Ethics, AICPA, *Opinion re: "Specialization"* (No. 17; New York: American Institute of Certified Public Accountants, 1965).
4. Joseph E. Lane, Letter to the Editor, *The Journal of Accountancy* (February, 1964), p. 30.
5. *Ibid.*
6. John L. Carey (ed.), *The CPA Plans for the Future* (New York: American Institute of Certified Public Accountants, 1965), p. 238.
7. Robert M. Trueblood, "To Improve Financial Reporting," Remarks to Council of the AICPA, Boca Raton, Fla., May 2, 1966.
8. Manuel F. Cohen, Address before the Seventy-Ninth Annual Meeting of the American Institute of Certified Public Accountants, Boston, Mass., October 5, 1966.
9. Arthur A. Schulte, Jr., "Compatibility of Management Consulting and Auditing," *The Accounting Review,* XL, 3 (July, 1965), 592.
10. John L. Carey and William O. Doherty, *Ethical Standards of the Accounting Profession* (New York: American Institute of Certified Public Accountants, 1966), p. 23.
11. *Ibid.*
12. John L. Carey, "How Can We Expect to Compete?" *The CPA,* October, 1964, p. 2.
13. T. A. Wise and the eds. of *Fortune, The Insiders* (Garden City, N. Y.: Doubleday & Company, Inc., 1962), p. 10.
14. T. A. Wise, "The Very Private World of Peat, Marwick, Mitchell," *Fortune* (July, 1966), p. 130.
15. George Mead, "Auditing, Management Advisory Services, Social Services, and Profit-Motive," *The Accounting Review,* XXXV, 4 (October, 1960), 659.
16. Kenneth S. Axelson, "Are Consulting and Tax Services Compatible?," Peat, Marwick, Mitchell & Co., *Management Controls* (July, 1963), p. 116.

17. "Are CPA Firms Taking Over Management Consulting?," *Forbes* (October 1, 1966), p. 27.
18. Kenneth S. Axelson, "The Development of Management Services in the Public Accounting Firms," Peat, Marwick, Mitchell & Co., *Management Controls* (January, 1963), p. 4.
19. John L. Carey (ed.), *The Accounting Profession—Where Is It Headed?* (New York: American Institute of Certified Public Accountants, 1962), p. 160.
20. Darwin J. Casler, "The Independence of the Public Accountant," *Business Topics,* XII, 1 (Winter, 1964), 54-55.
21. Francis W. Pixley, *Auditors: Their Duties and Responsibilities* (8th ed.; London: Henry Good & Son, 1901), p. 17.
22. Paul Grady (ed.), *Memoirs and Accounting Thought of George O. May* (New York: The Ronald Press Company, 1962), p. 94.
23. Adolf A. Berle, Jr., *Power Without Property* (New York: Harcourt, Brace & World, Inc., 1959).
24. Kenneth E. Boulding, *Organizational Revolution* (New York: The Federal Council of Churches of Christ in America, through Harper & Brothers, 1953), pp. 136-37.
25. *Supra,* p. 172.
26. Paul O. Gaddis, *Corporate Accountability* (New York: Harper & Row, 1964), pp. 77-78.
27. James Allen (ed.), *William O. Douglas, Democracy and Finance* (New Haven, Conn.: Yale University Press, 1940), p. 49.
28. *Ibid.,* p. 53.
29. *Ibid.*
30. Kenneth S. Axelson, "The Development of Management Services in the Public Accounting Firms," *op. cit.,* p. 6.
31. Kenneth S. Axelson, "Management Services and Audit Independence," Peat, Marwick, Mitchell & Co., *Management Controls* (January, 1963), pp. 1-2.
32. Morton F. Moss, "Management Services and the CPA Examination," *The Accounting Review,* XXXVII, 4 (October, 1962), 733-34.
33. Clinton W. Bennett, "Management Services by CPAs," *The Accounting Review,* XXXIII, 4 (October, 1958), 610.

34. John L. Carey, "Practical Ethical Problems in Accounting," *Proceedings of the Eighth Annual (1961) Institute on Accounting* (Boulder: University of Colorado, 1961), pp. 64-65.
35. Carey, *The Accounting Profession, op. cit.,* p. 88.
36. Robert M. Trueblood, "To Improve Financial Reporting," Remarks to Council of the AICPA, Boca Raton, Fla., May 2, 1966.
37. Boris I. Bittker, *Professional Responsibility and Federal Tax Practice* (New York: New York University, 1965), pp. 69-70.
38. Special Committee on the Federal Conflict of Interest Law of the Association of the Bar of the City of New York, *Conflict of Interest and Federal Service* (Cambridge, Mass.: Harvard University Press, 1960), p. 98.
39. *Ibid.,* p. 108.
40. Clinton Rossiter and James Lare (eds.), *The Essential Lippmann* (New York: Random House, 1963), p. 313.
41. Izette de Forrest, *The Leaven of Love* (New York: Harper, 1954), p. 65.
42. Martin Buber, *I and Thou* (2nd ed.; New York: Charles Scribner's Sons, 1958), pp. 132-33.
43. *Supra,* p. 177.
44. Machiavelli, *The Prince* (Baltimore, Md.: Penguin Books, 1961), p. 30.
45. Theodore C. Sorensen, *Decision-Making in the White House* (New York: Columbia University Press, 1963), from Foreword by John F. Kennedy, p. xiii.
46. Theodore C. Sorensen, *Kennedy* (New York: Harper & Row, 1965), p. 309.
47. Marion D. Folsom, *Executive Decision Making* (New York: McGraw-Hill Book Company, 1962), p. 4.
48. *Ibid.*
49. American Accounting Association, *A Statement of Basic Accounting Theory* (Evanston, Ill.: American Accounting Association, 1966), p. 50.
50. A. C. Pigou (ed.), *Memorials of Alfred Marshall* (London: Macmillan & Co., Ltd., 1925), pp. 167-68.
51. *Supra,* p. 180

52. Carey, *The CPA Plans for the Future, op. cit.,* p. 417.
53. *Ibid.*
54. Delmer P. Hylton, "Are Consulting and Auditing Compatible?—A Contrary View," *The Accounting Review,* XXXIX, 3 (July, 1964), 670.
55. Abraham J. Briloff, "Needed: A Revolution in the Determination and Application of Accounting Principles," *The Accounting Review,* XXXIX, 1 (January, 1964), 15.
56. "New Watchdogs—Or A Longer Leash," *The Economist,* September 10, 1966, pp. 1037-38.
57. *Supra,* p. 152.
58. *Supra,* p. 147.

Chapter 7

1. E. H. Carr, *What Is History?* (Hammondsworth, Middlesex: Penguin Books, Ltd., 1964, originally published 1961), p. 30.
2. Marc Bloch, *The Historian's Craft* (New York: Vintage Books, 1964; originally published 1953), p. 27.
3. Hans Meyerhoff, *The Philosophy of History in Our Time* (Garden City, N. Y.: Doubleday & Company, Inc., 1959), pp. 18-22.
4. Charles Frankel, *The Case for Modern Man* (Boston, Mass.: Beacon Press, 1959), pp. 133-35.
5. Ernest Nagel, "The Logic of Historical Analysis," *The Scientific Monthly,* LXXIV (March, 1952), 162ff. *passim.*
6. Karl Mannheim, *Ideology and Utopia* (New York: Harcourt, Brace & World, Inc., 1936), p. 5.
7. *Ibid.*
8. *Ibid.*
9. Carr, *op. cit.,* pp. 39-40.
10. Robert Aaron Gordon and James Edwin Howell, *Higher Education for Business* (New York: Columbia University Press, 1959).
11. Frank C. Pierson, *et al., The Education of American Businessmen* (New York: McGraw-Hill Book Company, 1959).
12. Committee for Economic Development, *Educating Tomorrow's Managers* (New York: Committee for Economic Development, 1964), p. 40.

13. Maurice Moonitz, *The Basic Postulates of Accounting* ("Accounting Research Study," No. 1; New York: American Institute of Certified Public Accountants, 1961), p. 4.
14. Weldon Powell, "Inventory of Generally Accepted Accounting Principles," *The Journal of Accountancy* (March, 1965), p. 32.
15. A. C. Littleton and V. K. Zimmerman, *Accounting Theory: Continuity and Change* (Englewood Cliffs, N. J.: Prentice-Hall, Inc., 1962), p. 4.
16. *Ibid.*
17. John Dewey, *Philosophy and Civilization* (New York: Capricorn Books, 1963, originally published 1931), pp. 15-16.
18. Abraham Kaplan, *American Ethics and Public Policy,* published previously as *The American Style,* Elting E. Morison (ed.) (New York: Harper & Row by arrangement with Massachusetts Institute of Technology, 1958), abridgment of pp. 36, 37, 39.
19. Arthur M. Schlesinger, Jr., "The Historian and History," *Foreign Affairs,* XLI, 3 (April, 1963), 491.
20. *Ibid.*
21. *Ibid.,* pp. 495-96, *passim.*
22. *Ibid.,* p. 497.
23. *The New York Times,* November 25, 1965, p. 8.
24. A. Whitney Griswold, *Liberal Education and the Democratic Ideal* (New Haven, Conn.: Yale University Press, 1959), p. 136.
25. Bertrand de Jouvenel, "The Technocratic Age," *Bulletin of the Atomic Scientists* (October, 1964), p. 29.
26. *Ibid.*
27. Introduction by Julian Huxley, Père Teilhard de Chardin, *The Phenomenon of Man* (New York: Harper & Row, 1959), p. 17

Chapter 8

1. John F. Kennedy, *Inaugural Address* as President of the United States, January 20, 1961.
2. Karl Mannheim, *Ideology and Utopia* (New York: Harcourt, Brace & World, Inc., 1936), p. 5.

Appendix A

1. Percy W. Bridgman, *Reflections of a Physicist* (2nd ed.; New York: Philosophical Library, 1955), p. 431.
2. Arthur Andersen & Co., *The Postulate of Accounting—What It Is, How It Is Determined, How It Should Be Used* (Chicago, Ill.: Arthur Andersen & Co., 1960), p. 28.
3. Leonard M. Savoie, "Accounting Improvement: How Fast, How Far?," *Harvard Business Review* (July/August, 1963), p. 144.
4. Arthur Andersen & Co., *Accounting and Reporting Problems of the Accounting Profession* (2nd ed.; Chicago, Ill.: Arthur Andersen & Co., 1962).
5. *Ibid.,* Table of Contents.
6. Financial Analysts Federation, *Membership Directory* (15th ed.; Auburndale, Mass.: The Financial Analysts Federation, 1963).

Selected Bibliography

Books

Anderson, Corliss D. (ed.). *Corporate Reporting for the Professional Investor.* Auburndale, Mass.: The Financial Analysts Federation, 1962.

Berle, Adolf A., Jr. *Power Without Property.* New York: Harcourt, Brace & World, Inc., 1959.

Cardozo, Benjamin N. *The Growth of the Law.* New Haven, Conn.: Yale University Press, 1924.

_______________. *The Nature of the Judicial Process.* New Haven, Conn.: Yale University Press, 1921.

Carey, John L. (ed.). *The Accounting Profession—Where Is It Headed?* New York: American Institute of Certified Public Accountants, 1962.

_______________. *The CPA Plans for the Future.* New York: American Institute of Certified Public Accountants, 1965.

Carr, E. H. *What Is History?* Hammondsworth, Middlesex: Penguin Books, Ltd., 1964. (Originally published in 1961.)

Frank, Jerome. *Law and The Modern Mind.* Anchor Books ed. Garden City, N. Y.: Doubleday & Company, 1963. (Originally published in 1930.)

Gordon, Robert Aaron, and Howell, James Edwin. *Higher Education for Business.* New York: Columbia University Press, 1959.

Grady, Paul. *Inventory of Generally Accepted Accounting Principles for Business Enterprises.* ("Accounting Research Study," No. 7.) New York: American Institute of Certified Public Accountants, 1965.

Kuhn, Thomas S. *The Structure of Scientific Revolutions.* Chicago, Ill.: The University of Chicago Press, 1962.

Ladd, Dwight R. *Contemporary Corporate Accounting and the Public.* Homewood, Ill.: Richard D. Irwin, Inc., 1963.

Mautz, R. K., and Sharaf, Hussein A. *The Philosophy of Auditing*. Madison, Wisc.: American Accounting Association, 1961.

Meyerhoff, Hans. *The Philosophy of History in Our Time*. Garden City, N. Y.: Doubleday & Company, Inc., 1959.

Pierson, Frank C., *et al. The Education of American Businessmen*. New York: Columbia University Press, 1959.

Storey, Reed K. *The Search for Accounting Principles*. New York: American Institute of Certified Public Accountants, 1964.

Whitehead, Alfred North. *Adventures of Ideas*. New York: The New American Library, 1955. (Originally published in 1933.)

______________. *The Aims of Education*. New York: Mentor Books, 1949. (Originally published in 1929.)

Monographs and Reports

Arthur Andersen & Co. *Accounting and Reporting Problems of the Accounting Profession*. 2nd. ed. Chicago, Ill.: Arthur Andersen & Co., 1962.

______________. *Establishing Accounting Principles—A Crisis in Decision Making*. Chicago, Ill.: Arthur Andersen & Co., 1965.

______________. *The Postulate of Accounting—What It Is, How It Is Determined, How It Should Be Used*. Chicago, Ill.: Arthur Andersen & Co., 1960.

Report of AICPA Special Committee on Opinions of the Accounting Principles Board. New York: American Institute of Certified Public Accountants, 1965.

American Accounting Association. *A Statement of Basic Accounting Theory*. Evanston, Ill.: American Accounting Association, 1966.

Other

Spacek, Leonard. "Are Double Standards Good Enough for Investors But Unacceptable to the Securities Industry?" (Address before The New York Society of Security Analysts, New York, September 30, 1964.)

Uniformity in Financial Accounting, published as the Autumn, 1965, ed. of *Law and Contemporary Problems.* Durham, N. C.: Duke University School of Law, 1966.

INDEX

ABOUT THE AUTHOR

Abraham J. Briloff, Professor of Accountancy at The Bernard M. Baruch School of Business and Public Administration of The City College, The City University of New York, has also been a practicing Certified Public Accountant for over thirty years.

Dr. Briloff has been a Director of The New York State Society of Certified Public Accountants and of The Estate Planning Council of New York City and a member of various committees of the State Society and the American Institute of Certified Public Accountants.

Articles by Dr. Briloff on accounting theory and practice have appeared in *The Journal of Accountancy, The Accounting Review, The New York Certified Public Accountant, Trusts and Estates, The Journal of Taxation, The Financial Analysts Journal,* and elsewhere. He was the coordinating editor and a contributing author for *Estate Planning and the CPA,* the text used by the AICPA's Professional Development Division.

Professor Briloff was educated in the New York City schools and received his Bachelor of Business Administration and Master of Science in Education degrees from The City College. He received his Doctor of Philosophy degree from the New York University Graduate School of Business Administration.